Corruption in Developing Countries

—◦⟨❧⟩◦—

RONALD WRAITH

AND

EDGAR SIMPKINS

Note
For the purposes of this study Britain
is regarded as a developing country until
about the 1880s.

London
GEORGE ALLEN & UNWIN LTD
RUSKIN HOUSE   MUSEUM STREET

PRINTED IN GREAT BRITAIN
in 10 *on* 11 *point Times Roman type*
BY SIMSON SHAND LTD
LONDON, HERTFORD AND HARLOW

CORRUPTION IN DEVELOPING COUNTRIES

CONTENTS

218648

Foreword

The first part of this book is largely about Nigeria, at any rate so far as practical examples are concerned. This, however, is both acci- dental and incidental. The only reason why Nigeria figures so prominently is that it is the country, outside Britain, where the authors have lived longest, and they think it is better to write of what they know than of what they have heard at second hand. There are, however, ample reasons for thinking that the actual situations described can be paralleled elsewhere. The authors have indeed come across them in other parts of Africa, but not having this book in mind at the time they failed to document them. They have also heard them discussed by students and civil servants from almost all the underdeveloped countries of the English-speaking world, and it is a fair supposition that the problems are universal.

The book is an attempt by two collaborators to examine a social situation sympathetically. The bulk of it will be a discussion of bribery and corruption in Britain. Its most significant aspect will be an attempt to explore ground which the authors think has not been adequately explored before—what were the factors which led Britain, a country as corrupt as any, to achieve in a particular century a standard of public integrity which is perhaps without precedent. Perhaps even more important, can any threads be traced in the pattern which are meaningful for Britain's former African and Asian dependencies?

It is hardly necessary to apologize to Nigerian readers for citing examples from their country, since the best elements in Nigerian society, at all levels, are themselves the most forthright critics of corruption there; and nothing is written in the relevant chapters which is not already public knowledge from newspapers or official reports.

Nevertheless, the authors wish to repeat with emphasis that the first part of the book is only incidentally about Nigeria, or indeed West Africa.

The Problem

—◦❧❦◦—

Throughout the fabric of public life in newly independent States runs the scarlet thread of bribery and corruption. This is admitted by everybody; very little can ever be proved about it.

The reaction of the educated citizens of these countries to this state of affairs is that of any other people; they are angry, ashamed, indifferent, cynical according to their different temperaments. What distinguishes them from people who live in a more fortunate atmosphere is that circumstances force even the angry and ashamed into a resigned apathy. Those who have tried to live as moral men in an amoral society have generally given way sooner or later under agonizing pressures; the pressure of legitimate ambition which can only be achieved by illegitimate means; the pressure from families, insatiable for help; the slow, insidious pressures of a society in which material success is adulated (even by the standards of the twentieth century), and where moreover material failure is ruthlessly mocked; the pressure of increasing defeatism, on realizing that public opinion stigmatizes the transgressor so lightly, and that so little seems to be gained from trying to swim against the tide. This is the general picture. Within it, some go on trying, a few with rare persistence; corporately they achieve little, since most of them are teachers or civil servants, firmly enmeshed in the system which they want to destroy, and silenced by the terms of their official employment.

The reactions of foreigners to the situation vary from shocked horror to wonderment as to what the fuss is all about. Visitors from several nations, including members of the Commonwealth, have expressed surprise to the writer that matters in West Africa where the writer lives should be considered serious, let alone scandalous, and have justified their attitude by stories of official peculation in their own countries which are certainly impressive in terms of the eminence of the people involved, and the size of the sums of money which change hands. But some of these examples are from business rather than public life (though it is the cross-fertilization of the two which offers the richest spoils) and occasional picturesque financial buccaneering, even when the public sector is involved, is less soul-destroying in itself than in combination with the pervasive, petty corruption of the poor and the quiet, cynical corruption of the influential; both of which tend to be common, not remarkable, in newly independent countries.

Some are naïvely shocked, but these become fewer, since standards elsewhere are not such as to make bribery and corruption a matter for surprise, and those who actually live in these countries have little alternative but to adjust to the prevailing atmosphere. Others, including some in the lower and middle ranks of the commercial world, give way to it without much of a struggle, since they must adapt or go under to less scrupulous competitors.

But aside from those who are too worldly-wise to be of any help in tackling the disease, or who are not sufficiently worldly-wise to live in such countries and be at peace, there are foreigners, and specifically British ones, who adopt an attitude which they believe to be both balanced and benevolent, and which they base upon their knowledge of British history. This has made them immune from shock, while not eroding their belief in public virtue as an attainable ideal.

Briefly, their argument is that the matters of complaint—the sale of office, the buying of votes, the rake-off on the contract, and the many subtle elaborations of these—can all be paralleled in the history of the British people in the eighteenth and nineteenth centuries; that their influence survives into the twentieth; and that they are worse today than they were twenty years ago.

The fact that all these statements are correct does not, however, dispose of the matter satisfactorily.

In the first place, it is the boast of these countries that they are telescoping the centuries. The greatest solecism that the European can commit is to say that in Europe a certain phase of development took 500 years, or the 2,000 years of the Christian era. What Britain did in 500 years Africans in particular are determined to do in fifty. This is legitimate; what is not legitimate is to be selective—to say that for certain purposes Africa will move at ten times the pace of her former guardians in education, the right to vote, parliamentary democracy and technological progress, but reserves the right to travel at a more convenient pace in public honesty.

Secondly, there was never a time in the history of corruption in the public life of Britain when there were not powerful forces fighting against it. In the end these won, and for half a century public integrity was as high as any outside the aboriginal tribe, where corruption does not exist because there are no temptations. These forces have lost some ground of recent years, but the integrity of statesmen, civil servants, the police, and the councillors and staffs of local authorities is still impressively high. In Africa corruption flourishes as luxuriantly as the bush and the weeds which it so much resembles, taking the goodness from the soil and suffocating the

growth of plants which have been carefully, and expensively, bred
and tended. The forces ranged against it are negligible; not negligible
in fire or indignation or idealism, but quite simply negligible in
weight. The calm and balanced attitude, which is held by those who
live in Britain rather than in new countries themselves, is, to say the
least, inadequate. It assumes that the situations in modern Africa
and nineteenth century Britain are comparable, which is untrue. It
amounts to little more than drifting and hoping for the best, in the
comforting belief that given a free hand Africans today will behave
like Englishmen a century ago. Paradoxically it is the same critics
who tend to mock the idea that Africans should do this in any other
field of social development.

Thirdly, in the century or so of struggle between corruption and
its foes Britain was a wealthy country, even if her wealth was ill-
distributed, and the supply of able and educated men from her
privileged class was sufficient to keep her in the forefront of the
nations. Many of these men were corrupt, and their inherited wealth
did not make them less so; but others, as public conscience grew,
helped to shape and lend it by the fortunate accident of their own
wealth and culture. The new African countries are poor, and are
trying to pull themselves up by their own bootstraps. The public
men on whom wealth has descended in a sudden and unimaginable
torrent are not heirs to a tradition of comfortable bank balances and
public responsibility; they are *nouveaux riches* tycoons of public
administration. Those who happened to be in the right place at the
right time were not all of them cultivated, educated or upright men.
They are not to be compared with the men on whom public responsibility descended, in Cabinet, civil service or town hall, in the rising
tide of Victorian prosperity in Britain.

Above all, young men from the secondary schools and universities
who enter the public service do not see a clear road ahead, along
which they will travel as far as their abilities will take them, in the
knowledge that merit will be rewarded and integrity will be their
greatest asset. They see a jungle of nepotism and temptation through
which they must hack their way unaided. The greatest imponderable
asset which these countries possess, in the field of public service, is
the enthusiasm of young men. That this enthusiasm should turn to
cynicism not only in their own formative years but those of their
country, is a dangerous and tragic situation.

The study is limited to Britain and a few countries which grew to
statehood under British tutelage. The study of corruption in the
Near East, in Asia, in Latin America, in America itself would no
doubt be fascinating, if unedifying. No one doubts that luxurious
and exotic blooms flourish in those jungles. The next few chapters
are simply about what used to be called 'British Africa'.

CHAPTER 2

Glimpses of Corruption

——o·❧·o——

It is frustrating to try to write, one's phrases wrapped in a cocoon of ambiguity, about something which everybody knows, which no one dares openly to acknowledge, which can rarely be proved and which may lead to serious trouble if one is in the least incautious. Perhaps that is why studies of contemporary corruption are rare.

What can be said about corruption among the mandarins, and in the high places, can amount to no more than a few careful generalizations. Of corruption among the common or less gifted citizens one may write a little more freely. It is only of muncipal corruption that one is able to write at large, free from the shadow of the law of libel; to write also with some precision, since the field especially in Nigeria has been admirably documented by successive Commissions of Inquiry, whose published works, now assuming a considerable bulk, are among the livelier contributions to contemporary Nigerian literature. It is a pity they are not better known.

Some years ago Dr Nkrumah shocked many Christians by permitting the base of his statue outside the Law Courts in Accra to be inscribed with the words—carved imperishably out of granite—'Seek ye first the Kingdom of Politics and all else shall be added unto you'. It is clear from subsequent events that this was hardly an overestimate so far as some of his own supporters were concerned, and the Osageyfo himself was courageous enough in 1961 to compel his own Ministers to declare their business assets and commercial interests, and to do a full-time job for a full-time salary. This is no final solution, since people cannot be compelled to be honest, and a man of influence in public life has many opportunities to circumvent the letter of the law, through relatives, agents and foreign bank accounts. But the Osageyfo's gesture gave hope to many Africans.

It is one of the regrettable assumptions among young West Africans today that Ministers are rich, and that they become rich by being Ministers. This is hard enough to bear; what the writer found even harder was to be told by a final year honours class in the University College, Ibadan, that the situation in Great Britain was identical, and that the Colonial Office had obviously been a particularly good field for plunder, since on leaving its highest office

Lord Chandos went to the chairmanship of Associated Electrical Industries and Lord Boyd to the chairmanship of Guinness; having, it was tacitly understood, bribed their way in from the spoils of office. Such is the context of thought in this matter, among the supposedly most intelligent—and, what is more serious, among the young.

The writer has been told in more than one West African country, however, that corruption among top people must be seen with an understanding eye. It is not necessarily concerned with personal enrichment, or at least only in moderation. The root of the matter is that political parties need money, and the small subscription from the average man is not available. The large subscription from the man of influence must therefore take its place, and the accession of certain large sums to the party funds represents something not reprehensible, but notably self-sacrificial, on the part of those who are the channels of this communication. An unofficial percentage on a contract (and there are some big contracts), the compulsory purchase of land at an unorthodox price, a little wise direction in the development of real estate—these must not be too hastily condemned. It may well be.

It is unfortunate that Ministers, among whom are men of ability and integrity, should almost gratuitously have made themselves a butt, defined by the Oxford Dictionary as 'an object of teasing or ridicule', by possessing motor cars of embarrassing size and living in houses which are commonly said to have cost the taxpayer well over £30,000. Anyone who happens to travel in a car of extravagant aspect is now liable to have the word 'Meenister' shouted after him by the local urchins. The writer was present on one occasion when Mr Creech Jones came to address a group of West African students at a country house in England. He was not at that time Colonial Secretary, but he had been until the very recent past. The great man's car swept up the drive; he emerged from it with difficulty, as it was a Morris Minor, stricken in years and driven by his wife. The burden of his remarks has no doubt been forgotten by everyone who was present, but the image of the car remains indelibly printed on the memories of some twenty-five West Africans, and was the subject of conversation ten years later. West Africa is sadly afflicted by the love of ostentation, and thousands of men on the middle and lower rungs are crippled financially because of it. Ministerial ostentation can perhaps be excused on the grounds of dignity of office, or more straightforwardly because Ministers can afford it; but it is an unfortunate example, and gives rise to cynicism.

How much is true and how much is false about corruption in high places nobody outside a small circle can ever know for certain. What *is* certain, and can be said without circumlocution, is that to wander through the corridors of power in these countries is to wander through a whispering-gallery of gossip, in which the fact of corruption at the highest levels is taken utterly for granted, and the only interest lies in capping the latest story with one that is even more startling.

There is of course an illicit glamour about alleged ministerial corruption which causes it to be talked about more perhaps than it deserves. It is certainly unfair to those Ministers who are free of it that they should be linked in the generic word 'ministerial' with those who are not.

It is indeed always unfair to speak of people in categories instead of as individuals. In the writer's experience the civil services in West Africa can, as a corporate whole and at the time of writing, be proud of their general integrity; on the other hand there is little doubt that the depredations of some civil servants are considerable. Those who deal direct with the public and are in a position to bestow benefits on individuals, or to influence their bestowal, are of course more vulnerable than the rest, and the known fact that some such men have avoided or declined promotion to higher salaried grades tells its own story.

The almost unbearable dilemma of such a man is described poignantly in Mr Chinua Achebe's novel *No Longer At Ease*. Obi Okonkwo is in a position to influence the award of scholarships— or people think he is, which amounts to the same thing. He is honest, he resists; he is not unusual in this. But pressures unknown and unimagined by his prototype in Whitehall wear him down, and the book opens as he stands in the High Court in Lagos. He 'appears unruffled and indifferent', but it is the apathy of defeat. Mr Chinua's book tells simply and directly the whole story of this section, without its unavoidable circumlocution. He could as well have been writing of a man in the office of a Loans Board, a Customs or Immigration Officer, or a policeman.

The problem has been openly and officially recognized in Ghana and Nigeria by the appointment of Advisory Commissions on the suppression of corruption in the public service, and more than one Government maintains an Anti-Corruption Officer on its normal strength.

*

The economic effects of all this on a country may not be very considerable. The sum total of illicit gains is no doubt small in relation to the revenue, and there is no evidence from more developed countries where large-scale corruption is common that corruption and inefficiency are necessarily correlated. The taxpayer is of course being robbed, either directly in cash or indirectly by unsuitable appointments being made on his behalf. But by far the more serious loss is the loss of self-respect and the growth of frustration and cynicism. It is above all a moral problem, immeasurable and imponderable. And politicians and civil servants who are guilty are more guilty only in degree than the mass of people whom they represent and are supposed to serve.

*

For while some of the corruption of which one hears in high places has at least a robust and buccaneering flavour, the corruption which one experiences oneself, or learns of at first hand through the tribulations of African dependants, is depressingly mean and squalid; and it is all-pervasive.

It is distressing that people who in the life of family, clan or tribe are generous with one another to the point of destitution should in the world of cash services, and among strangers, become so mean that the simplest service is extorted, quite illicitly, for a 'dash' or rake-off.

It is incongruous that in the merciful professions of nursing and medicine the out-patient must find his twopence for admission, at the head of the queue, to his rightful place; that in the most ignominious of human emergencies the bed-pan can only be secured for a penny; that the pound note is looked for under the pillow of the consulting room of the Government doctor.

To put a man in the way of a job at £5 a month ought, one would have supposed, to be a simple human kindness among people so underprivileged that to have a job at all is to be an aristocrat. To spoil it by the demand of a rake-off of several shillings a week for a year seems grasping and callous.

To learn of the messenger who admits the 'applicant'[1] to the presence of the clerk who may help him onwards to the boss, but only in return for a series of illicit tolls, is not to learn of human nature at its best.

The foregoing facts are too well known to need documentation. Other practices, revealed for example in an official Inquiry into the Lagos Town Council, (a Report which will be more extensively cited later in the chapter) include the exaction of a fee by produce inspectors for every bag of produce that is sealed and graded, and a deduction by pay clerks from the wages of daily paid staff. In another Report, from the Northern Region of Nigeria (which will be cited in the next chapter) there is an interesting note on Veterinary Assistants. The suggestion is made that cattle owners should be warned that it is not necessary to make a 'gift' either to *avoid* cattle inoculations, for the benefit presumably of the superstitious who do not hold with such things, or alternatively to *secure* cattle inoculations, for the benefit of the enlightened. This would seem to suggest

---

[1] An applicant is a man who belongs to a growing profession. It means an unemployed person seeking work.

B

that cattle inoculators have established something which mortal man has never previously achieved—a profession in which it is impossible to go wrong. There are dark warnings also against the payment of a 'gift' to avoid a sanitary inspection of one's compound, to win an early hearing of one's case in court, to get one's vouchers cleared and cashed quickly at the Treasury or to get preferential treatment from agricultural extension workers. Other occasions for human frailty seem to relate to children at school, either in avoiding the experience altogether, getting permission for them to leave early, or securing some special favour, of a kind unspecified; this is already somewhat dated, as the attitude to education has changed recently and rapidly, but it leaves certain questions lingering in the mind.

There is much to be said in mitigation and explanation, and it is said in the next chapter; but the stark reality is unpleasant.

With the police the matter is more serious, for to live in a country where the police are corruptible is to live on a quicksand. For the British in Africa, bearings so familiar that they have never noticed them disappear, leaving them bewildered and insecure. In this kind of insecurity the average African lives his life. In fairness it has to be recalled that the comfortable classes in Britain take a different view of the police from that which is taken by the underprivileged; but even at their least engaging the police in Britain are not systematically corrupt. Again it is unjust to categorize, and there are many good policemen in West Africa in whom the idea that the police are public servants is taking root. But to ignore the other side of the picture would be to bury one's head in the sand, and to show less sympathy than an exploited public deserves.

There are innumerable ways in which the police of any country can use extortion, and it can be argued that if people give way they are as guilty as the police themselves. What matters is the extent to which extortion *is* accepted as normal, or possibly even as reasonable, and in parts of West Africa matters have gone rather far.

The European knows little of what is going on around him, but the evidence of his eyes and ears, and his reading of the newspapers, makes even him familiar with the commonest of rackets—that of the Traffic Police. It is not difficult to find something wrong with the average passenger lorry in Africa. It may be overloaded, or unroadworthy, or unlicensed, or without lights; it may well be all four. It is correctly stopped by the police; after an interval for formal exchanges, during which five or ten shillings is unobtrusively slipped under the wheel, or at the foot of the trunk of a nearby tree, it is allowed, incorrectly, to proceed, sometimes to the common danger.

By coincidence, as these words were being written an article appeared in a Nigerian daily newspaper, by a well-known Nigerian journalist, on 'Cheap Deaths on Nigeria's Roads'. Its closing paragraph was featured in a panel:

'Let bribe givers among vehicle drivers and bribe takers among the police earn the death penalty.'

The coincidence, however, is not far-fetched, for it is a common matter for journalistic comment.

In general, there is little that cannot be bought, and little extortionable that is not extorted.

In local courts it is virtually impossible for the foreigner to pierce the fog; all he knows is that the fog is thick.

These are unrewarding matters about which to write, not only because of their inherent unworthiness, but because every reader, and certainly every African reader, will know so much more about them than the author; though he might be unwilling to be even as explicit. For there is, except as between trusted friends, an inevitable conspiracy of silence.

It is often said that Africans are among the happiest of people, and it is true that a walk through an African village will show more laughing faces, a more obvious contentment with the simple joy of living, than a walk from the Marble Arch to the City, or from Times Square to the Bowery. But for the struggling civil servant, the local council treasurer, the applicant, the unemployed schoolboy, the flotsam and jetsam of the towns, and all others who have been sucked into the stream of competitive twentieth century life, the natural and endearing African happiness has become tarnished by rapacity and graft.

*

One turns to corruption in local government with a mixture of relief and dismay—relief because the actual facts have been more precisely investigated, and can be quoted; dismay because as matters stand at the time of writing local government in the southern Regions of Nigeria[1] has reached the point of being a conspiracy against the public, so riddled is it with bribery, nepotism, politics and corruption.

For many years the critics have been pointing to the folly of the colonial administration in forcing a veneer of British local government on West African territories, supposing in their blindness that a plant which has only been known to flourish in the temperate, misty and kindly atmosphere of England and Wales could be transplanted to the harsh, exotic climate of the African tropics. They happen to have been wrong in their facts, because the colonial administration, from the Colonial Office to the District Officer, has done its best to restrain West African governments from adopting *in toto* a system that they knew could never work; the pressure for its adoption came

---

[1] The North is less well documented.

from within West Africa, and was based on the suspicion that differentiation meant discrimination, that modification meant the second best. (A glance at neighbouring French territories, where fellow Africans assumed that local government as in metropolitan France was the natural order, would have adjusted their thinking on this point.) But with the critics' conclusion no one would quarrel, and no one as far as is known has ever quarrelled; the critics have been fighting over a battlefield already won.

The adoption of British local government, with ultimate power in the hands of elected councillors, but shorn of the restraints of British convention, compromise and mutual respect between elected representative and paid officials has amounted to an open invitation to corruption, an invitation eagerly if incredulously accepted.

The only supposition on which the English kind of local government can rest is that elected councillors are people who for one reason or another wish to serve the community. It may be due to the inherent goodness of their natures alone, or this may be fused in varying degrees with the love of power, the satisfaction of public regard, or an inability to mind their own business; but whatever the motive it could hardly be financial. In West Africa the position is otherwise. A government, presumably in its right senses, proposed to confer on councillors, with minimal constraints, the right to allocate market stalls, to control paid appointments and to award contracts. Even if the bribe required to get on the council in the first place were increased many times over, it would still become a sound investment. Its beneficial results, from the councillors' point of view, are set down in the Reports of a Series of Commissions of Inquiry concerning maladministration and corruption in most of the larger urban authorities in the Eastern and Western Regions of Nigeria. There is no reason to suppose that the position is any different in the smaller rural councils, but open scandals of the kind recorded in these Reports are perhaps more serious, and certainly more difficult to conceal, in the large towns than elsewhere. The councils were given their enhanced powers in the early 1950's; the peak year for Commissions of Inquiry was 1955, though they continue busily at the time of writing.

It may seem strange to an English councillor that the allocation of market stalls should be of such importance to serious men, but among market-minded people in West Africa the possession of a stall in a big market means a comfortable income, of a strategically placed stall comparative wealth, and the control of a number of stalls for illicit sub-letting an enviable unearned competence. It was a principal theme of the wide-ranging Port Harcourt Inquiry,[1]

---

[1] Report of the Commission of Inquiry into the Working of Port Harcourt Town Council, February 1955.

and in the town of Aba it warranted a special Inquiry in itself.[1]

The tendency of councillors to allocate stalls to themselves, their wives, their relations, and then to the highest bidder can only be described as pronounced.

If a man has spent a month, as the author of the Aba Report did, in investigating such a highly specialized racket, he may presumably lose a little of the calm and detachment proper to an administrative officer. At any rate his language was more forthright than that of some of his colleagues working in the same general field, though with their wider opportunities and more varied interests. He was moved to say in his conclusions that he could

'only gasp at the entirely shameless conduct of the councillors and the executive staff. No moral principle and no prick of conscience appears to have entered their minds at any stage. . . . I find that all the councillors must be held jointly responsible for their decisions and actions. Not one has resigned in protest, and not one has asked that his name be recorded as voting against the scandalous allocations of . . . The Chairman of the Council is principally noteworthy for his sanctimonious announcements, deliberately calculated to deceive the public. This makes his deeds even more intolerable . . . My impression of Mr . . . , as a witness and as Chairman of the Markets Committee, is that he is without scruple.'

Although the language is slightly exceptional, the facts, regrettably, are not. There is even a silver lining to his Report, as he postulates the possibility of an honest council:

'Unfortunately, a policy that, in the hands of an honest council, operates satisfactorily and with justice may become an instrument of evil and oppression in the hands of a venal council. One needs two policies: one for the honest council and one for the corrupt council. Regrettably however it is not possible to devise any policy which can wholly defeat the depredations of a dishonest council. At some stage, when it comes to allocating market stalls, it is essential to separate the sheep from the goats if genuine traders only are to be allocated stalls. That means interviews and that in turn means opportunities for corruption.'

Others working in the sphere of local government find it difficult to grasp the concept of an honest council, since such a thing has never come their way; they have grown up with the racket and they assume—who can blame them?—that that is what local government means.

[1] Report of the Inquiry into the Allocation of Market Stalls at Aba, March 1955.

There is no silver lining, in this matter at any rate, in the Report of Mr E. W. J. Nicholson,[1] in ordinary life the Town Clerk of Abingdon, Berks, who in 1956 investigated the affairs of the Ibadan District Council, guardians of the largest African city south of the Sahara. He was satisfied that two councillors interfered directly, and in person, in the letting of stalls in a profitable motor park in Ibadan. The Chairman of this Council said at one point that there was no reason why councillors should be denied the rights of ordinary citizens, and from his own behaviour, as recorded in other parts of the Report, this might be called an understatement.

The control of paid appointments and the award of contracts are less exotic phenomena, and touch a universal chord. The distinguishing features in local government are their pervasiveness and their blatancy.

At the lowest level—the appointment of unskilled labourers—there is no actual evidence that money changes hands. The Port Harcourt Report tells us that

'the Caretaker Council found in the office (i.e. the Town Hall) twenty-one persons who were paid as labourers but known and treated as "office helps", although not so provided in the estimates. Most of these have been newly employed on the recommendation of various councillors, who evidently regarded this minor patronage as one of their perquisites.'

There was an even odder episode in Onitsha, where on one occasion a councillor on his own initiative and authority engaged a gang of labourers and set them to work.

A little higher up the social scale, however, it appeared that a labour overseer might have to pay some £15 for his job, and a case is quoted of a cemetery keeper being mulcted of £23 for a £33 a year rise (*ibid.*):

'It seems to have been almost a recognized practice that junior members of the staff had to pay for any unusual increase in their pay, and that there was no effective means of redress.'

A more sinister trend is the tendency of councillors not only to demand bribes for securing employment but for retaining it—what is known in more conventional gangster circles as protection money. The fact that influential councillors have been to council employees 'in the night'[2] and said that if they do not produce a given sum

[1] Report of the Commission of Inquiry into the Administration of the Ibadan District Council, by E. W. J. Nicholson, LL.B., December 1955.

[2] A phrase widely used in Nigeria to cover a shady transaction; it does not necessarily mean that the deed was done after the hours of darkness, though these are favoured, but indicates rather a state of mind.

within a given time they will be sacked, has long been known to students of local government, who are grateful to Mr Nicholson in his Report on Ibadan for bringing it into the light of day. A considerable section of this Report (p. 20 onwards) is devoted to the almost incredible case of councillors who, to the Commissioner's satisfaction, blandly informed four 'revenue collectors' at the same car park that failure to pay £10 each would result in their dismissal. It is an interesting reflection that the councillors had no doubt that people who collected money on car parks, although presumably earning a bare living wage, would be in a position to pay this money.

'This was perhaps the worst single case brought before the Commission. Taken as a whole it presents an unpleasant picture of corruption and maladministration, containing conspiracy to get rid of the four temporary revenue collectors.'

'Perhaps' is an important word here, for some would think that the case of Mr X was, if possible, more nauseating still. Mr X was a man with a dubious record for trustworthiness, who, having once been dismissed from the Council's service for his behaviour in a case of embezzlement, was reinstated, but only in a position which did not involve the handling of cash. But

'he politely objected to this posting because he had been out of a job for some time *and his reinstatement had cost money*, and he had been promised he would be sent to Dugbe Market. The Treasurer asked him to put his objection in writing, and sent a letter to the Chairman with a minute asking *him* to confirm that Mr X should return to his old job. *The Chairman* endorsed the latter with instructions to the Treasurer to place Mr X in his former job, *which was the collection of market tolls*.' (Author's italics.)

In a lesser known Council[1] it appeared that the Secretary had seized a good deal of what is more usually the councillors' initiative, since evidence was given that he was not only appointing his own relations to posts of sanitary labourers and clerks, but that clerkships outside his own family circle were commanding the respectable price of £80 to £100; though his own appointment was said in evidence to have cost £400, which is above the average for a council of that standing, and reveals that the councillors also were alive to their responsibilities.

The point is introduced because it is common at conferences concerned with local government for the staff to complain that they are hamstrung by the corruption of councillors. Councillors, on the

[1] Report of the Inquiry into the Administration of the Affairs of the Igbo-Etiti District Council, September 1955.

other hand, complain of the nefarious practices of the staff. The harmonious councils are those where councillors and staff are hand-in-glove.

The writer has for many years had personal experience, from first-hand testimony, of the size of bribes payable to local councils for the award of a scholarship or a course in the United Kingdom, which may be between £25 and £50. Only in rare cases does an award seem to be secured without payment.

The point needs no further labouring, and the tale is endless.

But it is the award of Council contracts which provides the richest field for the chosen representatives of the people. It is clear from a perusal of the Reports, as it is from everyday gossip, that a bribe of 10 per cent—a little more, a little less—payable by the successful tenderer to members of the Council is fairly standard practice, as it is indeed in loftier realms. The incompetence, irresponsibility and general fog surrounding many of these contracts is perhaps not strictly relevant to the theme of this book, except in so far as contracts are awarded for considerations other than, or in addition to, the standard 10 per cent; the extra dash, or the tie of blood, can be influential in securing some awards which are not merely stupid but wholly fantastic.

The author of the Igbo-Etiti Report, writing under the euphemistic heading of 'Perverseness in Awarding Contracts', observes that

'it was rare for their the lowest bid to be chosen or the most experienced and competent contractor. In some cases contracts were awarded to tenderers who had never been contractors, e.g. the contract for staff quarters was awarded to . . . , a bicycle repairer.'

A charming case of 'perverseness' is quoted over the award of a tailoring contract, the total value of which was £16 7s 0d. A certain councillor extracted £3, or over 20 per cent, from a tailor for the promise of this contract, in blissful ignorance of the fact that two of his colleagues on the Council had done the same in respect of other tailors. The resultant necessary division of this contract into three, to the value of £5 12s 0d for each part, was scarcely worth the layout of £3, as the tailors bitterly complained.

'What we have here is not merely corruption, but corruption with cheating added.'

This tendency of councillors to claim to be the correct recipient of a bribe, without, as one might say, giving satisfactory credentials, has more than once been a source of embarrassment. It was so for the unfortunate Mr J., a Syrian, who aspired to be awarded a licence to run buses in Lagos, and whose vicissitudes are described by Mr

Bernard Storey, the Town Clerk of Norwich, to whom it fell to investigate the maladministration of the metropolis as early as 1952, and whose report is a classic of dry humour.[1]

Having, according to evidence accepted by the Commissioner, paid £100 in notes to two councillors without result, and having unsuccessfully (one is glad to note) tried to bribe the Mayor, he put himself, to the tune of another £50, into the hands of a self-styled expert in these matters, who appears to have been a sort of professional contact man between the Council and those who sought its favours, and who at least puts himself in a class above the councillors by giving a quite splendid receipt for the money, over a twopenny stamp. But the Syrian emerged unsuccessful from these bitter experiences, as a decision in favour of his rivals was reached by a meeting of the Highways Committee, which was 'attended' incidentally by seven members of the Town Council whose only right to be there was that they represented those rival interests themselves. At this meeting 'pandemonium reigned—everybody shouting the wares of his protegé'.

But out of evil comes good:

'I think that the duplicity of the dishonest councillors was so great that ultimately they deserted those who had bribed them and joined the honest councillors in arriving at a decision which on the whole left little to criticize.'

The award of contracts to firms in which councillors have an interest was later investigated by Mr Nicholson in Ibadan, who singles out not the largest but the most venal of the various cases before him for special condemnation. It concerned, immediately, the supply of chairs for the Town Hall, though the enterprising contractor appears to have been equally ready to supply cutlasses, books and stationery and to remove the Council's night-soil, at terms agreeable to himself and his friends on the Council. The sum to be carved up on the chairs amounted to 12s 6d per chair, or 12½ per cent above the price for which they could normally have been bought retail in a shop. Chicken-feed, no doubt, but of a blatancy so marked as to be called distinguished.

*

The local government Reports, from which a few extracts have been culled merely to give something of their unique flavour, confirm that a monumental miscalculation was made. What was contemplated as public service became private plunder. The public is now paying for this, but as with corruption at higher levels what matters is not so

[1] Report of the Commission of Inquiry into the Administration of the Lagos Town Council, by Bernard Storey, O.B.E., 1953.

much the financial cost as the cynicism which has been bred and the ill repute into which local government as an institution has fallen. Few men of substance and integrity would wish to be associated with it; its staff can only be retained by giving them the status of Regional civil servants, in a so-called 'Unified Local Government Service', thus protecting them from the irresponsibility of councillors. The public, or such of them as know what is going on, shrug their shoulders in fatalistic disgust.

*

The word corruption, as usually employed, means the illicit gain of money or employment, and that is the principal sense in which it is discussed in these pages. A reference to corruption in local government would however be incomplete without some mention of political jobbery, which is corruption of another kind.

Local councils in Africa have tended to become extensions of national or regional political parties; they may be said to combine in one body what in Britain would be found in the local authority, concerned with the administration of services, and the local constituency organizations of the political parties, concerned with winning the next election. This has resulted in some painful situations; dismissal of council staff who were not politically acceptable; the appointment of party men with minimal qualifications for the job, or sometimes less; and the suppression of conscience.

In the higher reaches of the Lagos Town Council Mr Storey felt compelled to write as follows:

'Looked at from whatever angle you will, the incident (of the appointment of the Town Clerk) is calculated political jobbery without a single redeeming feature. It shows a callous disregard for the principles of honest local government, and is a matter of which the Democratic Party in the Lagos Town Council may even now feel ashamed. I condemn it without reserve.'

*

An election is traditionally the *locus classicus* of bribery and corruption, and it is impossible that Nigeria should escape the general infection. On the other hand one does not contemplate the conduct of an election in Nigeria with any great sense of outrage; it is the grotesque rather than the venal that weighs upon the spirit.

At the approach of an election considerable numbers of people lose their heads, and even leaders of ability and standing revert to a tender mental age. Wild and intemperate accusations fill the air. All sense of shame evaporates. The conduct of a campaign is, to put it mildly, uninhibited. This pandemonium, however, is caused by a few people and by the newspapers. Small stage armies of party agents, supporters and hangers-on, concerned more to draw attention, *fortissimo*, to the huge delinquencies of their opponents than to disseminate a creed, roam the streets and tear along the main roads, filling them with sound and fury. The newspapers, who must sell to an unsophisticated public (the lesser ones being themselves barely literate) treat all this as if it were an adult activity. It signifies, in fact, very little.

It has an occasional ugly side, since from time to time the police will find an electioneering van with weapons of a murderous kind. Their investigations generally reveal small parties of thugs on the loose, disowned by their parties, execrated by the mass of the people, and even they themselves whipped up not so much by a lust for blood as by an obsessional conviction that their opponents are doing the same thing; they are beastly, but in the total picture unimportant.

To see the picture in perspective, one has only to consider election day itself, when the melodramatic curtain-raiser is over and the general public takes the stage for the play itself. Almost invariably, election day is calm, level-headed, mature. The ordinary man and woman, unaffected by the vapourings that have gone before, behaves like a textbook citizen. It is a pity that the parties do not rise to the level of the people.

The serious thing from the point of view of national self-respect is the unquestioned assumption that opponents will cheat, and the inordinate effort that goes into the prevention of remote and improbable types of fraud. That fraud takes place, and that some of it is of a wildly improbable kind, is not to be denied; but that it has any significant effect on the results of an election is equally improbable.

In the fevered imaginations of party organizers their opponents plan to insert ink, glue or nitric acid into their ballot boxes,[1] to tear off their names and symbols from them, to forge ballot papers (in which they over-estimate their technical proficiency), to bring in lorry loads of illicit voters, to bribe polling officers.

In cold fact, very few specific allocations are ever made, and most of these dissolve into a mist at the touch of the precise, searching question.

The common allegation that one's supporters (though never one's opponents) are prevented from registering on the electoral roll is answered by the fact that in 1959, for the Federal Election preceding Independence, 87 per cent of those entitled to register actually did so, a high figure by the standards of any country in the world where registration is voluntary and not automatic. To the allegation that they were prevented from going to the poll, the answer is that 79.8 per cent did so, a figure which it would be interesting to compare

[1] Each candidate has his own, with his name and the symbol of his party pasted on it.

with that of the United Kingdom. There may be added the further fact that the ballot was secret, and that no serious complaints were made that it was otherwise. From these uncontrovertible facts it seems that an unusually high proportion of the people both registered and voted, and that the result of the election represented the wishes of the people.

Within this generally satisfactory framework there is undoubtedly bribery and corruption. At the outset of the operation, after nine million people had been issued with registration cards, there was a brisk sale of them. The fact that these transactions were wholly pointless—since the cards were intended as a mere convenience to assist identification on polling day, that people could vote without them, and that they could in fact get a reminder of their identity number nearer the date—is perhaps irrelevant. Here was something which was illegal, the assumption was therefore made that there must be some point in doing it, and the law was broken. Corruption took place. This can be stated categorically, since a number of arrests were made and offenders punished.

Another type of fraud which was almost certainly committed, and which is virtually impossible to prevent under the prevailing voting system, was the illicit sale of ballot papers. The keen minds of party agents realized many years ago that there was nothing to prevent a voter from taking his ballot paper into the booth, inserting it not in the ballot box but into his pocket, emerging with the righteous air of a citizen who has done his public duty, and repairing to the house of a willing buyer; who would towards the end of the day, being himself a voter in good standing, present himself to the polling officer, virtuously draw his own ballot paper and insert it into the box, along with those which he had accumulated during the day. This system was first explained to the writer in 1953, and it has been popular ever since. It cannot be prevented as long as the voter goes into a booth, which is a secret place, and puts an open ballot paper (i.e. one not containing a candidate's name) into the box of his choice—unless he is searched; and it is a gloomy commentary on electoral morals that the Regulations do in fact provide for voters to be searched, and that presiding officers have to arrange for a searching booth, and for a male and female searcher to stand by. Little, if any, use was made of this provision in the Federal Election.

In this matter a pessimistic view is taken of human nature—no doubt justifiably—in the Gambia, where ingenious minds devised the fool-proof way of stopping a man from voting more than once—or at least more than once in any one visit to a polling booth. It could be called the audible method of voting, and provided one could swallow the indignity was simplicity itself. In place of the ballot box was an empty oil-drum, the bottom of which was occupied by a large bell. Instead of a ballot paper the voter was furnished with a small missile, in the nature of a child's marble, which he dropped into the drum and on to the bell. To vote twice was automatically to draw attention to one's transgression, unless one were sufficiently skilful to ensure that missiles hit the bottom simultaneously; for at the second 'ping' the listening representatives of the law would pounce. It is difficult to see any flaw in this, except that it would perhaps be better not to have an election at all than to resort to such indignity, even if its alternative is a modicum of cheating.

It is strange, however, that African leaders, almost morbidly sensitive to criticism from abroad, seem not to appreciate the low stature to which their countries are brought in the estimation of the observer by ignominious practices. Their reply to this admittedly sweeping judgment would be that elections are important, and that acceptance of even a modicum of bribed votes is irresponsible. People will judge the matter differently, and it cannot be resolved. Perhaps what matters most in the present discussion is a sense of proportion. Well over seven million people voted in the Nigerian Federal Election, and most majorities were large. Returning Officers suspected a few cases of the fraud which has been described, for occasionally there were ballot papers which looked suspiciously as if they had been put in the box in a bunch; but proof would have been virtually impossible and no election was validated on this ground. Does one take a steam-hammer to crack a nut, or an oil drum and its fantastic accompaniments to defeat an unknown but probably modest measure of dishonesty?

Another regrettable necessity is the marking of the finger with indelible ink, so that a voter may not present himself more than once, either at the same polling booth or another. In some countries—though not in West Africa—this is treated so seriously that the finger is marked with a silver nitrate pencil, which really leaves a small brand or burn upon the skin, and thus has the advantage over the more conventional indelible ink of being in fact indelible. It may please the connoisseur of the esoteric that a British firm engages in the manufacture of these pencils for use in developing countries, an unknown and unacknowledged service to representative democracy. The indelible ink rarely justifies the enthusiasm of its manufacturers, for if dealt with at once it can be removed by vigorous rubbing in the hair, and if this fails some specific of the type of Milton or Dettol is known to give good results; so that electoral officers are reduced to the degrading necessity of giving instructions that the nail of the finger must be covered with this liquid, experience having shown the nail to be retentive. It would perhaps be simpler to rely on the vigilance of polling agents, who ought to know everybody in a station where only 500 may vote. In any case the removing of the ink is largely done for fun.

These precautions, disagreeable though they are, show that

corruption is taken for granted by those who make the laws, and it cannot be seriously doubted that a lot of it exists. The question is whether the remedy is not worse than the disease. The electoral laws of any country naturally provide against fraud and error, but the question of degree has some importance, and elaborate precautions against bare-faced and deliberate cheating may seem to suggest that the whole process of democratic election may be somewhat premature.

Furthermore, a number of practices are common which, while not amounting to corruption in the venal sense, are nevertheless a corruption of the forms or procedure of democracy.

Electoral regulations, broadly following the United Kingdom pattern, provide an opportunity for anyone left off the roll by accident to claim inclusion, and for anyone to object to the presence of a name on the roll because he thinks it should not be there. The intention of such provisions is to correct *bona fide* mistakes, and in Britain it is largely the registration officers themselves who take advantage of them, to put right their own errors. In parts of Nigeria the matter was regarded in a somewhat different light. According to the published Report of the Federal Electoral Commission, more than 20,000 objections were lodged *in one constituency*, on the assumption that this was a legitimate electoral tactic. The sheer organization of clerical work must have been impressive; the fact of doing it at all, while not corrupt in the strict sense of this inquiry, was nevertheless discreditable, since thousands of those objected to were life-long residents in the place, and according to one newspaper the mass-production of objections, whereby the labour of filling in the name objected to, the reason for objecting to it, and the signing of the objector's name were divided among a team, working at high pressure, resulted in some people objecting to themselves. It was done in the expectation that those objected to would have to prove entitlement, rather than that those objecting should have to prove disqualification, and this is obviously approaching sharp practice. In the end the affair fizzled out ignominiously.

In less extreme cases, large numbers of objections were made because of the belief, rarely proved, that political opponents were drafting supporters to a marginal constituency, either to register themselves falsely as residents or to satisfy some formal requirement of residence which would carry them over polling day and allow them to vote improperly. This belief was not without some foundation in fact in previous elections.

Finally, there was great commotion about the appointment of electoral and polling officials, it being widely alleged that the obvious people to do this work, the staffs of local authorities, were all politically engaged. It seems likely that a good many of them were, and this stems from the largely political nature and purpose of local government in West Africa.

But—and it cannot be too often repeated—all this activity, often degrading, sometimes farcical, is largely carried on by a few people whose professional business it is to do so, and in whom the electorate is not interested. It does not fairly represent the temper of the people, who are on the whole very sensible about elections.

It may be that the most venal aspect of elections, and the most harmful to the national interest, is that about which no vestige of proof can be offered—the purchase of candidatures and seats by bribery. It is rare that anyone who bribes or is bribed reaches the point of saying so, and the chances of ever discovering the facts about this matter are remote.

On the fringe of the problem, light relief is occasionally afforded by the hopeless independent candidate, who invests his deposit in the full intention of withdrawing at the last moment, as some regulations allow, and accepting a consideration from the rival who is in most fear of his vote being split. Occasionally also there are engaging arguments as to whether a 'feast' or any other form of the customary, almost obligatory, African hospitality constitutes 'treating', a cold and inappropriate word for an alien concept.

But the central and troubling question of what proportion of the candidates bribe, how they do it and how much they spend are unanswerable. There are not lacking those who claim to know; but when it comes to the point they will not say. It is clear that a high degree of corruption in government and administration makes candidature a sound and profitable investment, and it is assumed by all that the investment is widely made.

And yet, as was said at the beginning of this section, the sense of outrage is not great. Few would deny that the wishes of the people are broadly represented in the result; the conduct of elections is efficient and on the whole impartial; the behaviour of the public admirable. Most of the complaints of the minority parties are of a political kind, in that they criticize not the conduct of the elections so much as the alleged suppression of basic electoral freedoms by the Government in power. They generally appear, upon investigation, to be exaggerated as the high figures for registration and polling show. And although the existence of bribery and corruption may be taken for granted the young Nigerian idealist does not inveigh against elections, or feel ashamed of them, as he does of the quiet continuing corruption which was discussed in the earlier part of this chapter. His opinion of elected persons is not high, but the manner in which they get elected is not a burden of his conscience.

*

This has been a necessary chapter, in that it would be peculiar to write a book about corruption and say nothing about its manifestations. But it is not a particularly useful one. Nobody who is sufficiently interested to read the book will have learnt anything that he did not already know. It has been wholly unconstructive. And by focusing attention on the bad it may have under-estimated the good. However, it has set the stage for more profitable considerations.

CHAPTER 3

Tout Comprendre c'est Quelquechose Pardonner

———⊶❦⊷———

To judge the venality of bribery and corruption in West Africa by the standards of contemporary Britain would be neither intelligent nor just. A fair judgment must take account of the *mores* of the two societies, a comparison of which will explain a good deal that appears to be culpable; and also of certain pressures within West African society, which will mitigate some of the rest. There remains much that is inexcusable.

The point is perhaps more clearly illustrated by nepotism than by bribery or corruption. Little was said about nepotism, except in passing, in the last chapter. There is really very little to say, except that public life is riddled with it, and that everybody knows this. A book written for publication cannot mention names and cases.

The concept of impartiality, and of appointment by merit, is embodied throughout Africa by the appointment of Public Service Commissions, and these have in fact done excellent work, and at the time of writing are not, in the writer's experience, the subject of malicious gossip. In their first years their Chairmen were expatriates who, being free from family and local pressures, and in every sense disinterested, would, it was hoped, assist these vitally important bodies to win respect. They have been replaced by Africans without any loss of such respect and they are, to use a cliché which puts the point well, bulwarks of the constitution. It is almost impossible to overstate their importance in the coming years. But although they have introduced and maintained objective and honest standards into the appointment of the bulk of the civil service, there is a limit to what they can do in a society which accepts nepotism not as something reprehensible but as a man's first and unquestioned duty.

Britain has had a hundred years to get accustomed to the idea that it is anti-social to advance the claims of relatives for public posts. A manufacturer or a shopkeeper may leave his business to his son, or get his nephew a job in the firm, and no one will think it improper, since he is free to do what he likes with his own. If he has shareholders to consider he will think carefully before recruiting his

C

relations, but except in large firms which have developed bureau-cracies of their own he is free to follow his own judgment, and in any case for the sake of his shareholders and his profits he is unlikely to appoint someone who is incompetent simply because he is related to him. In her public life Britain has enjoyed her golden age of patronage and nepotism, but since the Civil Service reforms of 1854 a distinction has become established between what a man may do with his own money and what he may properly do with the taxpayers' money; and though there have been interesting survivals of patronage into the present century it has become accepted by and large that in recruitment to the public service, including the service of local authorities, entry is by competition, or by merit impartially judged, and that the pulling of strings by influential friends and relations will not merely not help but will disqualify.

This distinction between private and public employment is only a mildly sophisticated one, but it is beyond the level of sophistication of a good deal of thinking in West Africa. There is much to excuse nepotism. Any man rising to a place of importance in politics will be surrounded by relatives and friends looking confidently to him for patronage; the tradition of centuries leaves them in no doubt that he will provide for them, and that if jobs do not exist they will be created. He may grasp the constitutional idea himself, but it is difficult for him to explain it to his kinsmen. Consequently the life of Ministers and other people of importance is made burdensome by nagging and uncreasing demands, as they find themselves enmeshed in the familiar net of family obligation. The writer has been told, in weary and oppressed tones, by Ministers both in Nigeria and Ghana, that a Minister's life seems to consist as to about half in getting people jobs, even down to the grade of messengers and office cleaners, a circumstance which might well surprise a Minister in Whitehall.

In a nutshell, nepotism in the public service in Britain would by now go against the grain of public opinion, and would cause a sense of guilt in both giver and receiver. In Africa uninformed public opinion would be surprised if anything different happened, the sense of guilt on the part of the giver would be mingled with a sense of family duty done, and the recipient would take it for granted. For why should a man become big and powerful except to look after his relations?

The absence of any distinction which is in the least subtle between public and private, or public and party, responsibilities is shown by the constantly recurring problem of the electoral activities of members of Government, who towards election times repeatedly travel at the public expense, as though on public duty, on journeys which are quite openly electoral campaigns. Some of them un-doubtedly know what they are doing, but this is not true of all, for some find the distinction genuinely difficult to comprehend. In the strict sense they are acting corruptly, but only in the context of the *mores* of Great Britain; and an act is presumably only corrupt if society condemns it as such, and if the doer is afflicted with a sense of guilt when he does it; neither of these apply to a great deal of African nepotism.

Public conscience and a sense of private guilt are however taking root in some aspects of public administration which are exceptionally well understood and where feelings run high, and notably in the award of scholarships. The machinery for awarding scholarships impartially is plain for all to see, but no one in Africa would seriously deny, not only that it has been one of the more fruitful fields for bribery, but also that it happens mysteriously that the young relations of the eminent gain scholarships in a manner which, if open and above-board, would destroy the beliefs of the behaviourists and prove the hereditary transmission of talent.

Even the Public Service Commissions cannot altogether swim against the tide of pressure from the highest quarters.

*

The point we wish to establish is that over wide areas of African society nepotism may be regarded as a virtue rather than as a fault; that in more sophisticated circles, where it is accepted as wrong, the pressures of society in general and of families in particular make resistance to it an almost superhuman feat; and that therefore we may regard it with some sympathy and indulgence. Similarly, there is a good deal to be said, not in defence of corruption as such, but in mitigation of the deed. It derives partly from anachronistic custom and partly from the exceptionally harsh economic pressures of a rapidly changing and developing society. It is perhaps unnecessary to say that it derives also from simple avarice.

*

Mr. Bernard Storey, in his Report on the Lagos Town Council, has this to say:

It is a custom of West African life (I am informed by those who have spent many years in the country and by Africans themselves) that a person in authority is entitled to expect (and not merely demand) and to receive some form of consideration (formerly a gift in kind but now usually cash) for something done, in the course of exercising his authority, to the benefit of the giver. . . .' (p. 49, para. 280).

He then goes on to cite, as illustrations of persons in authority doing something in the exercise of that authority, the dreary chronicle of nurses, clerks, police and produce inspectors. This was written in

1952. Ten years later it can be said with confidence that the custom of exchanging gifts, regarded as a courtesy of life between the high and the low, or between host and guest, is fast diminishing.

Ten years ago it was a familiar embarrassment to overseas visitors, travelling with one suitcase and moving on by air the next day, to be presented with a splendid bowl of eggs, a brace of live chickens, or as happened to the writer in Togoland on one occasion, a magnificent ram. The embarrassment used to be twofold—what to do with these indigestible gifts without causing offence, and how to return them, also in kind, but to a value appropriate to the presumed relative importance of host and guest, from the contents of a night-stop bag. This dilemma is largely over and done with, at any rate on the beaten track. This may be partly because visitors now come not as single spies but as battalions of spies, so that even African customary hospitality has had to bow beneath the weight of expense; but it is more probably because general sophistication has spread, and people have realized that this sort of thing is not customary, and indeed would be highly inconvenient, in the wider world.

That this is not just the narrow view of an expatriate visitor, but does genuinely represent a trend of opinion, is shown in a Report—of which more use will be made presently—the Report on the Exchange of Customary Presents in the Northern Region of Nigeria, written as long ago as 1954, which says at one point:

'There is no doubt that the scale of compulsory gifts . . . has decreased considerably in recent years with the growing enlightenment of the *talakawa*'
and again
'The payments also appear to be decreasing in extent and it may, therefore, be assumed that the public are becoming more sophisticated in their attitude to gifts of this kind.'

If a social trend has penetrated the consciousness of the *talakawa* of the Northern Region it is unlikely that the wide boys of Lagos will have been unaware of it, and a defence of their depredations based on custom and tradition cannot have much weight in 1962.

Furthermore it is difficult to accept the implication that a cash payment, in lieu of the customary gift, has the venerable sanction of native custom. The exchange of gifts, in its pristine innocence and in its traditional setting, took place between men who had hardly entered the competitive, literate, busy western world. At its best, it is difficult to imagine the £5 note being substituted for the ram, or five shillings for the bowl of eggs. It is at best a debasement of native custom.

The matter is admittedly debatable, and involves odd subtleties. If we may revert to the traveller from overseas, it is not so many

years since there was no scale of overnight claims for official hospitality, and those who wandered round from one District Commissioner to another did so at their host's expense. Common
courtesy demanded that one acknowledged this, and it was acceptable
to native law and custom as between expatriates that a bottle of whisky
should be presented on departure. To carry six bottles of whisky in
one's baggage, apart from the fact that it could be misinterpreted, is
less convenient than to carry six pound notes (alas, the equivalent
value at the time); yet to present one's hostess with a pound note on
leaving her house would not have been easy. The difference between
the pound note and the bottle of whisky, which probably had the
price indelibly stamped upon it in any case, was subtle to a fantastic
degree, yet it was important. There are many occasions in British
social usage when the gift of flowers or fruit, or the present bought in
a shop, would be acceptable, while the offer of their cash value would
be offensive in the extreme. Similarly it is an odd circumstance that
one may stay in a man's house and consume his food and drink to
the value of several pounds with a clear social conscience, but
should you require a threepenny stamp for him custom demands that
you give him exactly threepence in exchange, stamps being too
closely associated with cash to make the gift acceptable.

Only a professional anthropologist, and a fairly specialized one at
that, could say what corresponding subtleties exist in African society.
But it is straining credulity to compare the offering of eggs, chickens
or a goat to a village personage whose office is hallowed by tradition
with greasing the palm of the nurse, clerk, produce inspector or
policeman. For one thing, the latter are not persons of inherent
dignity but minor functionaries in a bureaucracy, and neither
bureaucracies or their functionaries form part of indigenous
tradition.

*

However, the existence of a bureaucracy, and the consequent growth
of a large number of people who are in a position to bestow favours,
has introduced one new subtlety, easy to comprehend if not to
define, namely the difference between a customary gift and a bribe.
To this problem the Government of the Northern Region addressed
itself in 1954.

The Report on the Exchange of Customary Presents, published by
the Nigerian Government Printer in that year, is an instructive and
possibly unique document. It began with a resolution in the Northern
House of Chiefs on February 26, 1952, moved by the Emir of
Gwandu, in these terms:

'That this House, agreeing that bribery and corruption are widely
prevalent in all walks of life, recommends that Native Authorities

should make every effort to trace and punish offenders with strict impartiality and to educate public opinion against bribery and corruption.'

The resolution, which was carried unanimously, resulted however in a somewhat different kind of inquiry—the study of the customary exchange of presents between 'Chiefs and District and Village Heads and their people'. The whole of the subsequent inquiry was of course conducted on the borderline of bribery and corruption; the reports from Residents which formed the basis of its conclusions dealt widely and deeply with these topics, and it is understood that some startling facts emerged, which are unfortunately classified as confidential and are not available to the student; but the actual Report was not about bribery and corruption as such, since these are already dealt with under the criminal law, but about the related topic of custom, its use and abuse, and its adaptation to the twentieth century. This makes it a more, not less, valuable source of information from the point of view of this chapter.

Two paragraphs identify the problem so succinctly that we quote them *verbatim*:

'12. . . . the view was expressed in one quarter that it would not be be possible to forbid the customary exchanges of gifts in any form on the ground that these exchanges were an integral part of social behaviour, that the gifts from the richer to the poorer were alms the giving of which was a religious duty and that many poor and aged people who at present lived in reasonable comfort would find themselves destitute if the giving of presents, which often in their case were return presents, was forbidden. This view, it should be emphasized, was an isolated one but it was one to which the Committee felt that it must give the most careful attention, if only because of the religious and charitable issues alleged to be involved.

'13. After prolonged and detailed consideration of the material at its disposal the Committee felt bound to say that, even though it recognized that customary gifts were far from a simple problem and involved the whole social system, it could not fully subscribe to the opinion put forward above. The evidence showed that only a very few customary gifts had origin in religious observance or charitable motives. The remainder were purely secular and ceremonial and in far too many cases nowadays (whatever may have been the case in the past) merely served the ends of *Neman Girma*, prestige, ostentation or avarice.'

What was required, therefore, was to distinguish between one kind of gift and another, and this could not easily be done since one category faded into the next, and there were no sharp edges. Nevertheless, the distinctions which the Committee made assist clear thinking.

The existence of 'legitimate gifts' is naturally acknowledged; they include the presents brought by guests to the party on the occasion of recognized ceremonials, and of course alms given out of compassion to the old, infirm or helpless (though a severe reference to parasites and hangers-on suggests that this is no simple matter). But 'legitimate gifts' fade into 'disguised bribes', and the problem becomes involved because the folk about whom this Report was mostly written were not the city slickers but the humble peasants, who are drawn into an evil system with no consciousness of wrongdoing. The offering of the guest, or even the tribute to the traditional superior, becomes an exaction by an official who has no shred of traditional entitlement to it; in other words a racket.

But most people, including the victims, are not aware that it is a racket, and public opinion does not react against it. There were—

'simple folk who genuinely believed that it was customary and legitimate for a labourer to make regular monthly contributions to those above him, or for a litigant to give a native court judge a thankoffering after a case was successfully over or for a candidate for clan headship to distribute money to every member of the clan. To the educated, however, these were obviously cases of bribery and extortion.'

It is at about this point, however, that the Committee was able to say that, looking over the years, the scale and extent of these gifts was decreasing, and as the Report was written in 1954 there is hope that the diminution has continued.

There was a further distinction of gifts which were in origin traditional and therefore 'legitimate', but which had grown to such ostentatious size as to constitute an abuse of tradition, and indeed to have become a burden on the community as a whole, including even the more enlightened recipients; but it seems that this problem, at any rate in its extreme form, may be local to the North of Nigeria —the Salla Festival being one of the great occasions for it—and it need not therefore be developed in this study.

The rest of the Report is concerned with proposals for reform, and specifically with propaganda and the education of public opinion. They are interesting, but as to whether they have been effective there is, according to recent inquiries by the writer, little evidence.

*

A factor which contributes to bribery and corruption among town dweller and peasant alike, and which increases its severity, is the ingrained and universal love of ostentation. On the whole the traditional education of the African—in extended family and age grade—was aimed at conformity; the individual only had meaning in as far as he fitted into a system of relationships, and independence of thought and action would have been discouraged, even if it had been comprehensible. But from time to time there would emerge the big man who surpassed his fellows in physical achievement and bravery in battle; to him excessive adulation would be paid, and songs of praise, embarrassingly sycophantic to modern ears, would be sung; retinues of admirers, or hangers-on, would surround him, and precede him on his journeys. The tradition of the 'big man' persists, but wealth and possessions have replaced valour in war as the criterion of bigness, and these generally come by way of politics. The praise-singers, the cheer-leaders and the sycophants remain, however, and this explains to fuss, so strange to western observers, which still surrounds politicians, and which could hardly be explained in terms of their political achievements. To act humbly even if you are a great man requires sophistication. It may of course be that this kind of sophistication is irrelevant to West African society, that one should not seek to strive for it, and that the sociologist would be surprised that one should even consider doing so. On the other hand it may be something which inevitably follows education, the change of spiritual values which this engenders, and absorption into other cultures. Most political parties in West Africa, and their importance and representativeness can hardly be denied, are anxious to claim that they are 'socialist', and though their interpretation of this word may legitimately differ from that of Keir Hardy or Professor Tawney, as indeed it does, it can hardly include extravagant living on the material plane, if it is to maintain any shred of its dictionary meaning.

That sophistication of this kind may eventually take root in Africa is also supported by the fact that it already exists. But those who have achieved it find themselves trapped in the curious dilemma that if they put their principles into practice they will lose face, and consequently lose money and career. The successful lawyer cannot afford to run a modest car or live in a modest house or he will cease to be successful. There is of course nothing new in this, as is seen from a glance at the habits of film stars or tycoons, or at the buildings of banks or insurance companies, in Europe or America, but the characteristic thing about ostentation in West Africa is its pervasiveness and degree.

The facts that the retinue of politician or District Head must resemble those of an oriental potentate; that the graduate on his first job must possess a motor car that his counterpart in Britain might aspire to on retirement; that the labourer must possess a wrist watch and a fountain pen—with every intermediate gradation among the classes—these represent financial burdens which were appropriate, *mutatis mutandis*, to a society which did not have to live on cash salaries, but which in modern West Africa lead many to corruption and some to the magistrate's court. Again, for an inside view of this, the reader is referred to Chinua Achebe's junior civil servant, whose final downfall was caused by the insurance on his unnecessary motor car and the replacement of its tyres. It may be answered that his motor car was not unnecessary, since the Government gave him an advance for it. The Government is wrong. There are far simpler ways of solving this problem, even in a country as lacking in public transport as Nigeria. But it is relevant to note that the Government assisted its servant on the downward path by perpetuating a colonial standard of life which had been fixed, for themselves, by an expatriate administration.[1]

Not that the average man appears to need assistance on this path. He plunges all too eagerly along it of his own accord, as is shown by the unfinished houses, built beyond the owners' means, and the fantastic imbroglio of debt in which so many live. A country which on any comparative world list is among the poorest has taken to itself a standard of living appropriate to the top bracket.

All this helps to explain and mitigate, if not to excuse, bribery and corruption.

*

Another mitigating factor is the carry-over into a wage-earning economy of a vast network of family obligation appropriate to a simpler age. This too is diminishing, but it tends to diminish at the top instead of at the bottom where men can least afford it.

The wide family obligations of Africans and the comparatively narrow ones of Europeans are sometimes contrasted as though human nature and family affection differed fundamentally between the two races. It seems more probable that one kind of obligation becomes gradually transformed into the other as a result of moving from a self-supporting and communal existence on the land to a wage-earning and individualistic way of life in towns.

Unfortunately in West Africa this has not happened gradually but suddenly. It has meant that a man living on an inelastic wage, in an inelastic house—in conditions that is to say in which his only reasonable family obligation would be to his children and his parents —is still having to assume the obligations appropriate to the village

---

[1] Cp. The Prime Minister of Nigeria—' "I wish I had the courage to downgrade all salaries to the levels which we can afford to pay." But with a deprecating smile he said that neither he nor his colleagues had or were likely to have such courage.' (*West Africa*—September 15, 1962.)

and the farm in the setting of the tribe; where food from the earth can be stretched a little further than a wage, and where the family is not hemmed in by walls and streets. There comes a point beyond which this quite literally cannot be done any longer.

In Britain a man has an absolute obligation to support his children and his parents; society would censure him if he failed in either duty —indeed the law would step in and compel him to fulfil his natural obligations. But his obligations would not necessarily go further than this. They may very well do so, as the strength of family ties varies from one family to another, but neither public opinion, nor the opinion of his friends, nor the law of the land would compel him to support his cousins or his nephews, or indeed his own brothers, in the same way that they would compel him to support his children or his parents.

By contrast in Africa most men—for only a very few are emancipated from this—have an unquestioned obligation to share money, food and house with a very wide circle; a young man, almost a boy himself, must pay for the education of younger brothers, and if he has himself moved into the stratum of modern professional employment, he must carry the double burden; if a man prospers and makes money he will often find that he grows no richer because the more he earns the more people he must share it with.

Several generations must pass before these obligations begin to accord with the everyday facts, including the facts of housing; for those who continue to flock to the towns, where they seek, and find, shelter with a kinsman, cannot imagine what the pattern of life there is like until they experience it. They do not know that there is, literally, no land on which food may be grown, and that every item of food must therefore be paid for; that there is no employment; and that the familiar props of existence will be knocked away. He cannot, or will not, return, and his kinsman, who cannot by custom fail him, must take on new and finally crushing responsibilities.

On a short view, we must be thankful that the net of family or tribal obligation is so strong, since it is all that there is to hold up the thousands of unemployed young men in the towns of West Africa. If this net were to break under the strain the results could be very serious; and it cannot go on taking added weight indefinitely. On a longer view we must hope that Africans will not for ever have to live in two worlds, either of which imposes burdens sufficiently hard to bear. For family obligations of a proportion now unimaginable to an Englishman add to the other pressures which keep pushing the swimmer under water. From his earnings, and his equally meagre perquisites, the average townsman simply cannot do what his own custom imposes on him. It is impossible to keep out of debt, and corruption thrives on indebtedness.

*

Lastly, there is simple poverty. Ostentation and the support of numerous relatives could by themselves make anybody poor, but quite apart from this there are in West Africa, two worlds perhaps even more distinct than the two worlds of Disraeli's England. There is of course no evidence from any age or country that the rich are less corrupt than the poor, and it would therefore be misleading to imply that if people were not so poor they would be less corrupt. The evidence points in fact the other way, for the appetite grows by what it feeds on, and when one thinks of corruption in West Africa the mind does not naturally turn to the masses of poor people, whose resources are indeed so slender that there is little about which they could be corrupt, but to the glossy and well-fed.

But the mere fact of living in two worlds, or even worse of living with one foot uneasily in each but with the obligations of both, is in itself unsettling, and inimical to the growth of private conscience and public morality alike; while the poverty of the lower world is poverty indeed for the urban wage earner. It is an ironical though familiar fact that whereas the African of the village and the bush is contented, his wants being few and his joys simple, his sons are so intolerably bored and discontented that nothing will satisfy them but to ex-exchange this frustration, which is at least well-fed frustration, for the frustration of the towns where it is not always easy to eat.

Nigeria is at the difficult stage through which all countries seem to pass, of suffering extremes of poverty and wealth, and of living in fact on two completely different levels. Even today, Edwardian England seems incomprehensible, though so many people are still living who saw it through adult eyes; the glaring contrast between the luxury and ostentation of, for example, the country house week-end of the upper classes, and the degradation of the slums; the fact that a family lived for a week on the price of one good lunch in a West End restaurant—these and a hundred other contrasts now seem extraordinary.

They exist, reproduced with remarkable exactitude, in Nigeria today. Young men from the universities start work at £1,000 a year, professional men earn many thousands, a meal and a bed at a hotel costs five or six pounds, an indifferent meal in a restaurant fifteen shillings. The wage of a labourer or servant is £5 or £6 a month; the salaries of clerks are reckoned in such figures as £84, £96 or £104 per annum. £10 does not go very far, is certainly not extravagant, for a dinner party for a few friends; the steward who serves it has that amount, if he is more than averagely well-paid, to support his wife and family for a month. The same thing, one assumes, may be found in Asia and the Middle East, and in other parts of Africa itself. The following words, written by the present author of East Africa, are not altogether untrue of the West:

'The most significant fact about urban East Africa is that no Government or employer can even make the assumption, that is taken for granted in most parts of the world, that a man's wage should be sufficient to feed, house, clothe and generally support himself and his family. One of the documents of major importance to East Africa is the Kenya Report of the Committee on African Wages (1954), usually known as the Carpenter Report, in which we read that "approximately one half of the urban workers in private industry, and approximately one quarter of those in the public service, are in receipt of wages insufficient to provide for their basic, essential needs". The Government of Uganda, in reviewing its own wages policy in 1955, laid down as a general principle that it should work towards a state of affairs when a man's wage would support himself and his family, while admitting that to do so immediately would be impracticable without a significant increase in the revenue, which could only come from higher taxation. This is the most important fact about the urban situation, and one which is not paralleled today in "western" societies. As a result of the work of the Carpenter Committee there has grown up a new comprehension of what a wages policy should be, and some of the lowest wages have improved, but only to the point when existence on wages is possible, not to the point when it is enjoyable or even tolerable.'

A wage policy of 7s 6d a day for the lowest paid workers in the public service has been advanced by West African political parties as an immediate step forward, though a figure as large as this is not by any means the rule at the moment. It is barely possible to support a family on this wage.

In Victorian and Edwardian England this does not seem to have been necessarily destructive of morality. The honesty, thrift and self-respect of the very poor was often striking, and the integrity and principle of the early working-class movements, trade unions, friendly societies and the like, seem more and not less impressive than those of the labour movement in the affluent 1960s. But the Nigerian urban proletariat today lives in a world of more expansive ideas about equality than did the Victorians, of less rigid sanctions in matters of personal behaviour, and in a society which has been more violently disturbed. The field of temptation is correspondingly stronger, and a word to which the Victorians gave a quasi-religious flavour—thrift—is seldom heard.

*

We have tried to put forward, so to speak, the case for the defence; the reasons why African bribery and corruption should not be judged by the standards of contemporary Britain. It is not pretended that it is a powerful case since the people whom it defends most strongly are those against whom least complaint is made.

The customary exchange of gifts has affected the general climate of behaviour, but is a declining force, and cannot be quoted as a defence against the more iniquitous practices of today; the love of ostentation is something which a nation with aspirations towards equality and welfare must control and overcome; family obligation is a heavy drain on the salary and wage earner, and forces many thousands into debt, and the existence side by side of two nations with two unrelated standards of living, with traditional pressures weighing more heavily on the poor than on the rich, makes corruption a matter for no surprise and only modified reproach.

The case, such as it is, is a defence of private corruption, which usually starts with debt, which in turn is caused by intolerable private pressures. It is not this kind of corruption which is lowering to national self-respect, which causes frustration and anger on the part of honest men, or which breeds cynicism and revolt. This is brought about by public corruption on the part of elected representatives or holders of well-paid responsible public office. For this, the case that has been made is no defence at all. The simple cause of corruption in public life has nothing to do with traditional values, with the African personality, or with the adaptation to western values; those responsible for it have no difficulty in adapting to western values if they want to. Its simple cause is avarice; the wrong that is done is done in the full knowledge that it is wrong, for the concept of theft does not vary as between Christian and Muslim, African and European, or primitive man and Minister of the Crown.

CHAPTER 4

A Question of Loyalties

The foregoing chapters have been depressing, and it is hoped in this one to do something to restore the balance, and to show African leadership in a more agreeable and responsible light. But first it will be appropriate to sketch in the background of the situation which has produced these disappointments, and has caused some men lacking in strength of character or social conscience to behave in the manner of Horatio Bottomley rather than as men responsible for a new nation and responsible to millions of poor and simple people.

For fifty or sixty years Nigeria was a British Colony ruled by foreigners, with the result that government was always 'they', and never 'we'; a friend up to a point, it was an enemy at the deepest level; commanding respect and esteem, it never won loyalty or affection. It was legitimate field for plunder, though the precautions which it took against being plundered were usually adequate. Its greatest fault was an inability to delegate, trust or train; to the very end colonial service officers worked themselves into the ground with a conscientiousness that would have been awe-inspiring if it had been directed towards producing capable successors; as it was, it was often pointless.

The results of this were, first, and somewhat nebulously no doubt, a habit of African irresponsibility towards those in power, carried over into the days when power came to Africans themselves; and second, an almost total absence of senior African civil servants who had themselves been trained in honest and responsible attitudes to public business. Instead of a second or third generation, with roots in a public service tradition, there was last-minute improvisation, resulting in young men of few qualifications and no experience leaping into positions which should have been held by their fathers before them, but which had in fact been held by devoted but mis-guided foreigners. Their youth had some bearing on the matter, since the members of the new legislatures and governments, often scarcely older or more experienced themselves, might have accepted advice and restraint from African civil servants of standing, old enough perhaps to be their fathers. Except at the highest level they would take neither from the few retiring British, or from African boys, as they considered them, straight from school. There was a missing generation of Africans. Accordingly, again except in a few of the highest positions, the new rulers moved into a framework that was pliant instead of rigorous.

Years before they had been preceded by a much larger body of elected representatives in the local councils, where of course there was no expatriate framework to the council staffs. The latter, ill-paid poor relations of the civil service, were even more pliable, subject to the will of ill-qualified and frequently unscrupulous councillors, and easily engulfed in party politics.

It is unjust to generalize about the early legislators, in whose ranks were men of ability and integrity. It would not, however, be unfair to say that they were generally younger or more inexperienced than their responsibilities justified, and that for the most part they were not men who, before representing their constituents in Parliament, had gained eminence in other walks of life, or who had continuing careers outside Parliament, or who had a business or profession on which to fall back—the sheet-anchor of the British politician and the source from which he derives a measure of independence. Britain, after a long parliamentary history, is being faced squarely with this question of the professional politician, who is not part of her tradition, and whose position is in important ways weaker than that of the amateur. The pressures of a parliamentary career tend to increase their number, and there is a school of thought which would uphold them in principle, but public opinion generally would regret their dominance in the British Parliament. In West Africa the professional politician took the stage from the beginning.

One aspect of the situation was that the financial rewards of success at an election acquired an inappropriate importance. Even the salary attaching to membership of a legislature, not usually a determining factor in the mind of a British MP, often represented a very much higher income than that to which his Nigerian counterpart had been accustomed. So much so that more than once an unusually naïve or unusually honest representative has complained how much the investment cost him!

All these factors in combination, together with those discussed in the last chapter, brought a materialistic element into a political career, in terms of simple financial gain. It would be absurd to suggest that politicians elsewhere are starry-eyed idealists, and indifferent to their pockets, since a career in politics is as tough and ruthless as any, and more uncertain than most. On the other hand, a distinction may be made between the struggle for power, influence and reputation on the one hand, gambling with success or failure, and cold-blooded personal financial gain on the other.

At the level of local government, as we have seen, there was even more personal avarice, sometimes of the crudest kind.

*

We turn to the more agreeable side of the picture, and first it is necessary to acknowledge that a book about corruption must tend to be unjust to those whose integrity is beyond question. Throughout this dismal narrative these men have not received their due. Their task is doubly hard, and their position doubly admirable, because of the corruption which surrounds them. At this point, therefore, let them be paid a warm and admiring tribute. That the ethic of integrity could govern Nigerian public life is shown by their example and by that of many colleagues in the professions, and especially on the Judicial Bench.

But this is proved even more strongly in another way, that is in the honest, unselfish and efficient administration of certain indigenous institutions.

*

The tribal unions of southern Nigeria, and especially of Eastern Nigeria, have caught the attention of a few wandering scholars[1] who have written about them, but on the whole they have not been publicized, and Nigerians themselves have been reticent about them, as they regard them with a certain ambivalence.

The use of the word 'tribe' reveals a deficiency in the English vocabulary. It is customarily used, as any dictionary definition will show, or pre-literate or even primitive people, and is inappropriate to the developing countries of the Commonwealth. The difficulty is to say what word *is* appropriate, to describe such people as the Yorubas or Ibos, for example, who possess a distinctive language, tradition and culture, of which they are proud and to which they are loyal, but whose numbers and whose position in the corporate entity of Nigeria make it difficult to describe them as nations, which otherwise would be a more appropriate word; in any case there are many smaller tribes which could never sensibly be described as nations. Accordingly, *faute de mieux*, we speak of tribes.

The tribal loyalty is immensely strong—stronger by far among the mass of people than loyalty to Region or Federation—and it bears fruit in extremely practical ways.

These associations have followed the diffusion, first of the Ibo people and then of others, which has come about as the result of better communications, urban employment and the transfer of civil servants and employees of commercial firms from one part of the country to another. Finding themselves exiles in a 'foreign' town, they have regrouped, like the London Welsh or the Society of York-

---

[1] Especially that of Professor James Coleman, of the University of California, to whom acknowledgment is made for much of what follows.

shiremen, but instead of merely playing Rugby football or keeping alive traditional songs and festivals (though they do this as well) they have become pioneers in social progress.

The first regroupings, which were as recent as the 1920s, were very local in character, being based upon 'the kinship group and the town or village where the lineage is localized', but with the passing of time they began to federate, firstly, and a little strangely, on the basis of the colonial government's organization of Division and Province, and later on an all-tribal basis. Thus, examples of the names of early pioneers were the Naze *Family* Meeting and the Ngwa *Clan* Union; of the middle period the Owerri *Divisional* Union; of the later period the Ibo *State* Union and the Edo *National* Union. Others took on names associated with the idea of progress, such as Improvement League, Progressive Union and Renascent Convention, which names they quickly justified. For although their first purpose when they get together as 'expatriates' in Lagos or Ibadan was mutual aid and comfort, and gatherings for local songs and dances, they soon took on serious responsibilities towards their rural homelands, where 'home' branches also began to be formed. Between them the 'expatriate' and 'home' branches have raised and administered considerable sums of money which have been spent principally on building primary schools, paying for scholarships to secondary schools and overseas universities, and improving the physical condition of the villages. They have also come to have a powerful influence, partly official and partly unofficial, in the local government councils, and have formed a training grounds for future political leaders—indeed the overwhelming majority of members of the first Eastern and Western legislatures were men who had been prominent leaders in their tribal associations. In the cities of their origin the unions have provided a substitute for state social insurance.

The material achievements are sufficiently impressive, but what is more to the point of this study is the voluntary and democratic nature of their organization. Clan or union meetings are held regularly and are well-attended, and include established professional men and traders as well as the daily paid labourer. The Englishman, reasonably enough, is apt to compare the debt which the state owes in Britain to the voluntary organizations, and the flexibility and human understanding which they still provide, with the suffocating atmosphere of bureaucracy in which corresponding social progress has to develop in Nigeria. He deplores the fact that voluntary organizations do not take root in West Africa, overlooking the fact that they are there in rich profusion already, but that on the whole the purposes which they serve are ancient and not modern purposes. The unions are a welcome exception, for even more to the point is their lively spontaneity and success in comparison with the dragging footsteps and exiguous achievements of the local authorities.

D

The latter, government-sponsored and copied from a foreign model, associated in their early years with the colonial administration, have, as was shown in a previous chapter, a sad record of muddle, corruption and strife. Although no accounts are published by tribal associations, and although no foreigner could be privy to their counsels, it is apparent from what they do that the unions are handling sums of money comparable to those of many local authorities, that they are spending it constructively, *and that they are handling it honestly.* Enough has already been said about corruption in local government, but this one point may be added—that whereas councillors bribe and council treasurers abscond with the cash without greatly shocking public opinion, the treasurers and committee members of the unions do not do so. . . . The writer cannot possibly know this from personal experience, and scandals would never get into the newspapers, but he has checked it sufficiently often with Nigerians from many walks of life to say it with confidence.

This is a point of crucial importance. To put your fingers in the till of the local authority will not unduly burden your conscience, and people may well think you are a smart fellow and envy you your opportunities. To steal the funds of the union would offend the public conscience and ostracize you from society. The ethic is there, but it has not yet been transferred from the seat of natural loyalty, which is the clan or tribe, to the new seat of loyalty which is the State.

The unions show that Nigerians are as capable as anybody of public as well as private integrity, provided that their deepest loyalties are engaged.

How soon loyalty to tribe will give place to loyalty to the Nigerian nation is a question on which much besides the abatement of corruption is involved—indeed the whole political future of the country in the next decade. Evidence from Nigeria's dealings with the outside world leaves no doubt that the transference has begun, for in the first year of independence Nigerians, irrespective of tribe or party, have shown pride in the part which the Federal Government has played in the Congo, in the Commonwealth Prime Ministers' Conference, and in the counsels of the United Nations. So long as it is a question of Nigeria *vis-à-vis* the rest of the world there is loyalty to national leaders, and the only serious dissensions that have arisen concern Nigeria's alignment in the grouping of other African states.

Internally, the position is not so simple. Political party leaders assent with their minds and pay tribute in their speeches to the ideal of nation-wide parties, separated by social and economic beliefs rather than by Region or by race, but it is difficult for them to cast off their own tribal origins, and more especially to win support among people in other Regions and of different origins. The British administration, and in particular Sir Arthur Richards, now Lord

Milverton, has often been blamed for dividing Nigeria by creating a federal state based on three somewhat arbitrary Regions, but since Independence the tendency has been towards further division and not towards integration; to the tribal factor is added the religious one, since Islam in the North has many stronger affinities with co-religionists outside the borders of Nigeria than with co-nationalists who are her southern neighbours.

Nigerians are well aware of this, and hence the ambivalence which was mentioned earlier towards the tribal unions. It is urgent from the point of view of national interest that tribalism should diminish, and that the tribe should take its proper place as a focus of cultural instead of political loyalty. It is not altogether palatable therefore that the achievements of the unions should be made known or their activities encouraged. The dilemma is a genuine one, and the ambivalence must not be treated lightly or critically.

On the one hand, the tribal unions are the most characteristically Nigerian political institution of the modern Nigerian State; yet their existence is in fundamental contradiction to Statehood. Their work is more effective than that of the local organs of constitutional government, and it is work of high importance; yet the longer it continues to be done tribally the more Nigerian nationhood is retarded. In the long run it would benefit the country if community development and education were channelled through local government and not through extra-constitutional organs based on kinship and lineage; in the short run their achievements are too valuable to be lightly cast aside. In any case the question of casting them aside hardly arises, since a state with pretensions to democracy cannot suppress or control spontaneous and useful work by voluntary organizations, even if it only benefits kinsmen or co-tribalists.

By what means the transference of loyalty from the tribal union to the local and Regional authority can be accelerated is outside the scope of this book. We revert to the point that ability to administer corporate affairs with integrity has been demonstrated by the unions, and that this may suggest that integrity in modern representative government is not an unattainable ideal.

*

We now turn to an examination of bribery and corruption in the recent history of Britain.

Postscript

On page 14 were marked that 'It is frustrating to try to write, one's phrases wrapped in a cocoon of ambiguity, about something which everbody knows, which can rarely be proved, and which may lead to serious trouble if one is the least incautious. Perhaps that is why studies of contemporary corruption are rare.' We were speaking then of 'corruption in high places'.

Since these words were written a Report[1] has been published which allows us to indicate a little more clearly, without offending against the law of libel, the scope and nature of the kind of transactions we had in mind.

It is the Report of a Commission of Inquiry, presided over by a High Court judge, and not the verdict of a court of law. No one stands convicted of any offence. Nevertheless, its observations are remarkably forthright, a provisional map of corruption has been sketched, and the Commission has recommended prosecution at a number of points.

A political party is alleged systematically to have transferred large sums of public money to its own use through the device of a so-called Investment and Properties Corporation. Between 1958 (when it was incorporated) and 1962 'over £4 million passed into the coffers' of the party concerned, 'a large part of which was spent on electioneering'. Other sums, running into seven figures, were, by such devices as the juggling of bank accounts, or the purchase of properties with public money at prices far higher than valuation, diverted to party or private use. Considerable personal benefits were obtained by highly placed individuals, who were able to obtain the money with little or no regard for the normal controls over public expenditure. Apart from these allegedly criminal acts, huge sums of money were spent on legitimate objects, but with incredible recklessness, extravagance and disregard of accounting procedures.

The findings of the Commission have been vigorously challenged by the party concerned as being biased and intemperate, and as exceeding the proper scope of a fact-finding Commission. It is interesting, however, that while the transfer of public funds to the

[1] Report of a Commission of Inquiry into the Statutory Corporations of the Western Region of Nigeria: Federal Government of Nigeria, 4 vols., January 1962, 20s.

party, and their use for election purposes, is not seriously challenged as a question of fact, many members of the party do not regard this as corrupt, since they do not draw a distinction between Party and Government, and accept without question that the Party, rather than Parliament, is supreme—a not unusual attitude in Africa generally. Others, who feel less comfortable on this issue, nevertheless regard it as a fine, and debatable, point of political ethics, rather than as a self-evident wrong.

PART TWO

BRITAIN, EIGHTEENTH
AND NINETEENTH CENTURIES

Corruption, the most infallible symptom of constitutional liberty.
(Gibbon: *Decline and Fall of the Roman Empire*, Ch. 21)

CHAPTER 1

The Background

—◦❦◦—

As Part I of this book has shown, bribery, corruption and nepotism flourish in Africa today. Their growth and prosperity south of the Sahara may comfort those who speak the language of moral superiority to people with different coloured skins; those who are anxious for the growth of democracy in the youngest countries of the world, and who know the dangers Britain has grappled with during three hundred years over this very problem, will be less easily satisfied.

It is not surprising that many people murmur in Britain when they read some of the names in the New Year or Birthday Honours List; what is surprising is that so little time has been devoted to studying the way in which British political institutions work manifestly for the advantage of certain people, and quite as clearly do not benefit others. Why, for example, are thirteen of our Prime Ministers and roughly the same number of Foreign Secretaries and Chancellors descended from Sir George Villiers, an Elizabethan squire? Why are so many cabinet ministers, bishops, judges and top managers drawn from such a small group of public schools? Many volumes are printed every year about British constitutional law and the institutions of government, with very little study of what actually happens from the working of these institutions in terms of the people who operate them.

Bribery and corruption, for example, which once stifled the life of British institutions in all departments of society, and today endanger the very existence of democracy in newly developed countries of

Asia and Africa, have received comparatively little study from British scholars. In America there have been several books on the subject, but in recent years there has only been one British survey, and that only on elections;[1] though of course examples of bribery and corruption are documented in many authoritative works on institutional government, and will be quoted in the course of this study.

For various reasons the old, complicated system of bribery, corruption and nepotism died out in Britain. Individual cases continue to occur, but the system as such, which had reached its peak in the eighteenth century, no longer existed at the start of the twentieth. The reasons for its decay in Britain may be usefully studied, not only for the benefit of the new-born countries of Africa and Asia on whose well-being the future happiness of mankind so largely depends, but also to ensure that the same old weaknesses do not once more corrode British life.

Bribery and corruption may involve no more than simple avarice, but this is usually by no means the only motive involved. Along with nepotism, they might be described as the acquisition, exercise and delegation of authority according to self-interest rather than merit. 'If you give me power, I will give you money', or 'Will you give me a peerage if I contribute to party funds?' In this way Bill Boodle may become Baron Boodle for social and political services if his party is in power; he may also become a director of some public or private enterprise because a peerage adds prestige, and other directors are willing to exchange some of their wealth for the power and status which it is hoped Baron Boodle will add to them.

Power, wealth and status are all involved in these transactions, and there is not always a clear dividing line between the three. Anyone who has travelled in developing countries knows the extent to which modern firms today can control or influence great organs of government; conversely, and notably in Soviet Russia, it is possible for great economic interests to be controlled by the fluctuations of the political barometer; elsewhere social status is still so important that it makes nonsense of the apparent facts of democracy.

Secondly, such things have been as long established in Britain as anywhere else in the world. For instance, in 1583, Philip Stubbes[2] describes how to enter an Oxford College: 'Except one be able to give the Regent or Provost of a House a piece of money, ten pounds, twenty pounds, yea a hundred pounds, a yoke of fat oxen, a couple of fine geldings, or the like, though he be never so toward a youth, nor have never so much need of maintenances, yet he come not there I warrant you.' Here is a classic case of corruption with its causes

---

[1] Cornelius O'Leary: *The elimination of corrupt practices in British elections, 1868–1911.*

[2] *The Anatomie of Abuses.*

and cure equally obvious and simple. A small group of men (the Heads of the Colleges) have near-monopoly of one form of status, an Oxford MA (which still has to be purchased today). So they demand in return a large entrance fee from anyone who wants this particular status symbol, and this should provide them with good dinners for several weeks to come. The obvious cure, apart from severe legislation which is not always effective, is to build more and better universities, so that the monopoly of the status symbol (and of learning) is no longer restricted to a few. This example of corruption is taken from early Reformation England, and clearly the same sort of corruption is likely to arise in the early history of many new nations. Given a shortage of any political, social or economic commodity, man's lust for power, wealth and status will do the rest. The cries of the French Revolution are the ultimate cures: Liberty will distribute power; Equality will disseminate wealth; and Fraternity will curb the passion for status.

English history is packed with examples of how these different forces interacted. Henry VIII and Elizabeth I, like most of the Tudors, did not insist too much on their own great status when they dealt with Parliament; they preferred to be polite, and concentrate on political power. Both James I and Charles I talked too much about their authority and status, but the day came when Charles was short of money and wanted it to fight the Scots, and then Parliament demanded a great deal of political power in return.

Perhaps because Britain is an island, her inhabitants have always been sailing away somewhere, thus upsetting the balance of classes and consequently the balance of powers. The Elizabethan adventurers who sailed the world in the sixteenth century drew such wealth from the slaves of West Africa and from the New World that by the seventeenth century the City of London was strong enough to break Charles I in the Civil War. The unknown merchants of the eighteenth century who sailed to the Indies were able to make such fortunes that they helped to destroy the apparently invincible Whig landlords who had power, wealth and status in abundance.[1]

The Whigs were also destroyed from above, in an interesting way. George III had status and wealth but wanted power as well, and used both to get it by destroying the Whig government. He himself was eventually stopped by the national disgrace of defeat in the American War of Independence, and by the onset of his insanity.[2] Coming from a German family he was very conscious of his status, and told his first Parliament 'I glory in the name of Briton'. It is often true that those who lack status in some sense are the most vigorous wielders of political power; the Jewish Disraeli encouraged Imperialism and made the Queen Empress of India; the Spanish-

[1] Basil Williams: *The Whig Supremacy*.
[2] Watson: *The Reign of George III.*

descended de Valera fought for Irish Independence; the Corsican Napoleon ruled France: the Austrian Hitler conquered most of Europe for Germany, and Maltese, Greeks, Spaniards and Italians blazed 'Algerie Francaise' on their car horns. In Central Africa today we have Sir Roy Welensky, the son of a Lithuanian Jew, declaring that he will keep the British flag flying in Rhodesia, while Mr Kenneth Kaunda, educated in Nyasaland, struggles for the rights of Northern Rhodesian Africans.

For various reasons which will be examined in another chapter, power, wealth and status have always been in slightly different hands since the sixteenth century in Britain. Those in authority have therefore had to go on raising the price they pay for their authority all the time. Britain has been extremely fortunate in this, and it is one of the factors which for three hundred years has forestalled the possibility of revolution and civil war. The opposition has always had something to offer, so to speak, which the government wanted, so a bargain has been struck.

If this analysis in terms of power, wealth and status is correct, then a great many problems become clearer. In many developing countries the new rulers have been starved of all three, and the sudden advent of democracy has merely offered the opportunity to purchase wealth and status, rather than use political power properly. In some territories, especially where Lord Lugard's influence was strong and his philosophy of indirect rule most strictly applied, the real power lay with the British, but the Chiefs retained their superior social status and frequently their wealth also. When political power has been handed over to them in the name of democracy and self-government, their countries have sometimes been called 'more stable' by foreign commentators, meaning that status, power and wealth were concentrated in the hands of one oligarchy. But this is hardly commendable from the democratic point of view. Something of the same sort has happened in many of the independent states of Central and South America, where all power—economic, political, social and military is vested in a small group of officers who seem to be overthrowing each other alternately in successive *coups d'etat*.

Apart from wealth, status and political power, military force is clearly an important factor in this discussion. 'Who will move if the Army does not?' wrote Colonel Nasser before the Revolution in Egypt. Who indeed? King Farouk successfully controlled political power, a vast fortune and any social prestige and status that was available. But as Israel developed, so King Farouk was compelled to hand over more and more power to the younger Army officers.

Are there any other factors that we should consider? The most obvious seem to be spiritual or religious force, as exemplified in a church or in a great spiritual leader; the working or labouring force, embodied in the trade unions; and possibly the rising force of technical knowledge;[1] the tyranny of the expert, however, although an absorbing subject, does not properly arise in this discussion.

The most important of these is undoubtedly spiritual power, or the power of a Church. It is probably as its strongest and most explicit in some South American states, in Spain and in certain Muslim countries. It can sometimes be exercised by a spiritual usurper, like Rasputin in Russia under the old Tsarist régime, in which instance the leaders of society, resenting his inroads upon their power and status, combined to murder him and restore the old order. It may be a great prophetic force like that of Mahatma Ghandi, breaking down the old political and social order, and not so successfully trying to reverse the new economic order. The political leaders in India at that time (the British) were ultimately prepared to tolerate Ghandi's challenge, but some devotees of the old social and religious order were not, and like many religious and spiritual leaders he was assassinated. For by their very nature true spiritual leaders do not trade their leadership for power, wealth or social status, and have therefore a tendency to disrupt any system from which they emerge, and to meet violent deaths themselves. Jesus is an even clearer example; the Devil put certain specific temptations to him in the wilderness, asking him to turn stones into bread (create wealth), jump off a pinnacle of the Temple (gain status as a prophet of miracles) or dominate the kingdoms of the world (political power), provided he would worship Satan.

In Britain the 'spiritual order' has been fairly closely tied to the social order, and those who have superior social status very frequently belong to the Church of England, while the nonconformist strength has usually lain in the middle and working classes. During the nineteenth century, the British radical nonconformists had to accept Gladstone, a strong Anglican, as their leader, and even today it is unusual for the leaders of society to be anything except members of the Church of England.

Britain has been fortunate in having enough religious diversity to prevent any one denomination from gaining absolute control, as the chapter on British religious life will show. Black Africa has had no such good fortune. Sometimes primitive animism reappears, as in Mau Mau, but usually it has been superseded by Christianity or by Islam or, regrettably, by a sort of negative western belief in the virtue of getting rich as quickly as possible. Unfortunately, the leaders or prophets of these faiths have mostly come from outside Black Africa, whether they be men like Albert Schweitzer, David Livingstone, Cecil Rhodes or the nineteenth century Fulani in Northern Nigeria. African Christian leaders have not always been opposed to

[1] Michael Young: *The Meritocracy*.

European imperialist influence,[1] and it is only recently that pro-foundly Christian Africans, often espousing the cause of non-violence, have risen on behalf of their fellow-countrymen in South Africa and Northern Rhodesia.

Many new African states are therefore in a difficult position. Under colonial rule no local armed forces had been developed much beyond the ranks—in Ghana for a long time after independence the head of the Ghanaian Army was a British General, and in the Congo there were no Congolese above the rank of Sergeant; and there has been little spiritual leadership which was truly indigenous, however many 'expatriate' missionaries there may have been. In the absence of indigenous military or religious leadership, and the frequent demoralization of those who have moved into towns to become an urban proletariat, the sudden advent of democracy has often left an inexperienced group of elected representatives in the tempting position of having political power to sell in return for money or social prestige. It is easy for people in the 'West' who have helped to create this situation to hold up their hands in horror, but Britain's own record is embarrassing.

For two hundred and fifty years before 1688, Englishmen had been killing each other to obtain power, and for a wide variety of other political and religious reasons. The settlements of 1660 and 1688 inaugurated the Age of Reason, and substituted a system of patron-age, bribery and corruption for the previous methods of blood-letting. After three hundred years without armed conflict on British soil, and the religious forces of the land so divided that none of them can completely dominate the others, Britain has almost wiped out political bribery, the buying and selling of office, and political corruption, the selling of privileges by those with power. Almost, but not quite. It is no longer customary to buy the electorate, although it is not uncommon to buy oneself a political position in a party. It is, however, still common practice to buy social status for oneself, or more usually for one's children. In Britain men are usually too old to change their accents or the habits of a lifetime when they have amassed sufficient wealth to do so comfortably, but they can still send their children to expensive schools to obtain the correct accents and status symbols, and they may still buy their way into the House of Lords by donating funds in the right quarters.

For in Britain, one of the main ways in which people are rewarded is not monetary but social. By the 1880s direct bribery of the electorate and of politicians was dying out, but a more sophisticated system of corruption was taking its place, and certain offices and professions are still the preserve of those whose wealth or social status counts for more than their ability. Some years ago a journalist

[1] For a very moving account of how an African Christian feels see Ndabaningi Sicolei: *African Nationalism*, 1959.

Member of Parliament coined the phrase 'The Establishment', which has passed into the language with remarkable speed; true, it is used in so many senses as to be almost meaningless, but in any of its senses it assumes the existence of a group (or groups) of men possessing wealth, exercising power and preserving status, responsible only to one another, the self-appointed arbiters, behind the scenes, of much that is important in the life of the nation. It may be that their existence is an illusion; but if so, why does the word seem to supply a long-felt need in the English vocabulary? Can Britain rightly feel proud of her achievement in wiping out the more obvious forms of bribery and corruption, when this system still exists after three hundred years of prosperity and peace at home? Africa, with pitifully low standards of living, has to grapple with these problems in one decade.

As this study proceeds many reasons for the collapse of bribery and corruption in Britain, as a system, will become clear. At certain times it was religious idealism, particularly among the nonconformist groups; at others the doctrines of Francis Place, Jeremy Bentham and the 'Utilitarians'. But it was not always for such honourable reasons. It may even be that Britain dealt with some of the problems of bribery and corruption during the nineteenth century because she was such a snob-ridden society, and because it was possible to trade social status for political power without allowing money to enter into the transaction. In the United States and some other countries, where social status was not until recently an important factor, there has been a much greater degree of bribery and corruption as the terms are usually understood. As several recent studies have shown, this is not the only cause of corruption in American politics, but it is one of them. America has always placed great emphasis on political liberty, but this is not enough to destroy corruption, for which economic equality is usually the best device. Presumably it will be the same in the new countries of Asia and Africa; it will not be enough to offer political democracy on a plate; most of these countries must gain economic equality for themselves as well. Even that is not enough. The other necessary factor to destroy corruption appears to be an expanding economy such as the Victorians possessed.

For in an expanding economy there are many alternative ways of making money. Most men value political power, however slender their portion of it, and in an expanding economy the price of votes that remain available for sale goes up considerably. Increasingly in the western democracies bribery can only be carried on by large party political organizations, and possibly the party machines can only be controlled by people who are millionaires, or who wear the purple of commerce. For example, the party with the biggest financial backing may benefit from advertising campaigns which, while not part of an electoral campaign (which would be illegal) none the less influence the result of an election. And so 'bribery' ceases, and passes into the sphere of 'influence', more or less legitimate.

Although a study of this subject breeds cynicism in the student, we approach it not dispassionately but with a 'value judgment'; namely that the transference of power, wealth and status for each other are all equally undesirable. To destroy them the French Revolution ideals of Liberty, Equality and Fraternity are all needed, but unfortunately these have as yet made no great headway among mankind.

How Victorian England succeeded in destroying the system of corruption which had existed in the previous century is now the subject of the following chapters. The analysis of corruption in terms of the exchange of wealth, power and status will carry us a certain way; the facts of the expanding economy, the growing population, the increasing ease of communication and the spread of education are continually important; but there are other and more elusive factors, more difficult to analyse and certainly more difficult to document—the personal integrity of individuals, or of a significantly high proportion of individuals, both in their private and public behaviour, and an attraction to public service the rewards of which were certainly not financial and which carried very little power; in other words a remarkable emphasis on status alone.

It seems that whatever may have been the political and economic reasons for the decline of corruption, the puritanical thread in the fabric of Victorian England was important. It ran through society from top to bottom, and it does not appear to have its counterpart in Africa and Asia outside the restricted circle of family and tribe. British standards of honesty have not of course fully survived two wars and a social revolution, but their influence persists, especially in the public service.

We must now examine whether the lessons of eighteenth and nineteenth century Britain can be of value to twentieth century Africa.

CHAPTER 2

Parliamentary Elections

'*Seat in Parliament.* To be disposed of, a property which commands sufficient influence to return a Member. Apply personally to Mr Witham, Solicitor, No 8 Gray's Inn Square, London; if by letter post to be pre-paid.' (*The Courier*, 1835, quoted by B. Keith-Lucas: *The History of the English Local Government Franchise.*)

'This trade of politics is a rascally business.' (George III quoted by G. M. Trevelyan: *Early History of Charles James Fox.*)

—◦❧❦◦—

Bribery and corruption in parliamentary elections, long established in Britain, became a carefully organized system in the seventeenth century, when Parliament grew to be important. At first Parliament, and especially the House of Commons, which quickly divided itself from the aristocratic House of Lords, seems to have regarded itself mainly as a taxing machine, and was singularly slow to grasp that this control of money enabled it to claim other privileges and powers. In those earlier days the value of electing and being elected does not seem to have been especially prized, and it may well have been their victory in the Civil War that so convinced members of their own importance that they began restricting the sort of people permitted to elect them.

Before the Reform Act of 1832 there was, of course, hardly an 'electorate' as we understand the word today, and members found their way into the House of Commons as the chosen representatives either of the rural counties or the urban boroughs. In the counties the voting usually took place in the County Court, and was restricted by an Act of 1430 to certain property-owning freeholders; but in the boroughs there were fantastic differences both in the size of the boroughs incorporated by Royal Charter and the kind of people within them who were entitled to vote.

There were perhaps three main types—the 'rotten' borough owned by an individual (such as Old Sarum, which consisted of a thorn bush marking the site of the old town), the corporation borough, which could be governed by a dozen or so self-elected councillors, chosen because they were compliant enough not to disagree with some local patron (they could indeed be illiterate, as at Malmesbury in 1807, when ten of the thirteen members were unable to sign their names); and lastly, the free or open borough, where there was a comparatively large number of voters, but which had the most arbitrary qualifications from one end of the country to another; it was these that were most subject to bribery at election times, as is shown by an incident at Rochester as late as 1831, when a young man on trial for assaulting his father thought it sufficient justification to plead that his father had refused to make him a freeman of the Borough, which would have been worth at least £60 to him as a voter.[1]

The Royal Commission on Municipal Corporations, writing in 1833, had this to say about their earlier development:

'The greater number of the governing charters of corporations was granted between the reign of Henry VIII and the Revolution; the general characteristic of these documents is, that they were calculated to take away power from the community and to render the governing class independent from the main body of burgesses. Almost all ths councils named in these charters are established on the principles of self-election. . . . There is little reason to doubt that the form given to the governing classes, as well as the limitation of the burgess-ship during this period, was adopted for the purpose of influencing the choice or nomination of members of Parliament.'

Charles II in particular had used his power to annul charters and to create new ones extensively for his own ends, even employing a certain Dr Brady to prove that the word 'burgesses' (the word for voters in the old charters) meant the corporations themselves. Between the reigns of Henry VIII and Charles II, 180 members were added to the House of Commons by the creation of municipal Royal Charters,[2] and from the later seventeenth century onwards, when the prerogative was taken away, bribery was given its head. Many of the created boroughs were too small to begin with, and as time went by they grew even smaller. Such a system allowed the easy control of Members of Parliament, and their consequent corruption, by whoever controlled the boroughs. In 1793 the 'Society of Friends of the People' were prepared to prove that seventy Members of Parliament were returned for thirty-five boroughs in which there were hardly any electors at all; that ninety members were returned for forty-six places at which there were under fifty electors, and that another thirty-seven were returned for nineteen boroughs having under 100 electors.[3] The growing new industrial centres of Birmingham, Leeds and Manchester were unrepresented, but the Duke of Norfolk had eleven Members of Parliament to represent him, Lord Lonsdale nine, and Lord Darlington, the Duke of Rutland, the Marquess of

[1] *The Cornhill Magazine*, May 1885.
[2] May: *Constitutional History*, i. 329.
[3] Ibid., 332.

Buckingham and Lord Carrington six each.[1] These will perhaps suffice as examples of royal or aristocratic control of a corrupt kind, though bribery, as such, scarcely entered into the question, for most of the candidates were nominated.

The counties, which could claim a rather more representative sample of English opinion among their voters, were apt to become involved in unconventional election expenditure of a somewhat different kind; they frequently became the tilting ground of rival noble families, and in Yorkshire in 1807, for example, the Fitzwilliam and Lascelles families appear to have spent about £100,000 on a single election.[2]

As the power of Parliament increased, and the verdicts of close corporations and of the Commons committees reduced the power of the people to choose their own representatives, the position became increasingly ludicrous. By 1832 144 peers returned close on 300 members, while 187 more were returned by private individuals, and only 171, less than a quarter, were even supposed to be returned independently.[3] (It was among this quarter that bribery was rampant.) Scotland was even worse off than England, for at the same date 4,000 electors returned all the MPs in Scotland, and in Edinburgh thirty-three electors returned the local Member.[4] In Ireland the position was even more absurd, for almost all the members were Protestants nominated by landowners, and then 'elected' by a few local inhabitants of the right sort. In the last general election before 1832, out of a total of 658 Members of the House of Commons, 487 were nominated and the rest usually elected with blatant bribery.[5]

*

Our purpose is to trace the reasons for improvement, and we must resist the temptation to spend too long in the fantastic jungle of bribery and corruption as it actually existed, and as it is revealed in the Journals of the House of Commons, the volumes of parliamentary history and the reports of various commissions. A few examples of corruption before the Reform Act of 1832 must suffice:

In 1768 the Mayor and Corporation of Oxford were sent to Newgate gaol for asking their two Members to pay £5,670 of the City's debt. They were only a few weeks in prison, but while there they completed the sale of the Borough to the Duke of Marlborough and the Earl of Abingdon on the same terms; unfortunately for them the Town Clerk carried off the official books with details of the

---

[1] Oldfield: *Representative History*, vi. 286.
[2] But estimates differ; Halevy (*History of the English People*, 1. 24) thinks £50,000 and Professor Coupland (*Wilberforce*, 352) £230,000.
[3] Oldfield, op. cit.
[4] Woodward: *The Age of Reform*, p. 25.
[5] Oldfield, op. cit. and May: *Constitutional History* (1837) 1. 362.

transactions.[1] It was at this time that Lord Chesterfield complained that the average price of boroughs had gone up from £2,500 to £4,000 or £5,000 'because of interfering people from the Indies', and that Northampton even cost 'at least £30,000 a side'.[2] At Shaftesbury in 1774, amidst a great deal of drunkenness, one of the alderman disguised as Mr Punch passed sums of twenty guineas through a hole in the door, for which each elector had to sign a bill to an imaginary character called Mr Glenbucket.[3] This was a device to circumvent the laws against bribery. In 1771 the electors of New Shoreham formed 'The Christian Society', which sold the seat to the highest bidder and then distributed the proceeds among the electorate.

In 1784 the poll went on for forty days, at Westminster, with much bribery,[4] and with Charles James Fox elected by a majority of 236. However, the Tory High Bailiff failed to make a return of the election on the ground that a scrutiny of the vote was needed, which he managed to delay for over a year at a cost of £18,000, with William Pitt the Younger and the Government helping him all the time.[5] As a result of this famous election, however, Parliament reduced the length of the poll to fifteen days. This was not the only example of partiality among polling officers, for in 1780 there was a petition to the House of Commons from Coventry, because the sheriffs had so constructed the polling booth that their friends could enter through the Mayor's Parlour, while their opponents had to climb up the booth by ladder.

Treating, as distinct from bribing, also flourished, as is shown, for instance, in the Northamptonshire County records; in 1748 two candidates' 'entertainment' bills totalled £4,176, and one publican claimed for 409½ gallons of ale; a typical instance of eighteenth century electoral hospitality.[6]

In Scotland, Lord Melville, who was Lord Advocate for twenty-five years at the beginning of the nineteenth century, used to boast that of the forty-five Scottish members he could return thirty-nine, and an example of this farce may be taken from Bute, which had a population of 14,000, with twenty-one electors of whom one was resident. During an early nineteenth century election only one person beside the sheriff and the returning officer attended the meeting. He took the chair, constituted the meeting, called out the names of the freeholders, answered his own name, took the list of candidates and chose himself, moved and seconded his own nomina-

---

[1] Walpole, *Mem.*, iii, 153.
[2] Letters to his son, 19.xii.67 and 12.iv.68.
[3] *Journal* of the House of Commons; xxxv. 118.
[4] The Duchess of Devonshire appears to have kissed some voters as a bribe.
[5] Stanhope: *Life of Pitt*; i. 207–11.
[6] E. G. Forester: *Northamptonshire county elections and electioneering.*

tion, put the question to the vote and unanimously returned himself.[1]
There appears to have been no vote of thanks to the chairman. This
scarcely left room for bribery, but there was a great deal of it in the
three or four constituencies where opposition obtained; but the
corruption of Scottish MPs was proverbial even at Westminster.
Erskine May[2] states that it was said of one such member 'his
invariable rule was never to be present at a debate, or absent at a
division, and that he only once in his long political life ventured to
vote according to his conscience, and that he found on that occasion
he had voted wrong'.

In Ireland, the Protestant landlords held such control over
elections that about two-thirds of the members were returned by
about fifty or sixty influential patrons.[3] In the seats where there were
any opposing candidates or free voters the bribery, corruption and
drinking were alike fantastic. One Dublin candidate recorded that
he had to go into training for three months in hard drinking before
submitting himself to the electorate.

*

How did change come about? In the period *before* 1832 there were
two main influences on this system of bribery and corruption, which
contributed to its ultimate downfall.

George III was determined to destroy the power of the Whig
Government, and to do this he had to become 'the first of the
borough-mongering electioneering gentlemen of England'.[4] But as
his personal power declined after the American Revolution, and his
own madness increased, the control of the boroughs tended to pass
to a new group, the 'nabobs'. These were the East and West Indian
merchants of whom Lord Chesterfield so querulously complained;
they had done well out of the great victories of the elder Pitt, had a
great deal of free capital to spend on their return, and like most
people wanted power in addition to wealth. Many of the merchants
who had gone out to India from Manchester found bribery to be just
as useful in the Commons as in Calcutta, and sometimes they
combined to purchase a borough.

Even in the seventeenth century this tendency had been discernible,
for a number of private citizens were beginning to grow wealthy
enough to compete on fairly level terms with the State in their own
constituencies (so far as bribery was concerned), and many rich
merchants could certainly hold their own with the great landowners.
Consequently the landowners represented in Parliament passed an
Act to discourage bribery and corruption at elections, although it

[1] Speech of the Lord Advocate, 23.ix.1831.
[2] *Constitutional History*, i. 357.
[3] Wakefield: *Statistical and Political Account of Ireland*, ii. 299.
[4] Namier: *England in the Age of the American Revolution*, p. 4.

was already an offence at Common Law, and the House of Commons had already condemned it by resolution.[1] Unfortunately as the century proceeded the landowners found that the Act was not working properly. Sir William Davenant[2] grumbles about 'utter strangers making a progress through England, endeavouring by very large sums of money to get themselves elected. It is said that there were known brokers who have tried to stock job elections upon the Exchange; and that for many boroughs there was a stated price.'

In the following century Lord Chatham was to declare with some bitterness that 'without connections, without any natural interest in the soil, the importers of foreign gold have forced their way into Parliament, by such a torrent of corruption as no private hereditary fortune could resist'.[3] Again Parliament, in its unavailing way, passed an Act against bribery,[4] imposing fines for those detected in the offence, but bribery continued worse than ever. From then until the end of the nineteenth century Acts continued to be passed with the same lack of success until the root causes of the system were destroyed.

The Bribery Acts did not, for example, discourage Sir Manasseh Masseh Lopes, a rich merchant who was convicted of offering £2,000 in bribes to the electors of Grampound. He was sentenced to two years' imprisonment and a fine of £1,000; meanwhile he was elected for the even more corrupt town of Barnstaple, where he paid £3,000, but he was unseated and again tried and imprisoned. On his release he sat for the pocket borough of Westbury.[5]

But in spite of this borough-mongering, and in the longer term, the influence of the merchants was a healthy one.

It is often believed that the great period of corruption in parliamentary elections was during the administrations of Walpole and Newcastle, but although members were thoroughly corrupt during those periods, the costs of electioneering do not seem to have been high. After 1760 and until 1878, the standards of members went up and the standards of the electorate tended to go down. As MPs improved in calibre they tended to carry out a certain amount of reform from above, so that as the nineteenth century progressed and the number of distinguished members of the House increased, so did the speed of reform.

---

[1] *Male's Election Law*, 339–45; Comm. J. ix. 411, 417; Macaulay: *History of England*, iv. 615 (1st ed.).

[2] *Works* iii, 326–8; 'Essay on the Balance of Power', quoted by May, *Constitutional History*, i. 334.

[3] June 22, 1770, quoted by May.

[4] 2. Geo. III, c.24.

[5] Quoted by B. Keith-Lucas: *The History of the English Local Government Franchise*. Oldfield, op. cit., iv. 300; thought Barnstaple the most corrupt English borough, for the 400 electors regularly expected to receive £10,000–£13,000 at each election.

There seem to be several reasons for this improvement. One is clearly that men like the nabobs, given to bribery though they may have been, had not made their money in India or the West Indies without great ability, and their work had also given them administrative experience and an understanding of power; secondly, the jealously of the landed interests at home, as exemplified in the trial of Warren Hastings for corruption, had the effect of discouraging the grosser forms of extortion; thirdly, during the series of wars with France from 1740 onwards, the captains of naval vessels who had shown skill and initiative had frequently gained a great deal of prize money which they were prepared to exchange for political power; these men, like the nabobs, were men of talent; fourthly, the ideals of the French and American Revolutions were exercising a profound effect upon what men believed.

These revolutions were to a great extent affairs of the middle classes; in America revolting against a distant administration which curbed them economically, and in France against the land-owning aristocracy and the monarchy. But revolutionary ideas need discontent to feed on, and the middle classes in England were doing far too well to want a revolution. The working classes, without middle class leadership, and with means of escape from injustice that the French did not possess, were not ready for a successful revolution at that time either. But the great landowners often did become discontented; not only were people of much lower birth becoming wealthy, but they were becoming powerful, as they bought more and more boroughs, and gained social status by purchasing peerages, 388 of which were created during the reign of George III.

Thus it is that many of the ideals of the French Revolution found their expression not through the mouths of English Robespierres and Dantons, but through the most remote and socially superior English aristocracy, with names like the Duke of Devonshire, Earl Grey and Lord John Russell. These men were opposed to corruption, and tended to bring into the House of Commons as well as the House of Lords more men of high ability and wide education, as well as noble birth. Much reform was due to enlightened legislation from above, rather than popular agitation from below.

The second change which came about, in the period before 1832, was because of advances in public health and medicine, which caused the population to expand at an enormous rate. In 1700 the population was about 5 million; in 1750 around 6 million; in 1800 9 million; in 1820 12 million and in 1850 18 million. Few of these enjoyed the vote—indeed, no significant proportion of them did so until 1867 and 1884, for the 1832 Reform Act only gave the vote to about one adult male in twenty-four. Nevertheless, even within the very restricted franchise it was becoming increasingly expensive to bribe the electorate and it was clear that even a modest measure of reform would soon make it impossible. Representative government was ceasing to be a cosy private affair.

*

The great Reform Act of 1832 is generally regarded as a kind of watershed, with the barbarities of rotten boroughs and wholesale corruption on one side and progressive and civilized electoral reform on the other. This is an exaggeration. Bribery and corruption in particular grew rather than diminished for fifty years after the Act. There being more voters, more money was spent, for bribery seems always to be one of the growing pains of democracy in its early stages. Even during the 'hungry forties' the wealth of most men likely to be candidates grew, while the needs of those they bribed was greater. In Stafford, for example:

'At the first election after the Reform Act the initiative in demanding bribes, as in so many constituencies, came from the electors themselves, and corruption among the new £10 householders was reported to be as bad as among the old franchise holders. Even before the election started 5s and 10s tickets had been distributed to about 800 electors. There was evidence that one side alone had paid out about £150 in 5s tickets a week before polling day. But this was chicken feed compared with what was to come. When the election actually started the price of votes began at £2 10s 0d for a single and £5 for a plumper, and gradually rose to £4, £7 and even £10 for a vote. One agent alone paid out over £1,000 in bribes to between 400 and 500 voters. Of the 1,000 odd voters it was calculated that 850 were bribed. A Parliamentary Committee of Inquiry that sat in 1833 found ample proof of open and extensive bribery by both sides in the Borough, "though probably not more so than any other", observed the editor of *Messe's Parliamentary Guide* for 1835 with no trace of cynicism, and although the election was not declared void, the Borough was recommended for disfranchisement.'[1]

Sudbury,[2] (1845), Yarmouth (1849) and St Albans (1853) were presumably considered worse than this, for they were disfranchised for electoral malpractices while Stafford, in spite of the Committee's recommendation, was not.

From another, less well-known, source[3] we have the position described in Horsham in 1847, where three candidates contested a

[1] Norman Gash: *Politics in the Age of Peel*, p. 158; the definitive study of this period, which is a mine of information on electoral bribery, corruption and violence.

[2] Probably 'Eatanswill' of Dickens *Pickwick Papers* (see H. G. Nicholas, op. cit.); the 600 electors were so corrupt that the local clergyman arranged with the agents that the oath should not be demanded.

[3] Albery: *A Parliamentary History of Horsham, 1295–1885*, p. 353.

seat which was reckoned in the past to have cost some £4,000–£5,000. On this occasion liquor was free for all six weeks of the poll, and 'most of the male population were frequently drunk, and some were continuously drunk, for the whole six weeks'. As this ocean of alcohol seemed to have insufficient effect the candidates and agents resorted to kidnapping. To protect their own men, a van load of Conservatives was driven to Brighton, kept and fed until polling day and then returned for voting. One elector promised his vote to both sides, but was captured by the Radicals, rescued by the Conservatives, recaptured by the Radicals, given £40, and then taken for a quiet trip into the country, dead drunk. The election probably cost the two wealthier candidates between £60,000 and £100,000 each.

Nearly all the guilty authorities were in the South of England. Undoubtedly this is because the older boroughs of the South had long had voters open to direct corruption, a tradition not enjoyed by the newer and unenfranchised industrial towns of the North. But from the 1830s onwards bribery increased in the North also, but conditions continued to be so severe that a much larger proportion of the electorate seemed prepared to forgo their bribes for the sake of reform.

*

With the steady improvement in the quality of Members of Parliament it was the electors rather than the candidates who were setting the pace in bribery; indeed, Parliament passed a steady succession of laws which were ultimately one of the factors in destroying the evil. It will be convenient here to follow this legislation to its conclusion, and then turn to other factors.

In 1841 Lord John Russell succeeded in passing a Bill to make the procedure of investigating committees more flexible. Previously it had been necessary to prove that a candidate or his agent had bribed the electorate; now it was sufficient to prove that bribery had taken place, the assumption being that the candidate or his agent had committed it. Lord Denman's Act of 1852 still further strengthened the investigation committees by amending the laws of evidence and allowing them to examine both members and candidates personally. Where actual bribery was shown to have taken place the Committees set up by the House were vigorous and sometimes severe, as *Hansard* and the Royal Commission Reports show, and the facts were sedulously reported.

The Corrupt Practices Act of 1854 prevented candidates from making payments except through authorized agents, and provided for the publication of their accounts. The Bribery Act of 1858 curtailed travelling expenses (at least in theory), and various schemes for shortening the seven-year life of a Parliament, which would have made bribes more expensive, were proposed without apparent progress. Support for the secret ballot seems to have varied with the economic outlook. The Radicals proposed it in the dark days of 1817;[1] in 1833 a motion was easily lost by 211 votes to 116;[2] as economic clouds appeared on the horizon the favourable vote increased, and by 1839 216 MPs voted for it;[3] during the successful financial reforms of Peel support declined,[4] but with the depression that followed his resignation support developed rapidly, and in the dread year of 1848 it gained a majority of five. Then times improved a little, and in 1849 it was lost by 51 votes, in 1852 by 102 and in 1860 by 107. By 1872 when an Act was finally passed new forces had come into play, and the atmosphere of politics was utterly changed.

With the death of Palmerston in 1865 and the political confusion which followed much of the old party structure had collapsed, and pressure groups agitating for a further extension of the franchise were clearly audible. Such pressure groups are today one of the mainstays of democracy in many lands, but in nineteenth century England they were an adventure. 'Public discussion and public agitation of every kind of question became the habit of the English people, very largely in imitation of Wilberforce's successful campaign. Voluntary association for every available sort of purpose or cause became an integral part of social life in the nineteenth century, filling up many of the gaps left by the limited scope of state action.'[5] Further reform was now close at hand, although no one would have guessed it from the election campaign of 1865.

The contest in that year involved 'more profuse and corrupt expenditure than was ever known before'.[6] Fifty petitions were presented, thirty-five were tried, thirteen MPs unseated thereby and four Royal Commissions set up to inquire into the proceedings at Great Yarmouth, Totnes, Reigate and Lancaster. In Yarmouth the Liberal candidate spent 90 per cent of his money on bribes, involving one third of the electorate, and at Lancaster the Liberal spent £7,459 on bribes and the Conservative £7,070.[7] At Totnes the Conservatives spent about £5,000, but were not returned because of the state of the registers, and had only been persuaded to stand for the sake of the electorate, over two-thirds of whom were involved in bribery transactions.[8]

But the Government of Disraeli pressed on with reform, and the second great Reform Bill of 1867 brought genuine democracy nearer and gave large numbers of working-class people the vote. The results

[1] *Edinburgh Review*, June 1818, p. 199.
[2] *Hansard* Ser. 3 xvii 608.
[3] Ibid., xlviii 422.
[4] May, op. cit., i. 477.
[5] G. M. Trevelyan: *England in the Nineteenth Century.*
[6] *The Times*, February 13, 1868.
[7] *Parliamentary Papers*, 1867 xxvii. 92.
[8] O'Leary, op. cit., p. 30.

were almost immediate, for the urban electorate was practically doubled, and the Liberal Government of Gladstone set about reforming some obvious abuses that even the electors were now beginning to dislike. Open voting was the first, for it was clear that little progress could be made towards ending bribery until the ballot was secret. Gladstone appointed a committee in 1869 to examine the methods of conducting parliamentary and municipal elections with the aim of restricting intimidation and bribery and limiting expense.[1] This committee reported favourably on the secret ballot, and despite opposition and delaying tactics from the House of Lords, and several mistakes in drafting, the secret ballot was introduced in 1872.

Meanwhile, another useful reform had been introduced in 1868, by transferring the adjudication of electoral disputes and malpractices from the House of Commons or its committees to the Courts. As long as private members acted as judges in cases in which their fellow MPs were concerned, and on offences which they had probably committed themselves, there was faint hope of progress. The judges, incidentally, were not pleased by this measure.

It might have been supposed that the Act of 1872 alone would destroy the system of bribery and corruption by making it quite impossible to tell which way any particular elector had voted. But if this were so elections in developing countries today would present no problem of bribery; the struggle had to go on, for Englishmen of the 1870s were as ingenious as Africans of the 1960s in circumventing the law. The exchange of ballot papers, payment by electoral results, the corruption of returning officers, the substitution of voters, may all be used if the electorate wishes. The Commissioners who inquired into the election of 1880 found to their surprise that the dragon had not yet been killed. An average of nearly £1 had been spent for every voter,[2] and in Montgomery the Member admitted to spending over £13,000.[3] But while the growth of population and wealth swelled candidates' expenses to an unprecedented level at this election the end of the system was at last in sight, for overwhelming forces were now moving against it. Radicals like John Bright and Joseph Chamberlain, almost very leading writer, practically every nonconformist preacher, the whole force of Victorian morality and a mass of political pressure groups were against it, for the 1880 election had cost nearly £3 million.

It was with general relief, therefore, that the House of Commons greeted the Corrupt and Illegal Practices Bill of 1883, brought for-

[1] A. B. Keith: *The Constitution of England from Queen Victoria to George VI.* In the 1868 election between £1¼ and £1½ million had been spent. (*Parliamentary Papers*, 1868–9 xlviii. 225–6.)

[2] O'Leary, op. cit., Ch. 3.

[3] Treating also continued on a large scale. In one town in 1879, 2,281 electors went on a treat and returned 'firm and enthusiastic supporters of Mr Disraeli's policy' (Seymour: *Electoral Reform in England and Wales*).

ward by Sir Henry James, who had already experienced plenty of corruption in his own constituency.[1] The Act imposed heavy penalties; they were still not likely to be heavier than committing the crime itself, and a man could now advance himself quicker by a contribution to party funds than by bribing the electorate.[2] Fines of up to £200 were imposed as well as the threat of hard labour; treating by candidates was taken to mean the offer of food, drink or entertainment by the candidate or any of his agents; while influence was defined as using force, violence or restraint or 'the infliction of temporal or spiritual injury' to influence the result of an election. No candidate found guilty, or whose agent was found guilty, was to be permitted ever to sit for that constituency again, or for Parliament at all for seven years. Candidates were further limited to £100 for personal expenses, and must have only one agent who was legally responsible for the conduct of the campaign. Paid canvassers and hired vehicles wee forbidden. Returning officers' expenses were restricted; Gladstone wanted them paid for out of the rates, but was defeated by the Conservatives on this point.

The Act was undoubtedly the chief legislative weapon in destroying bribery and corruption in parliamentary elections, and the cost of the 1885 election was only £780,000 compared with £3,000,000 five years earlier. This was the more remarkable because Gladstone had still further increased the size of the electorate by Acts of 1884 and 1885 from about 3 million to 5½ million. The average cost per vote dropped from 18s 9d in 1880 to 4s 5d in 1885. The old system was virtually dead, and it only remained to drive a few more nails in the coffin.[3]

*

We have traced the legislation dealing with bribery and corruption and there can be little doubt that the legal destruction of the system took place between 1867 and 1885, and mainly in the last five years of that period. But Acts of Parliament are not in themselves the *cause* of any social improvement; rather they are the expression of the public mind and will, which has been prepared for their reception by other, more imponderable, forces. True, some of the Acts seemed to be ahead of their time, as is shown by the fact that large minorities were prepared to break the new laws; but they could not have been introduced at all had not public opinion already been moving in their general direction. What, then, were these deeper influences?

[1] O'Leary, op cit.
[2] J. F. S. Ross (*Parliamentary Representation*, 1948) estimates that up to 1939 a Conservative candidate had to subscribe £250–£1,000 to his constituency party and about half the election expenses, usually around £750.
[3] See Gwyn: *Democracy and the Cost of Politics* for much useful information. Gladstone's 1885 redistribution Act wiped out most of the small borough electorates where bribery had been most rampant.

Probably the most immediately effective was the growth of responsible political parties—those much abused institutions—which were compelled as time went on to put more positive and comprehensive programmes before the growing electorate.[1] William Pitt the elder was probably the first statesman of the eighteenth century to appeal to the general public. With many set-backs the custom developed throughout the nineteenth century and came to its first full flowering after the death of Palmerston, with Gladstone and Disraeli. It was only under a fully developed party system that bribery and corruption, as an accepted system, received their *coup-de-grace*. The more that parties were able to communicate a serious sense of purpose, and a programme that affected both the nation and the individual in important ways, the less the ordinary person was disposed to treat an election as an amoral orgy; putting it somewhat lower, the great national parties had, in the moral climate of Victorian England, to appear virtuous at all costs, and this may have helped them to support, as they did, the great Corrupt and Illegal Practices Bill of 1883.[2]

This is interlocked (as all these influences are interlocked) with the next great influence—communication. The leading voices of English literature were turning against *laissez faire*, a philosophy which justified some election excesses.[3] True, many of them did not appear particularly worried about the actual buying and selling of votes. Writers like Peacock (*Melincourt*), John Galt (*The Member* and *The Radical*), Dickens (*Pickwick Papers*) and even Disraeli (*Coningsby*) all appeared to think the matter mildly amusing; their fury was concentrated on other types of corruption and on bureaucracy (e.g. Dickens's Circumlocution Office). But Dickens, Ruskin and Matthew Arnold detested the *laissez-faire* school of thought; Charles Kingsley, Charles Reade and Mrs Gaskell were exposing the conditions of the towns; and George Eliot, Anthony Trollope and above all George Meredith (*Beauchamp's Career*, 1875) showed what was happening at elections. But apart from literature, there was during this period a great expansion of the popular press. More and more of the electorate could read what their respresentatives were thinking and saying, and the shock was sometimes as considerable as with contemporary televised press conferences. The new popular press also created a readership for scandal, and there was a lot of scandal to read about. Apart from the revelations of poverty made by heroic figures like Mayhew, Charles Booth and William Booth,[4] the news-

[1] S. Ostrogorski: *Democracy and the Growth of Political Parties.*

[2] As elections became national more seats were contested. In 1865, 293 were still uncontested, but in 1868 only 130.

[3] See *To the Hustings* (ed. H. G. Nicholas). Bribery was sometimes depicted as an example of the law of supply and demand.

[4] *London's Underworld: Life and Labour in London: In Darkest England and the Way Out.*

papers began to spread news of such conditions to the public, and also of what occurred at elections, and this hastened the growth of national platforms and programmes of reform.[1]

Interlocked with this—indeed largely the cause of it—was the spread of elementary education, and the surge forward in mass literacy given by the Education Act of 1870.

These were the three most easily identifiable influences; but just as they were interlocked with one another so all of them were interlocked with other influences operating further in the background, and whose proper discussion is in later chapters of this book—the reform of the legal system, a well-trained and incorruptible civil service, more efficient methods of accounting in Parliament and business, the development of the trade union movement and of professional bodies with high standards, and at the deepest level a religious influence which probed not only into private but into public morality.

*

When the time came for systematic bribery and corruption in elections to depart hardly anyone was sorry to see it go, and there is perhaps only one regret. Between 1832 and 1885 the bribery, the colour and the drinking at elections provided many great writers with the opportunity for memorable election scenes. Since then, hardly any novelists with the exception of Hilaire Belloc[2] appear to have had anything to say about the complications and the devices by which men can still exchange wealth and status for political power, without actually breaking the laws which have so carefully been passed against corruption.

[1] The Salvation Army and the nonconformists made temperance a vital social issue, and this helped to destroy 'treating' at elections.
[2] *Mr Clutterbuck's Election*, 1911.

CHAPTER 3

Influencing Members

'Corrupt influence, which is itself the perennial spring of all
prodigality, and of all disorder; which loads us, more than millions
of debt; which takes away vigour from our armies, wisdom from
our councils, and every shadow of authority and credit from the
most venerable parts of our constitution. . . .'
Edmund Burke: Speech on Economical Reform, 1780

The previous chapter was concerned with the bribery of the electorate
for the benefit of candidates; this chapter is concerned with the
bribery of Members of Parliament for the benefit of the Crown, or of
political parties. It took such forms as the conferment of offices and
pensions, the direct payment of money, participation in Government
contracts and shares in loans raised by the Government, and it
increased steadily from 1660 to 1780 or thereabouts,[1] after which it
declined. The reasons for its decline were not dissimilar from those
we have already discussed in the chapter on elections—the growth of
a responsible party system, the increasing supremacy of Parliament
in the affairs of the nation and the consistently improving quality
of Members of Parliament; the difference was that corruption in
this particular sphere came to an end a hundred years before it was
finally extinguished in elections. We are discussing an eighteenth
rather than a nineteenth century problem, and we shall be more
greatly concerned with the relations between Parliament and the
monarch.

We have said in a previous chapter that the party system only
reached its full flowering after the death of Palmerston in 1865, but
its origins can be traced back another two hundred years. The
Puritans were perhaps the first people to show the main characteristics of a modern political party. During the reign of Queen
Elizabeth I they opposed the prerogative of the Crown, and their
opposition grew consistently until the outbreak of the Civil War.[2]
Regular parties began to emerge from about 1670 onwards, and

---

[1] Sir W. Anson, op. cit., i. 373.

[2] 'It was to this sect whose principles appear so frivolous and habits so ridicu-
lous that the English owe their whole freedom of their constitution.' David
Hume, quoted by Kenneth Mackenzie: *The English Parliament*, p. 108.

although it took them many years to consolidate, the system which could contain both Government and Opposition had begun. Those who supported the Earl of Danby, who became the King's Principal adviser after 1673, eventually formed the Tory Party, and those who followed Shaftesbury and the 'Country' Party became known as the Whigs. Since both of them owned great wealth, prestige and power they relied considerably on 'gifts' to maintain their following and during the reign of Charles II bribery and corruption grew steadily worse.[1] It was the folly of his brother James which finally united Parliament and evicted the Stuarts, but the parties' unity did not last long after the accession of William III. He and Queen Anne both wanted to keep control of affairs in their own hands, but were compelled to recognize the growing power of Parliament. They both therefore increased the number of Royal Offices for their parliamentary supporters,[2] as well as the amount of money available for bribes.

Both parties in Parliament were however anxious to resist the enroachments of the monarch on their obviously growing power, and so a number of important measures were passed the limit the corruptibility of Parliament by the Crown; one Bill made some State appointments ineligible to Members, though with great difficulty, being rejected by the Lords in 1693 when the Commons had passed it, rejected in 1694 by the King when both Houses had passed a Bill, and not enforced until 1700, when the Commissioners of Revenue Board were disqualified from being MPs.

In recalling the struggle between Parliament and the Crown it is perhaps relevant to remember that Parliament has from early times excluded certain categories of people, whereas the Crown has been open to all if they happen to have been born at the right time and to have selected the right parents. Parliament now excludes children, lunatics and aliens, and the eighteenth and nineteenth centuries excluded women, but some of the greatest constitutional advances have been made when the Throne has been occupied by a child, woman, lunatic or foreigner, or by someone needing or appearing to need great help in government. Britain has been fortunate in having a series of monarchs throughout the eighteenth and nineteenth centuries who possessed one of these qualifications. France was not so lucky.

The first steps in constitutional progress in these matters were taken under the alien monarchy of William III, and even more under the feminine rule of Queen Anne. An Act of her reign[3] stipulated that nobody should be elected to Parliament who accepted a Crown post after October 25, 1705; anyone in the House accepting such a

---

[1] Burnet: *History of his own times*, ii. 144.
[2] Macaulay: *History of England*, iii. 541.
[3] Keith, op. cit., i. 304.

post before that date had to vacate his seat, but could be re-elected.[1] Under George I, a foreigner, further progress was made, and incapacity to sit was extended to pensioners of the Crown. But, by 1721 Walpole was fully in the saddle, and from then until about 1780, when George III's lunacy was becoming apparent, a system of bribery to maintain a ministerial majority was fully exploited, for it was undoubtedly the realization that a parliamentary position meant power which could be sold very profitably which attracted some people to it.[2] On the other hand, it was the growth of the sovereignty of Parliament over all other institutions which was slowly attracting a higher quality of men to the Commons and eventually into office.

Meanwhile, Honourable Members were doing very well for themselves. 'A bribe is given for a particular job; a pension is a constant, continual bribe' said Lord Halifax in debating one of the six Bills which wandered through the Commons but were all thrown out by the Lords.[3] As an example, Mr Rose Fuller, a prominent Whig MP, began supporting the Government early in the reign of George III and it was not discovered until after his death that he was in receipt of a secret pension of £500 a year.[4] Mr. Fuller, if he had known about it, would have approved of a letter written by Sir Robert Walpole after his retirement from office to Henry Pelham, whom he wished to be his successor: 'You must be understood by those you are to depend on, and if it is possible they must be induced to keep their own secret.'[5]

George III was determined to break up the party machines which were now developing, and used bribery even more extensively than it had been used before. Lord Rockingham went further than most of his colleagues in attacking his methods: 'The great number of offices of more or less emolument which are now tenable by parties sitting in Parliament, really operate like prizes in a lottery. An interested man purchases a seat upon the same principle as a man buys a lottery ticket. The value of the ticket depends upon the quantum of prizes in the wheel.'[6]

The system was attacked by Burke in a notable speech.[7] Reform of the Royal Household was thwarted because 'the turnspit of the

[1] This was a contributory reason why ministers were usually wealthy men in the eighteenth and nineteenth centuries; they could afford re-election.

[2] 'Walpole . . . knew that it would be very bad policy to give the world to understand that more was to be got by thwarting his measures than by supporting them. These maxims are as old as the origin of parliamentary corruption in England.' (Macaulay.)

[3] *Parl. Hist.* viii. 789: ix. 369: x. 1510: xii. 591.

[4] May, op. cit., i. 371 and Rockingham, *Memoirs*, i. 79n.

[5] Coxe: *Life of Pelham*, p. 193.

[6] Rockingham, *Memoirs*, ii. 339.

[7] Burke's *Works* (OUP, 1906, Vol. II). Speech on presenting to the Commons a plan for the better security of the independence of Parliament and the economical reformation of the Civil and other Establishments.

King's kitchen was a Member of Parliament;' the Board of Trade is a 'sort of intemperate bed of influence; a sort of gently ripening hothouse where eight Members of Parliament receive salaries of a thousand a year, for a certain given time, to mature at a proper season, a claim of two thousand for doing less, and on the credit of having toiled so long in the inferior laborious department'. In this speech Burke proposed to abolish the 'Principalities', including Lancaster and Cornwall, with all the separate offices (such as the Chancellor of the Duchy of Lancaster) which had grown attached to them; secondly, he proposed to abolish all the offices which had grown up around the landed estates of the Crown, and thirdly the extraordinary offices available at high salaries for Members of Parliament in the King's Household. These included men looking after the royal table-cloths, the Officer of the Great Wardrobe, the Groom of the Stole, the Keeper of the Jewel Office, as well as three useless treasurers to pay them all. Eventually these principles were embodied in Lord Rockingham's Act of 1782,[1] and from then on the Crown's power to offer pensions and sinecures in England was rapidly reduced.

This may clearly be seen from the figures. In George I's first Parliament 271 Members held offices, sinecures or pensions of some kind; in the first Parliament of George II there were 257; during the reign of George III until about 1780 the total rose again, but by the first Parliament of George IV in 1820 there were only 89 and by 1833 there were only 60.[2]

*

Another form of corruption that was frequently employed was the award of some kind of contract to Members, such as providing supplies to the Army and Navy, and this could sometimes produce considerable bitterness when the supplies turned rotten.[3] A great deal of naval history during the eighteenth and nineteenth centuries revolves around this question of corrupt suppliers to the Forces.[4] Partly owing to the shock of the American War of Independence, and partly owing to the rising cost to the Crown as its direct revenues grew fewer, this form of corruption also began to diminish around the same period. It is only worth bribing people if they are intelligent enough to be a nuisance, and the growth of bribery in Parliament was a testament to its growing power; when, however, any members

---

[1] Rockingham *Mem.*, ii. 334 and 22 Geo. III c.82. Burke became Paymaster in Rockingham's Government, and not only helped to abolish thirty to forty useless offices but received a fixed salary of £4,000 instead of the large unaudited emoluments of his predecessors.

[2] May, op. cit., i. 374. *Reports on Returns* made by Members; and *Hansard* Ser. 3 ii. 1188n.

[3] Anson, op. cit., 1. 372.

[4] *Parl. Hist.*, xx. 123–9 and xxi. 1333–4.

were so incompetent as to endanger the country then the other members of the Club felt moved to act, and this seems to have been what happened about 1782 with regard to naval and military contracts.

*

But if corruption in awarding contracts is likely to recoil on itself and be easily found out, corruption by awarding shares in loans, which was often practised by George III, is one of its most expensive forms. It was developed extravagantly by the Earl of Bute, the Duke of Grafton and Lord North, and meant that certain Honourable Members lent money to their country on very excellent terms to themselves. One loan brought out by Lord North[1] cost the country nearly £1 million; in one of Bute's loans in 1763 Members made a profit of £385,000;[2] in 1767 sixty Members were implicated in a fraud which involved the Chancellor of the Exchequer;[3] in 1769 and 1770 widescale corruption appears to have followed a Government lottery; and a motion against this by Seymour was refused, although 20,000 tickets were said to have gone to MPs;[4] two days later another member, Cornwall, who claimed that fifty MPs had been bought, was again refused leave to bring a motion.[5]

These forms of corruption were both expensive to the country and fairly easily detectable. Even Lord North was unable to continue them indefinitely, and they were more or less abolished by William Pitt the younger, who introduced what is virtually the modern method of dealing with tenders. He opened the tenders in the presence of those concerned and accepted the lowest tender, and 'was able to assure the House that not a shilling had been reserved for distribution to his friends'.[6] This was in 1784, the year in which Lord Rockingham's Act to abolish other forms of bribery came into force.

*

But the worst and most degrading system of all was direct payment for Members' votes. The early Stuarts had enough power to do without it, but once Charles I's head had been cut off matters changed; if the same thing were not to happen again, Parliament must be kept quiet. By the time of William III and Queen Anne this kind of bribery was customary, but it was Walpole who first developed the system which dominated the eighteenth century House of Commons. As its power grew under the House of Hanover, so did the amount of corruption.

[1] Anson, op. cit.
[2] *The North Briton* No. 42: Bute ms. in the British Museum.
[3] Walpole *Mem.*, ii. 428.
[4] May, op. cit., i. 384 and *Parl. Hist.*, xvii. 174.
[5] Ibid., 185.
[6] Stanhope: *Life of Pitt*, i. 219.

F

One of the difficulties of bribery and corruption lies in proving that it has ever taken place at all. Everybody appears to be united in believing that Sir Robert Walpole first created the direct payment for votes into a system, but there also appears to be very little that can be proved, and the proceedings against him had to be dropped by his enemies,[1] as nobody would give evidence. Parliament had gained supremacy over the Crown but was not yet itself responsible to anybody else,[2] so that to control Members the Government was even more inclined to resort to wholesale bribery for votes.[3]

In 1762 Bute entrusted the office formerly known as 'the management of the House of Commons'[4] to Henry Fox. Horace Walpole describes the methods: 'A shop was publicly opened at the Pay Office, whither the Members flocked, and received the wages of venality in bank bills even to so low a sum as £200, for their votes of the Treaty (of Utrecht—1763).' £25,000 was issued in one morning, as the Secretary to the Treasury, afterwards admitted, and in a fortnight a vast majority in the House had been purchased to approve the peace.[5] The climax came with the Ministry of Lord North. The King, George III, was fully involved and took a close personal interest in the proceedings, working generally through the Secretary to the Treasury, Robinson, who had the management of the House of Commons. 'Mr Robinson sent me a list of the speakers last night and of the very good majority. I have this morning sent him £6,000 to be placed to the same purpose as the sum transmitted on the 21st August.'[6] Usually the King employed the secret service money and the savings out of the Civil List; in 1782 the King writes:[7] 'I must express my astonishment at the quarterly accounts of the secret service only being made up to the 8th April, 1780. No business ought ever to be the excuse for not doing that.' In his answer to the King, Lord North explains that 'he has a heart full of the deepest affliction' over the delay. 'The secret service list was always ready after every quarter, so that no delay is imputable to him. Mr Robinson, whose list is of a nicer nature, never omitted entering every sum he paid the moment he paid it, that every article of his account is kept in perfect order.'[8]

*

[1] *Parl. Hist.*, xi. 1027–1303: Macaulay, op. cit., iii. 541 and iv. 146.
[2] Macaulay: *Essay on Chatham.* The Septennial Act of 1716 made matters worse by lengthening the life of Parliament to seven years and making it more independent of the electorate.
[3] Dicey: *Law of the Constitution*, p. 41.
[4] May, op. cit., 378.
[5] Walpole, *Mem.*
[6] George III to Lord North; Lord Brougham's *Works*, iii. 157.
[7] Correspondence with Lord North, ii. 144.
[8] Anson, op. cit., i. 374.

This form of bribery also stopped more or less with the end of Lord North's government. Why is it that parliamentary, as distinct from electoral, corruption 'is generally supposed to have ceased about the termination of the American War?'[1] In other words, between 1780 and 1784.

There are a number of possible reasons. The first is the clear failure of George III to break up the party system. With the defeat of the British by the Americans at Yorktown in 1781 Britain suffered a national disgrace, which roused the people and their MPs and forced the resignation of Lord North as Prime Minister. George III was forced to accept the Whigs in office and this, with his increasing insanity, virtually marked the end of his personal government. Charles James Fox wrote at the time 'provided we can stay in office long enough to give a good stout blow to the influence of the Crown I do not think it much signifies how soon we go after.'[2] Fox was proved right, although for many years after he wrote it looked as though the King's power would persist, for George continued to interfere, notably in the dismissal of William Pitt in 1801; but his own power and health had been fundamentally broken. Writing in 1789 at a time when he still controlled appointments in the Army, Navy, Church and House of Lords, he said 'I must decline entering into pressure of business, and indeed for the rest of my life I shall expect others to fulfil the duties of their employments, and only keep that superintending eye that can be effected without labour or fatigue'.[3]

Rockingham's Ministry passed successively a Contractor's Bill, a Revenue Officers' Bill and a Bill for the Reduction of Offices,[4] and although he died the King continued to be faced with unpleasant ministries. So much so that he told the Lord Advocate that 'sooner than yield he would go to Hanover, and had even prevailed upon the Queen to consent';[5] he was told quite clearly that it would be easy to go but not so easy to come back. He stayed, but the price of his remaining was that William Pitt the Younger became Prime Minister, and the King was scarcely able to rule without him for twenty years. George may have broken the Whig oligarchy, but the unexpected result was the growth of political parties to which the Crown ultimately became subservient. He may also in a sense have won his battle with the House of Commons, but it was through a Minister who kept a majority in the House with very little bribery, although Pitt did give offices and perquisites to his friends and colleagues.

*

[1] Hallam: *Constitutional History*, ii. 428.
[2] Letter to Fitzpatrick: *Mem.*, i. 317.
[3] Stanhope: *Life of Pitt*, ii. Appendix vii.
[4] May, op. cit., Ch. vi.
[5] Ibid., i. 64.

If the first reason for the great reduction of bribery was political the second was basically economic. Besides being a political and military defeat the American War was an economic disaster that had to be paid for. During the quarter of a century after 1789 the country was again in a state of national emergency, and continued the war against France by a policy of naval supremacy and large financial loans to other countries prepared to fight the Revolution and Napoleon. That Britain was able to do this was partly due to recuperating economic strength but also to the financial reforms of William Pitt. Even at best bribery and corruption is an extravagant and expensive form of government, usually indulged in by countries whose rulers have suddenly acquired wealth. One of the best but unkindest cures for corruption is undoubtedly a severe national crisis of some kind which will either abolish a weak government or reform it, and will anyway make it so short of money that it can no longer afford the luxury of bribery. The American and French wars had to be paid for by people just beginning to enjoy affluence, including the merchants and nabobs who were increasingly represented in the House of Commons; such people are usually impatient of wasteful government expenditure, and they were fortunate enough to be granted two great boons—a gospel for their beliefs in Adam Smith's *The Wealth of Nations*[1] and a great financial administrator in William Pitt. The freeing of trade, the abolition of government sinecures, the reduction of government economic control and the ending of parliamentary corruption went hand in hand. Furthermore, the newer Members of Parliament were more and more men who were already rich when they arrived at Westminster. Just as the rise of prices helped to destroy bribery and corruption at elections, so the rise in the wealth of Members helped to destroy it in Parliament itself.

*

The third reason was the development of political journalism, political oratory and serious political controversy.

The first to make full use of the opportunity offered by the printed word was John Wilkes. It is not relevant to enter into his story here, but this struggle had decisive results for the liberty of the press. From about 1771 onwards, although parliamentary reporting was still theoretically illegal, it was carried on successfully in practice and the public could read what their Members were saying. The press itself rose to new heights with the founding of the *Morning Chronicle* (1760), the *Morning Post* (1772), the *Morning Herald* (1780) and *The Times* itself in 1788, and another important factor in bringing Parliament under popular control was Fox's Libel Act of 1792, a

[1] First published in 1767.

great advance in allowing public criticism of governments. In addition Britain was fortunate in her propagandists. Hogarth perhaps drew attention to elections rather than to Parliament with his painting, but his later followers developed the art of the cartoon, so that Members of Parliament became well-known figures to the general public. Gillray in particular made Fox and Lord North unpopular during their coalition ministry.

By the later eighteenth century well-known journals like the *Rambler*, the *Spectator* and the *Tatler* appeared, and it became a commonplace to publish letters on particular political evils. Swift had shown the way by campaigning against the grant of minting Irish coinage to William Wood, and public correspondence continued throughout the century, helping to publicize the behaviour of Members and politicians generally.

By 1800 not only had the ferment of the French and American Revolutions produced numerous writers expounding political ideas, but people appeared to be entering the House of Commons to gain power or to express ideas rather than to seek social status or to make money. Perhaps this is one reason why it was a golden period of English political oratory, with Burke, Charles James Fox, Sheridan and Pitt illuminating the pages of English history. But another reason for the decline of corruption was improved publicity. The growth of newspapers and periodicals had enlarged the reading public, and the new circulating libraries of the mid-century increased it, and contributed to the rise of the late eighteenth century novelist and the writers of theoretical works.[1]

*

One other reform was partially inaugurated, which although it did not become normal practice until 1826, was another step forward against bribery; that was the publication of division lists, to show how Members voted. Macaulay states that lists were issued at the dissolution of 1689, but in 1696 the House of Commons declared that it was a breach of privilege to print the names of the minority, as being destructive of the freedom and liberties of Parliament.[2] With the increase in bribery under George III a movement began to publish details of how Members voted, which Burke[3] and many of the reformers of the time supported. In 1782 the Opposition freely published division lists with the ministerial names in red letters and the others in black, and this practice helped to kill the bribery of Members in the secrecy of the lobbies.

[1] London circulating libraries started in the mid-eighteenth century, and were opened in Birmingham in 1757 and Leeds in 1768. George II and III greatly enlarged the British Museum Library.
[2] *History of England*, iii. 535.
[3] *Comm. Journ.*, x. 572.

Another new public force which began to compel both Court and Parliament to behave itself more in accordance with popular wishes was the pressure group, which is dealt with in a later chapter, and the new use of the public meeting and the mob. These had always existed, but two conditions helped to increase their importance at this time. To begin with more Englishmen were living in towns, which is why the mob was becoming powerful at the time of Wilkes and during the Gordon Riots against Roman Catholics in 1780. Not only were people drifting to the towns, however, but the population itself was rapidly increasing, as medicine and economic opportunity both improved. The effect was to strengthen the power of the demagogue and of the untutored mob, but it also alarmed honourable members, several of whom had been captured by Lord George Gordon's rioters; during the years of the French revolutionary wars it led to a number of repressive Acts by a frightened Legislature, but in time the mass democratic meeting came to play a valuable part in English politics.

To sum up, the ending of bribery and corruption in the Houses of Parliament took place during the years after the end of the American War of Independence in 1781. It was partly due to legislation, but more fundamentally it was caused by political, economic and social forces. Politically, the defeat of the Crown in several spheres at home and abroad, and the growth of a party system based more on principles and less on interest; economically, the disasters of the two revolutionary and Napoleonic wars, coupled with the financial reforms of Pitt, who was almost unassailable in the House of Commons; and socially through the greater publicity given to the behaviour of Members and their voting. The reform of Members themselves played a great part in the eventual reform of the elections which returned them to power.

CHAPTER 4

Administration and the Civil Service

'The entire business of government is skilled employment.'
(Edmund Burke)
'A system of out-relief for the British aristocracy.'
(John Bright)

—◦❧❦◦—

The last chapter gave some account of reforms affecting parliamentary corruption which were made by the Rockingham Ministry and the Whigs between 1780 and 1784, largely because of the defeat of George III's policies and the disaster to the country of the American War. An equally vital series of reforms stemming from the same period was the transformation of government service which took place mainly between 1782 and 1832. It is still widely believed that the reform of the Civil Service began with the Northcote-Trevelyan Report of 1854. This is a gross exaggeration, since state intervention was a growing reality throughout the second quarter of the century.[1] Indeed, in some ways the Trevelyan Report was 'a biased abuse of his position'.[2] There were already 21,000 'civil servants' by 1832; by 1852, before the Report, the number had already almost doubled to 39,000, and this had not happened without some corresponding improvement in their organization.

The 'Civil Service' in Britain was originally a group of the King's servants, sometimes his domestics, and its growth was assisted by the Church, which had a virtual monopoly of education and provided most of the public servants before the Reformation.[3] After Henry VIII's dissolution of the monasteries the civil service gradually became secular, personified perhaps a century later by that most

[1] Prouty: *The Transformation of the Board of Trade*, 1830–55, p. 1.
[2] Sir John Craig: *A History of Red Tape*, on which this chapter relies for many of its details.
[3] We have used the phrase 'Civil Service' in inverted commas, because there was in fact no such thing as the Civil Service until after the Northcote-Trevelyan Report first adumbrated it in the nineteenth century, but we are so accustomed to the expression that it is convenient to use it in describing the multiplicity of offices which existed in the service of Parliament, or for the patronage of its members, during the previous centuries. 'There were "civil services", but no Civil Service; the question (in 1854) was whether to create one' (Mackenzie and Grove: *Central Administration in Britain*, p. 6).

famous of all civil servants, Samuel Pepys.[1] Many of the outdated useless offices once performed by the King's domestics remained well into the eighteenth century, and it was these (which we discussed in the previous chapter) which were filled by the place-men of George III and the Whigs. This arose from the implications of the Act of Settlement of 1707, which will be mentioned later in this chapter, for it was this and other measures which helped to distinguish ministers from civil servants; before that time the distinction was largely invalid.

Horace Walpole thought that the sinecures and ill-earned pensions which existed for Members of the eighteenth century House of Commons represented a thoroughly good system, on the principle that men who inherited titles might be stupid, but that people who bought sinecures were not. The evidence for the second part of this theory seems to be lacking, and many of those posts were filled by the duller family connections of leading men. Not long after the Scottish Lord Bute became Prime Minister there were sixty-three Macs, twenty-five Campbells, an uncertain number of Hamiltons and many other Scots to be found on the Pensions List.[2] This applied not only to Ministers' relations but to Members' relations as well, and was one of the reasons why the price of parliamentary seats was rising so high. 'Every appointment to the regular civil service was initiated by a Member of Parliament according to a system by which each Member of Parliament voting with the Government had a certain section of the public patronage handed over to him, and the more inefficient his nominee, the more grateful were the relatives of the nominee.'[3] We have already mentioned some of the more ludicrous offices at George III's disposal, and how Burke attacked them and Rockingham abolished some of them. But many of them lingered on into the nineteenth century, and in 1814, after their number had been added to in war time, Patrick Colquhoun estimated that £8 million, or nearly 3 per cent of the national income, was paid out in the form of State Service and Pensions.[4]

*

A glance at some individual departments will give an idea of how normal and acceptable this system of corruption was.

During the eighteenth century, with the rise of the Treasury and the appointment of Paymasters to the individual Forces and Departments of State, the Exchequer became a mere book-keeping section —'a museum of archeological antiquities'.[5]

[1] Arthur Bryant: *Samuel Pepys, Saviour of the Navy*, gives a good idea of staffing and numbers in Restoration days.
[2] Cole and Postgate: *The Common People*.
[3] Graham Wallas: *Public Administration*, January, 1928, p. 4.
[4] *Wealth, Power and Resources of the British Empire*, 1814.
[5] Craig, p. 38.

As a result of the application of piece rates to the enormous sums nominally passing through the Department and its books the 'Writer of Tallies' was getting £7,000 a year instead of the £10 he received 300 years previously, when he actually did the work. The 'Clerk of the Pells' took £7,600 a year during the American War, and a whole list of such offices was in the hands of the First Lord of the Treasury. But in 1783 the 'Chamberlains' were disposed of for a pension of £2,000 a year, and the 'Usher and Tally Cutters' ' offices were abolished, indented cheques being substituted for tallies. The 'Auditors of Prests and Imprests', with their staffs, were abolished in 1785 and replaced by two Commissioners, and although they had a staff of thirty the salary bill dropped from £33,687 to £8,650. The duties themselves were not altered. The Exchequer continued its shaky existence until 1834, using Roman numerals in Tudor script, on parchment rolls and frequently in Latin. Edmund Burke in his speeches and during his period as Paymaster did a great deal to reform these methods, but his efforts were not always successful; and although he disdained most of the emoluments and perquisites of office himself, he reappointed two clerks who had been dismissed for embezzlement, who, thus suitably encouraged, embezzled another quarter of a million pounds before they were caught. The Clerk of the Pells was reduced from £7,600 to £3,000 after the American War; the 'King's Remembrancer' averaged £1,633 in fees but left all the work to his deputy, the two posts being combined in 1823 at a salary of £1,000. Among the more archaic officers, the Clerk of the Nichills, the Surveyor of Green Wax, the Foreign Opposer, the Clerk of the Pipe and the Controller of the Pipe were all abolished in 1834, when the Exchequer's work passed to a Comptroller General of Receipts and Staff. The cost to the nation fell from £40,500 to £6,800.

Another remunerative employment during the eighteenth century was in the office of one of the Secretaries of State, as officials could hold several posts and therefore several incomes at once. A certain William Fraser, for example, who was an Under-Secretary from 1782 to 1789, drew not £500 a year but £2,255, because he was also German Translator, writer of the London Gazette, Clerk of the Signet and a Customs Writer.[1]

One of Dr Johnson's most remarkable definitions is that of excise —'a hateful tax levied upon commodities and adjudged not by the common judges of property but wretches hired by those to whom the excise is paid'. This may not be very good as a definition, but it certainly appears to have been justified emotionally. Excise receipts rose from £½ million in 1687 to £7 million in 1787,[2] and a lot of money was made by a few senior officials. The Solicitor received

[1] Craig, p. 71.
[2] Ibid., p. 101.

£2,246 a year but the work was done by a deputy on £500; but the Receiver-General, who received a salary of £3,050 had to pay out as much as £1,200 a year to other people to do his work.

The Post Office was another rewarding service for the unscrupulous. Henry Bishop, the inventor of the postmark, paid £21,500 a year to be Postmaster-General for seven years; Lord Arlington paid £25,000 for the next seven and the price eventually rose to £40,000. In the eighteenth century most of the senior officials did well for themselves; Anthony Todd, who was Secretary from 1768 to 1798, nominally received £200 but in fact got about £4,000, as did his successor until 1836. But decisive reforms were made from that time onwards by William Maberley, the next holder of the office, and by Rowland Hill, who introduced the penny post in 1840.[1]

The Board of Trade is one of the most interesting of all government departments in this context, as it bears on both the points we are at present considering—it was an example of vigorous reform before the Northcote-Trevelyan era, and it appears to have been less affected by inefficiency and corruption than most.[2] It began in 1640 as two separate committees of the Privy Council, one dealing with commercial treaties and weights and measures, and the other with 'plantations'; they were fused in 1671 and after several shaky starts got working in the eighteenth century. In 1779 the Presidency was separated from the remainder of the work to provide the Earl of Carlisle with a job after his failure in America. It was this action more than anything else that sparked off movements for economic reform, and Burke in his speeches made particular fun of the Board of Trade and the 2,500 volumes of reports it had produced. When the Whigs came into office in 1782 they abolished the Board, but with the revival of trade after the American War it was restarted in 1786 with its present constitution; in 1830 its staff numbered twenty, in 1840 thirty, in 1853 sixty-six, and in 1914 7,500.[3] The Board was steadily transformed from an advisory committee of the Privy Council into an administrative Department of State. When he reported in 1854 Trevelyan could say 'There is probably no department of the Government to whose functions so many and such important additions have been made as the Board of Trade . . . of late years, a large amount of executive business, very important and very serious in its nature, has been assigned to this Department. Thus in 1832 it was charged with the duty of collecting and publishing statistical information; since 1840 it has exercised a more or less minute control over the Railway Companies; about the same time the Government School of Design was placed under its superintendence; the Office for the Registration of Designs and that for

---

[1] H. Robinson: *The British Post Office.*
[2] Prouty, op. cit.
[3] Sir Hubert Llewellyn Smith: *The Board of Trade.*

the Registration of Joint Stock Companies have also been attached to it, and within the last two years a new and most important addition had been made to its functions by the Act for the Regulation of Merchant Shipping of the country, for the winding up and determination of the Merchant Seamen's Fund and for the inspection of our steam navigation.'[1] It was precisely because the Board of Trade was growing, and adding constantly to its functions in the early nineteenth century, that it had to be efficient; it was not saddled with archaic sinecures and could not afford corruption. The number of civil servants was small and they had a great deal of work to do in the growing governmental activity brought about by the radical social and economic changes of the industrial revolution. A dedicated oligarchy grew up that helped to remove antiquated laws and procedures so that business, local government, the money market, education and many other branches of society might grow, and the major reforms took place before 1850; otherwise nineteenth century Britain would never have been able to leap ahead of the rest of Europe as she did.

The War Office and the Admiralty were other examples of Departments in which both corruption and administrative reform can be traced in the early nineteenth century, but it will be more appropriate to say something of this in a later chapter on the Armed Forces.

*

We have departed somewhat from the reform of corruption to that of administration, and we must now return to examine the reasons why corruption was declining in government service during the late eighteenth and early nineteenth centuries. First, the Whigs' success in curbing George III and reducing the Crown's power of patronage; second, the financial reforms of Pitt, secure in power and possibly needing the weapon of bribery and patronage less than his predecessors; third, the stringency involved in nearly a quarter of a century's wars with France; and fourth, the fact that after Lord Liverpool's long period of office closed in 1827 there were frequent changes of government, with Canning, Goderich, Wellington, Grey, Melbourne, Peel, Russell, Derby and Aberdeen as Prime Ministers within the period of twenty-five years. The old practice of changing the principal officers of state each time had to be abandoned because it would have been unworkable, and as a result there emerged the modern type of civil servant with plans for nationalization in one file and denationalization in another, prepared to implement either with equal fidelity according to the political persuasion of his master. If he were non-partisan he would be rewarded with security; if he were

[1] *Parliamentary Papers*, 1854, xxvii.

partisan or corrupt the next ministry would almost certainly dismiss him.[1]

Later, in Victorian England, corruption declined as central control spread in spheres where efficiency, impartiality and technical knowledge were essential. The appointment of the first Inspectors of Schools in 1849, of Factor Inspectors and of Poor Law Commissioners were examples of this; so were the Charity Commissioners, appointed in 1853 to overhaul the grinding, creaking apparatus of centuries-old trusts and charities, many of which were being corruptly misapplied.[2] Another important but unheralded agency of central control was the General Register Office, founded in 1836 under the influence of Edwin Chadwick, who took records from the local 'Guardians' (the embryo local authorities) of all births, marriages and deaths. From 1839 to 1877, William Farr, FRS, published an Annual Abstract of Statistics, which helped to draw attention to disparities in local conditions of health and poor relief. These were the beginnings of a scientific approach to the problems of administration, and corruption does not flourish in this atmosphere.

There were other, more political, reasons. An amendment to the Act of Settlement in 1707 had prohibited MPs from holding offices of profit under the Crown if those offices had been created after 1705, which is the main reason why during the eighteenth century they held posts with such antiquated titles. The Act did not stop the flood of office distribution which took place during the rest of the century, and which, as we have seen, overflowed into the nineteenth, but at least it contained it within bounds.

One other problem was dealt with during these reforming years of 1780–84. One of the fears expressed by Members and by the public during the eighteenth century was that excise men would always vote for the Minister and use their office to further his purposes as well as making money for themselves. In 1782 the simple expedient was adopted of disenfranchizing civil servants completely, and they did not obtain the vote again until 1867. All through the eighteenth and the first half of the nineteenth century, however, there remained a large number of posts which could be held by Members who were not ministers, and these were widely used as an inducement to Members to vote the way the minister required.[3]

As to nepotism, it would be possible to give almost endless examples in the civil service, especially of how Walpole catered for

[1] The 'spoils system' in American administration may help to explain why there are more complaints of corruption in Washington than in Whitehall.

[2] The usefulness of this reform is shown by the fact that by 1894 £154,000 was coming to elementary schools and nearly £750,000 to secondary schools from this source.

[3] Craig, p. 174.

his family, and how offices in the Law Departments were multiplied to provide for the relatives of Ministers and Members; but eventually the question returns of how and why the system died. Some reasons have already been suggested and they accord well with the actions of the House of Commons. After the American defeat, the Commons set up committees to investigate unnecessary offices and they did this again in the Napoleonic Wars, and during the tide of reform in 1834. Some of the major reforms took place in 1810, however,[1] when fifty-five sinecures fell vacant and disappeared. In spite of this the Select Committee of 1810[2] reported that there were some 240 offices which ought to be abolished, and which cost just under £300,000 a year, regardless of the cost of deputies. There is an interesting contrast between the Reports of Select Committees in 1797 and 1834; the first stated that 'smaller persons (i.e. minor civil servants) should have adequate salaries and pensions instead of small sinecures, but that the large sinecures, which were connected with the great Offices of States, might be continued as they helped those who had given worthy service to their country when they retired'.[3] By 1834 the mood had completely changed:[4] 'Anything in the nature of a sinecure office ... is alike indefensible, pernicious as a means of influence and grievous as an undue addition to the general burden of the nation.'[5] Of course they were right to say this, but what had changed peoples' minds so completely in thirty-seven years?

We have tried to give what we consider the immediate reasons, but the fundamental reasons probably lie deeper.

Firstly, the industrial revolution had begun to make its effects felt. Business expanded and the business community, having obtained power with the vote, wanted much greater efficiency in government. During the second quarter of the nineteenth century Government was essentially an ally of business and commerce, as we have seen in a brief glance at the Board of Trade. It was the Government and the Government alone which could sweep away the waste of the antiquated system of the eighteenth century, which was now positively hindering the great leap forward in commerce. Men with some understanding of commerce, often the second generation of prosperous industrialists, like Gladstone, Peel, Cobden and Bright, began to appear in the House of Commons.

But not only had the people changed; the work had also. In the eighteenth century there was little real work and so much real wealth that inefficiency did not matter very much, and nobody hurls dia-

---

[1] Craig, p. 177.

[2] Report of the Commons Committee on Sinecure Offices, June 20, 1810.

[3] Select Committee on Finance, 1789–98.

[4] Report of the Commons Committee on Sinecure Offices, 1834, pp. 25–27.

[5] See Norman Gash, op. cit., Ch. 13; and Foord: *The Waning of 'The Influence of the Crown'*, lxii. 484.

tribes at the civil service of the eighteenth century as Dickens did in the nineteenth. Up to the early nineteenth century there were hardly any administrative or executive decisions to be made by 'civil servants'. Most offices were only open for two or three hours a day, though they kept a reserve of staff in case there should be a sudden onset of work. There were no vacations, but there were twenty-eight holy days and individual departments added what they wanted. The Customs only had forty-four days off a year, but the Stamp Office had fifty-two and the Excise Headquarters fifty-six. In case of a shortage of saints, holidays were added for the anniversary of Elizabeth I's accession, Guy Fawkes Day, the Great Fire, the landing of William III, the accession of the three Georges and four other Royal Birthdays.[1] By the time of Queen Victoria's accession, all this was changing and a large growing population had to be governed. The machinery of government was becoming so complicated that administrative decisions could no longer be taken by Ministers and Members of Parliament, and Departments and their specialists were expanding. Doubtless 'Parkinson's Law' operated equally well in those days, and increasing numbers of staff increased the amount of work, supervision and administration that had to be done.

Secondly, the pressure of population was being felt in the civil service in another way. The population of all social groups was rapidly increasing, but with the advent of new schools for the upper and middle classes, such as Haileybury, Rugby and Shrewsbury, Victorian England faced a dangerous surplus of well educated men of the 'governing class'.

*

This brings us to the era of the Northcote-Trevelyan Report and the emergence of a more systematic and uncorrupt Civil Service.

The origins of the modern British Civil Service were in India. The attack upon Warren Hastings by Burke was a valuable lesson to all proconsuls against accepting bribes, and after his indictment the Viceroys and Members of the Council were men of high standing, and were succeeded by an administrative service of almost mythical rectitude. Nevertheless, dislike and envy of the East India Company's monopoly grew, and in 1833 Macaulay recommended to Parliament an arrangement whereby four candidates were to be nominated to each vacancy in the Company's training school at Haileybury, and final selection was to be made on the basis of competitive examination.[2] 'Look at every walk of life, at this House and the other House,

---

[1] Perhaps this deal of leisure may explain the extraordinary literary ability of the civil service and the time they had for writing. Sir John Craig gives a list of 109 eminent writers who were civil servants.

[2] Ogg: *English Government and Politics*, p. 221.

at the Bar, at the Bench, at the Church and see whether it be not generally men who were distinguished in their academic career . . . the persons who became the greatest proficients in those languages (Latin and Greek) . . . will generally be the flower of the youth, the most acute, the most industrious and the most ambitious of honourable distinction.'[1]

Here is foreshadowed the popular image of the colonial administrator of later years, trained in Christian character and the Classics. These men, by their class and upbringing, were insensitive to the latent political aspirations of the people they governed, and it is fashionable today to denigrate them. But whatever their limitations may have been, they represented personal and public integrity at its highest.

Macaulay's system for India was soon suspended in 1837, but in 1853 nominations were finally swept away and replaced by open competition. In the same year Gladstone, as Chancellor of the Exchequer, appointed Sir Charles Trevelyan, Macaulay's brother-in-law, and Sir Stafford Northcote, to investigate the civil service at home. Their famous Report was in fact violent and unfair. 'It is only for the unambitious and the indolent or incapable that (entry to the service) is generally desired. The certainty of a pension furnished strong inducements to the parents and friends of sickly youths to endeavour to obtain for them "government employment".' At higher ages 'the dregs of all other professions are attracted to the public service as a secure asylum'. Trevelyan talked of numerous instances of the appointment of 'men of very slender capacity and perhaps of questionable character'. He gave no indication of where they were employed.

On the evidence of civil service reform that has already been given, and of some of Trevelyan's own statements, these comments are nonsense. The civil service then numbered about 53,000 and Trevelyan only claimed to have investigated 16,000, whose whereabouts are not mentioned.[2] When the Report was first published it was laughed at by most people, and according to Macaulay had little support in the House of Commons.

But the proposals of the Report were ultimately adopted and were, briefly, that admission should be by open competition, that there would be a sharp division between routine and intellectual posts (in the new 'administrative' grade), and that for the latter examinations should be academic. The whole process was to be supervised by a 'Civil Service Commission'. (Incidentally, examinations were not new. The Customs had tests before 1700 and by the early nineteenth century they existed in the Treasury, Audit, Admiralty, Emigration, Ordnance, Pay, National Debt, Privy

[1] Speech on the Government of India, House of Commons, July 10, 1833.
[2] R. Moses: *The Civil Service of Great Britain*, Ch. 3

Council, Registry General, Inland Revenue and Works;[1] but it was admittedly normal for the Treasury to write to the MP for the area concerned who voted with the Government, to see if he had a recommendation.)

From the viewpoint of this book, which is concerned with bribery and corruption, this was a tremendous advance, since the men who survived the process of 'open competition' were of the highest integrity. From another point of view, however, bribery and open nepotism were succeeded by influence of a different kind, since open competition meant in practice that the top posts went to those whose parents had been sufficiently wealthy or influential to get them to public schools and to Oxford or Cambridge. It ensured a large fund of lucrative jobs for intelligent, conscientious men from upper-class England. The Civil Service became what John Bright described as 'a colossal scheme of out-relief for the upper classes'. But they have left their mark on the Service to this day and are largely responsible for the recent tradition of honesty and incorruptibility in public life. (In the eighteenth century men from many classes had made their way to the top, whether it was by ability, corruption or nepotism.)

Trained in schools where strict morality was rigidly instilled, they played their games, spoke in their university unions and gained their first-class honours, everywhere being treated as superiors and masters of other mortals; as indeed in some senes they were, for their combination of intellectual, athletic and moral excellence was unique. Those who went overseas to serve the British Empire were subject to the temptation of power, brought about by their immense authority and effortless superiority. For this the British Empire later paid. But they were not subject to the temptations of corruption in the material sense. They had power and status beyond the dreams of an Indian prince—such indeed that Indian princes and rich men were desperately anxious that their sons should go to English public schools and endeavour to gain something of the same glamour. Their wealth was sufficient for their needs. Their ingrained integrity apart, how could they be corrupted?

'One of the greatest improvements in public affairs ever proposed by a Government,' said John Stuart Mill of the Report, but that was not the opinion of other men. The Treasury used to declare it had no vacancies, and then when the lists were closed, took men who had been tried out in other Departments,[2] and Trollope, who organized the Post Office in the provinces, could see no benefit in the competitions.[3] A Select Committee of 1860 declared that the Commission's Order in Council had been largely evaded and that its competitive examinations were 'shams' and 'a fertile source of abuse'.

[1] Craig, p. 188.
[2] Ibid., p. 188.
[3] Trollope: *Autobiography*.

In 1859 a Superannuation Act was decisive, because it provided that nobody appointed after that date should be eligible for a pension unless he had a certificate from the Commissioners on admission to the Service, and in 1870 the system of competitive examination was made universal and compulsory.

These measures were the final death-knell of patronage and privilege in the Civil Service, but it seems wrong to regard them or the Northcote-Trevelyan Report as direct and sudden inspirations from heaven; they were the end of a process which began in the 1780s and gained momentum in the second quarter of the nineteenth century. Its underlying causes, to sum up, were the industrial revolution and the population changes which followed it; the entry into Parliament of a new class of men, with adequate wealth, power and status of their own, frequently high-principled and not self-seeking; and the dominant philosophy of the time, expressed by the Utilitarians Bentham, Chadwick and Mill, which was against patronage and in favour of efficiency. The example of Napoleon had shown how a great Empire could be efficiently administered, and the new teachings of economic science were coming to be applied to government and the Civil Service. Corruption was swept away and many advantages followed. Whether there were any consequent disadvantages in having senior public servants drawn from one sector of society only is outside the province of this book.

CHAPTER 5

Local Government

'As the old ones drop off they are sure to choose none in their room
but those they have marked for their purpose beforehand; so rogue
succeeds rogue, and the same scene of villany is carried on to the
terror of poor parishoners.'

(Daniel Defoe, 1714)

'God expresses himself in many ways, even by local government.'

(G. K. Chesterton)

During the nineteenth century a radical change took place in local
government as it did in most other spheres of authority. In 1834
there were hardly any elected councils throughout the country, but
when Gladstone left office sixty years later every village, town and
county had one. The immediate results of this advance in democracy
were similar to those in parliamentary democracy—an increase in
bribery because of the larger number of electors to be bribed, and an
increase in corruption because of the expanding work of local public
bodies and the expanding opportunity this gave for graft in the
award of contracts and the sale of property. Towards the end of the
century, however, local self-government taught the British people to
govern themselves, and produced municipal councillors and administrators who had a profound influence on honest government
nationally. As in national government, reform reached its climax
in the 1880s, but its causes were somewhat different.

Hitherto there had been two principal elements in British local
government—the rural Justices of the Peace and the corporations of
the Boroughs, each a law unto itself, to whose shortcomings, to
use a mild expression, some reference has already been made in
Chapter 2.

In the country at large local government from about 1600 until
1760 was controlled by the County Justices, that is to say the
administration of justice and of the public services (such as they
were) were in the same hands; the unit of administration was the
ecclesiastical parish. The changing conditions of the industrial
revolution set their authority on its decline and strained the parish
system to the utmost, but their administrative function was not
finally abolished in the towns until 1835 or in the countryside until

1894. Their power had been steadily growing since the day of the Tudors, who sought to lessen the power of the nobles and barons by giving more of it to the justices. With the social revolution of the sixteenth century and the growth of roads and bridges, as well as with the dissolution of the monasteries, the JPs increased their local dominion, although they were formally under the control of the King's Council and the Court of King's Bench. Then in 1642 Parliament (containing many local magistrates) abolished these methods of control in order to reduce the power of the Stuart monarchy, and the mass of people came automatically under the direct and often harsh rule of the landed gentry. Throughout the eighteenth century their power continued to grow, and by 1760 they were responsible for law and order, the Poor Law, the control of the liquor trade, highways and bridges, labouring conditions and the general regulation of production and distribution.[1] Wealth, power and status were all concentrated in the hands of a few men in most areas of local government.

By 1832 there were over 15,000 separately administered parishes,[2] whose areas varied fantastically for reasons going as far back as the first invasions of England, and whose powers, wealth and population varied correspondingly. All the inhabitants had the right to participate in local business and the duty to perform the various offices of the parish, but in practice a small oligarchy, usually the tenants of the squire and the wealthier employers, presided over by the vicar of the parish and dominated by the local JPs, controlled their affairs.[3] The name Vestry was used to describe these bodies, the name being taken from the vestry of the Church, in which they usually met; most of them were 'open', i.e. everybody who lived in the parish could take part, but in the larger and also in the newer parishes they were 'closed' or 'select', like the closed corporations of the Tudor and Stuart boroughs. In some parts of England, particularly in the south, the system could work well either in the open or closed vestries, and they could carry out one vital purpose of local government, the training of citizens in its participation. By the end of the eighteenth century one keen observer could already note that 'the first attempt towards a democracy in England would be the common people demanding an admission and a voice in the Vestries and voting themselves whatever rates they thought to be appropriate'.[4] As their duties increased, however, with the growth of population and the development of transport, the work became too complicated to be done by mere rotation of office, even in the stable rural com-

[1] E. O. Dovell: *A Hundred Years of Quarter Sessions.*
[2] K. B. Smellie: *A History of Local Government*, p. 12.
[3] Sidney and Beatrice Webb: *Statutory Authorities for Special Purposes*, Chs. 5 and 6.
[4] Arthur Young: *Travels in France.*

munities of the south. It became common practice for those in control of the vestries to receive a sum of money from those too lazy or too busy to do the work they were supposed to do, and to make even more money by farming out the work to a contractor or some other official.[1] 'It is well known that when any person who has received a good education and whose habits are those of a gentleman settles in a Parish, one of his first objects is to exempt himself from parish office.'[2] These were possibly the more honest citizens, for those who did take office expected to fleece the community; 'every parish officer thinks he has a right to make a round bill during his year of office' wrote an observer in 1796, referring to their habit of awarding themselves contracts, according to their trade, for parish work. 'Accountable to no one for how they spent the parish funds, they abused their powers in many ways, but particularly in spending the rates, levied for the relief of the poor, on the feasting and refreshment of the vestrymen.'[3] It is remarkable how deep-seated was the habit, in vestry and borough alike, of feasting oneself at the public expense.

It was even worse in the swelling, heaving areas of London and the industrial North, for there the vestry system which was legally supposed to be in force often broke down completely. Occasionally the equivalent of the modern 'city boss' would arise to organize corruption as a system, as in Bethnal Green, where Joseph Merceron held power over a local political machine for nearly fifty years from 1787, although he was imprisoned in 1818 for misappropriating public funds.[4] It was bad enough where there was an open vestry, for these were often at the merch of the demagogue and mob rule. When the vestries were closed, i.e. restricted to a few members either by statute or custom, there was more often arbitrary rule and corruption of the worst kind.

Great towns like Leeds and Manchester, which were growing rapidly in the latter part of the eighteenth century, still had their vestries, their overseers and their constables on the rural pattern, but the country gentlemen who controlled such cities were careful not to come too close, except when their rents were in danger. In some places there were no vestries at all, closed or open, because the parish was a complete sinecure, and no one had ever carried out any Church duties for the stipend which he was doubtless drawing all the time. In many parishes too, funds which had been created

---

[1] Smellie, op. cit., p. 14.

[2] Report of the Poor Law Commissioners, 1833.

[3] B. Keith-Lucas: *The English Local Government Franchise*; frequent reference will be made to this book, which is a mine of information on the waywardness of human nature.

[4] Woodward: *Age of Reform*, p. 440.

originally for relief or education were merely used to line the pockets of privileged individuals.[1]

But perhaps the worst corruption existed in the 246 towns with Charters of Incorporation, where self-elected irresponsible corporations did largely what they pleased, wasted the ratepayers' money on private needs or on feasting, and were frequently insolvent.[2] 'The twenty-four shall be instead of the whole commanalty, and no other of the commanalty to meddle on pain of five pounds,' said a minute of the Romney Marsh Corporation in 1604. This was the sort of privilege which not only gained the self-appointed members of the Corporation a good solid income, but which gave them immunity from parliamentary reform. They were the real stronghold of parliamentary privilege and corruption, and especially of bribery, because they had charged for their votes and it was difficult for Members of Parliament to bite the hand that had fed them. Sometimes they were largely of one family, and they often sold their parliamentary representation to the highest bidder. Where freemen had the franchise, corporation trust funds were often used to bribe them, and when they had an exclusive right to the vote a large addition was frequently made to their numbers.[3]

In many boroughs the right to elect to Parliament was the sole function that was being exercised at the end of the eighteenth century, but in others the financial corruption and misuse of funds was incredible to modern eyes. The notion that corporate funds should be spent on the welfare of the inhabitants as a whole, and not on the private purposes and pleasures of the controlling body, had not dawned upon them. The Royal Commission which was appointed to look into this fantastic situation in 1833 reported an 'erroneous but strongly rooted opinion that the property of the Corporation was held in trust for the corporate body only, and not for the local community as a whole'. Expenditure of the latter kind would be 'a spontaneous act of private generosity, not the well-considered application of the public revenue'.[4]

But even before the revolutionary wars with France, thinking men could see that the Justices from an agrarian age were quite incompetent to deal with the new towns.[5] The best of the Justices were men whose interests had been rural, and in the government of rural England they often displayed knowledge, enthusiasm and public

---

[1] In one case, Bishop Pretyman Tomline, tutor to the younger Pitt, was found embezzling funds, but this was not generally thought to be discreditable to him. (Cole and Postgate: *The Common People*.)

[2] Report of the Commission on Municipal Corporations, 1833, p. 16.

[3] Ibid., pp. 33–4 and 45.

[4] Redlich and Hurst: *The History of Local Government in England*, ed. B. Keith-Lucas, pp. 127–8.

[5] 'Such an infinite variety of business has been heaped upon them that few care to undertake and fewer understand the office.' (Blackstone, 1765.)

spirit. It was too much to expect them to grasp the tedious and increasingly technical problems of an urban proletariat, still less to be in sympathy with its growing political consciousness.[1] But if one may sympathize with the best of them, and salute their achievement, there were others with whom it would be difficult to sympathize at all. For 'others were worse than useless, they were corrupt. The Justices of Middlesex are generally the scum of the earth ... notoriously men of such infamous character that they are unworthy of any employ whatsoever.'[2] By the system of making up for low wages by payments out of the rates which they developed at the end of the eighteenth century—the so-called Speenhamland system—they encouraged employers to pay low wages and put up the cost of poor relief. There were also many bigots among them: a member of the Municipal Corporations Commission in 1838 referred to 'the refusal of the County magistrates to act with a man who has been a grocer and is a Methodist', but added that this was 'the dictate of genuine patriotism'.

*

The first era of local government reform in the 1830s had a very great influence on the suppression of corruption. Corruption in national politics seemed to many people to be wrong in principle, but corruption in local politics was wrong in an even more embarrassing place—the pocket. As local government in England became increasingly democratic the ordinary ratepayer could not but note with fury the way in which local councils spent his money on themselves; when legislation suppressed the more blatant abuses his watchfulness continued. Legislative reforms in this sphere came from two directions:

First, the Poor Law, with which local government had been closely bound up since Elizabethan days, and on the foundations of which its administration had always rested, a fact which puzzles many people in today's developing countries where the relief of the poor is a family responsibility, and can hardly be thought of in any other terms. In the late eighteenth and early nineteenth centuries the Poor Law was getting seriously out of hand, both because of the amount of the national revenue that it was consuming and because of its inefficient and often corrupt administration. The industrial revolution, the drift to the towns and the economic depression after the Napoleonic Wars had so increased poverty and destitution that expenditure had risen from £1,912,000 in 1785 to the intolerable sum of £7,870,000 in 1817. This was derived from the local rates and administered by the parish vestries as their most important responsibility.

---

[1] A somewhat parallel situation arose 150 years later among the more patrician and paternal of colonial administrators *vis-à-vis* the urbanized Africans.

[2] Burke, 1780.

During the first thirty years of the nineteenth century a number of Acts of Parliament were passed[1] whose object was to bring some better order into the membership and method of voting in both the open and select vestries, and though these were aimed at reforming local government in the vestries, rather than corruption or maladministration of the Poor Law, they had the effect of restraining some of the old abuses, for example the favouring of relatives and dependants in the award of relief. More especially they put a sharp brake on some of the excesses of the select vestries, simply by providing for more equitable representation and proper voting.

But the new Poor Law of 1834 had more far-reaching effects on parish vestry government. Its provisions belong more properly to the story of local government reorganization than to the fight against corruption, but they are important to us for the centralizing principle which they introduced, and which is undoubtedly a deterrent to corruption in the raw stages of democracy. The Act removed the administration of the Poor Law from the parishes altogether and devised a new unit of administration, embracing many parishes and based upon geographical and administrative convenience; in other words upon utility; it devised new representative bodies to administer poor relief, to be known as Boards of Guardians, comprising the local Justices together with others elected on a ratepayers' franchise; established a national board of control called the Poor Law Commissioners; placed the actual executive work of relief in the hands of paid officials known as overseers, responsible to the Commissioners as well as the Guardians; and provided for proper audit and the surcharge of improper expenditure. It set the tone for later administrative reforms in other fields, and foreshadowed the peculiarly English relationship of central and local authorities.

The Commissioners were certainly successful in a financial sense, for the rate per head of expenditure for poor relief dropped from 9s 9d in 1831 to 5s 6½d in 1851;[2] but—alas for human nature— they were soon complaining that the new overseers used their office for private profit, let some people off the rate altogether or used the surplus for private business.

As for the Poor Law Guardians, the manner of their election continued to be both corrupt and grotesque for many years to come.[3]

*

If the Poor Law had as its main object the diminution of expenditure by more rational and efficient administration, which would incidentally diminish corruption, the Municipal Corporations Act of the

---

[1] Associated with the names of Sturges Bourne and John Cam Hobhouse.
[2] C. B. Fay: *Great Britain from Adam Smith to the Present Day*, p. 338.
[3] For details of this, see Keith-Lucas, pp. 126ff.

following year (1835) was more explicitly concerned with destroying corruption as such. Its purpose was to clean up abuses and anomalies in the administration of the boroughs, rather than to reorganize their powers and duties. We have already seen that there was plenty to clean up, and it will perhaps be sufficient to quote the stately concluding words of the Report of the Royal Commission of 1835 on which the Act was based:

'In conclusion, we report to your Majesty that there prevails among the inhabitants of a great majority of the incorporated towns a general, and, in our opinion, a just dissatisfaction with their municipal institutions, a distrust of the self-elected municipal councils, whose powers are subject to no popular control, and whose acts and proceedings, being secret, are unchecked by the influence of public opinion; a distrust of the municipal magistracy, tainting with suspicion the local administration of justice, and often accompanied with contempt of the persons by whom the law is administered; a discontent under the burthens of local taxation, while revenues that ought to be applied for the public advantage are diverted from their legitimate use and are sometimes wastefully bestowed for the benefit of individuals, sometimes squandered for purposes injurious to the character and morals of the people. We therefore feel it our duty to represent to your Majesty that the existing municipal corporations of England and Wales neither possess nor deserve the confidence or respect of your Majesty's subjects, and that a thorough reform must be effected before they can become, what we humbly submit to your Majesty they ought to be, useful and efficient instruments of local government.'[1]

The main provisions of the Act as they concerned maladministration were a ratepayers' franchise which greatly broadened the control of municipal affairs, some Treasury control to avoid financial abuses, the admission of the public to meetings and the separation of justice from administration.

The Act made history by explicitly prohibiting bribery and imposing severe penalties for it, but—again alas for human nature—these were not effective.[2] 'In some boroughs it appears that a considerable class of voters will not vote unless they are paid; this fact is so well known that the pure portion of the constituency, aware that the corrupt element is large enough to be able to turn the election, holds aloof altogether. Treating is also practised at municipal

---

[1] *The Report*, p. 49, quoted by Redlich and Hirst (ed. Keith-Lucas), p. 121.

[2] Details of its continuance will be found in Keith-Lucas, p. 173ff. The example quoted by Mr Keith-Lucas and reproduced above is from the Report of a Select Committee of the House of Commons on Parliamentary and Municipal elections in 1870, thirty-five years after the Municipal Corporations Act.

elections to a great extent. In some instances the bribery takes the form of payment for drink tickets instead of money; and more frequently the election is accompanied by an amount of drinking which is described as demoralizing to the town.'

The Bill met with strong opposition in the Lords and some of its provisions were modified. The most interesting compromise to emerge from the tussle between Lords and Commons was the institution of Aldermen,[1] a concession to the idea that democracy must not be overdone, but must be 'stabilized' by retaining a considerable proportion of councillors who are not subject to the discipline of the electorate.

Under the stimulus of this legislation municipal government prospered, and the towns steadily acquired responsibilities for sanitation and public amenities which had been withheld from them in the old corrupt days, and had been borne by numerous *ad hoc* bodies of commissioners. Slowly the system coalesced into the kind of multi-purpose authorities that we know today, the rural structure being completed by Gladstone's Parish and District Councils Acts of 1894. Once more, regrettably, human nature lagged behind, for bribery and corrupt practices continued among councillors and staff alike; it only ceased to be a major problem with the passing of the Public Bodies Corrupt Practices Act of 1889.[2]

This, however, was not the only side of the picture, for the years which followed the legislation of 1834 and 1835 saw the emergence of a new kind of councillor, and, more slowly, of a rudimentary 'service' of qualified officials. They were of a higher calibre than their predecessors; though there were many exceptions, the qualities of ability and integrity were beginning to establish themselves, and the big industrial cities like Birmingham and Manchester led the way.[3]

Parliamentary and municipal representation under the Acts of 1832 and 1835 would hardly be recognized today as being democratic. These Acts enfranchised only the middle class, and until 1882 a higher qualification existed for councillors than electors. But this was not without advantages, for many were successful manufacturers or merchants, which made them intolerant of inefficiency; many were rich, which put them beyond the temptation of bribery; and a remarkable number of them were practising Christians of an uncompromising kinds, and pillars of their local churches (or more often chapels, since the nonconformist influence in the reformed municipal government was strong).

[1] Aldermen are indirectly elected by the Council itself and hold office for twice the normal period.
[2] For brief details, see R. M. Jackson: *The Machinery of Local Government*, p. 329.
[3] Lady Simon, in *A Century of City Government*, vividly describes the municipal progress of Manchester.

There were of course others of a different kind, notably those whose vested interests were threatened by municipal reform, and whose main purpose in submitting themselves to the electorate was to keep down the rates, a motive which persists strongly to the present day. But the important point is that a bridgehead had been established in local government by the type of man whom the country came to associate with the civic virtues.

Meanwhile, the other side of the human partnership on which British local government is based—the partnership of unpaid councillors and paid officials—was beginning to take shape. In the more modern era, but before the reforms of the 1830s, local government staff first began to be employed in the various town commissions that preceded municipal reform, and which had been made necessary by the industrial revolution—the Commissions for Improvement, Lighting, Paving, Watching, etc. The 1834 Poor Law Act had added to their number by appointing overseers of the poor, and the 1835 Municipal Corporations Act, although it did not greatly extend the *functions* of the municipal councils, controlled their proceedings and established the beginnings of a municipal bureaucracy. Gradually many of these officials passed into the employment of local government as it took shape between 1835 and 1894. 'But not even at the turn of the century could this body of paid servants be called a service.'[1]

The local government service as we know it today is a twentieth century creation, and its establishment derives from the acceptance of standards by professional bodies, a common practice in recruitment, pay and pensions and the formation of a professional union.[2] But the formative work was being done in the second half of the nineteenth century. The background was unpromising, for local government, in so far as it could be called an embryo profession at all, could certainly not be called a reputable one. Most officials had no qualifications, and senior and junior posts alike continued to be filled by patronage and nepotism, and the status and working conditions of the junior and clerical staff were deplorably low.

Others, however, with considerable devotion, were laying the foundations of a profession which blossomed after the turn of the century. There were some Town Clerks of outstanding legal and administrative ability, most of whom were solicitors (though not necessarily full-time) and therefore members of a profession guided and disciplined by the Law Society.[3] But it is even more relevant to

[1] J. H. Warren: *The Local Government Service*, Ch. 3.
[2] The National Association of Local Government Officers.
[3] This had been founded under that name as far back as 1831, though it had existed under a more exotic name for nearly a hundred years before that; the Society of Gentlemen Practisers in the Courts of Law and Equity was founded in 1739.

note that during the half of the century we are discussing there also came into existence the Institution of Municipal Engineers (1873), the Rating and Valuation Association (1882), the Institute of Municipal Treasurers and Accountants (1885) and the Institution of Public Health Engineers (1895). Associations of this kind have an honourable place in the history of the war against corruption, and we shall return to a discussion of them in the final part of this book.

*

It is not easy to sum all this up, as there are many contradictions and cross-currents in a story of gradual improvement.

In the Reform Act of 1832 and the Municipal Corporations Act of 1835[1] an attempt was made to put voting on a solid property qualification so that a responsible middle-class electorate would be produced. In parliamentary elections, as we have seen, the immediate result was that the price of the bribe had to go up, and it was not until the advent of the working-class vote in 1867—indeed until after the effects of the Education Act of 1870—had made themselves felt that an electorate arose that was too large to be bribed. On the face of it, it should have been easier still to go on bribing the local, as distinct from the parliamentary, electors, for they were smaller in number, political parties were not yet heavily involved in local government, and the power of the local patrons continued to be considerable. As we have seen, bribery *did* quite frequently take place in local elections, but there were also influences tending to destroy it. One of the themes running through the Victorian era like a thread is the idea of technical progress, and one of the characteristics of the new machines that were constantly being developed is that they were not corrupt. As the power of the landlord declined and that of the factory employer increased, so did the values of the two change. Instead of a rural autocracy, for whom there were seldom elections in the nineteenth century, there emerged the industrial employers, wanting power locally, and with wealth with which the landlord could not compete; this tended to increase bribery and corruption. On the other hand, the market was growing, and employers' interests were becoming national rather than local, so that the tendency to corruption was slowly counter-attacked. By 1870, the year of the first great revolution in education, the employer was wanting an electorate literate and intelligent enough to buy and sell a wide variety of goods, and with sufficient prosperity to afford them; not one which could be bought and sold with a few pints of beer and a few shillings. Again, by 1894, when Gladstone was introducing his Parish Councils Bill, a greater proportion of the population was becoming an urban proletariat; the town was where they worked

[1] The franchise resulting from these two Acts was different but not widely dissimilar.

rather than where they lived, and although there was no great commuter population as there is today, an increasing number of people were living outside their place of work and were not so subject to their employers' influence. Even the rural areas of the south were being affected by social changes, for there was a great growth of seaside resorts, to which the older middle classes often retired; in the 1871 census forty-eight such places were listed and by 1901 another eighteen had been added.[1] Such citizens could not be threatened with the loss of their jobs, for they had none; they usually owned their houses and could not be dispossessed; they usually had too much money for it to be possible to bribe them, and often as a hobby they participated in the work of local government themselves.

These, then, were the currents under the surface of social life which were flowing against corruption. They were strengthened by two forces—the force of a revived religious faith with a social interpretation, and the force of legislation. We have said earlier that legislation often reflects rather than initiates social change, but the centralizing tendencies of the Acts of the 1830s, reflecting the philosophy that was common to the theories of Bentham and the practical administration of Chadwick, worked against corruption. It may seem a paradox that local government should be improved by making it less local, but in the circumstances of the time control of financial irresponsibility, and inspection of the stewardship of locally elected bodies, was an urgent necessity. This desire for central control and efficiency, so characteristic of the utilitarians, accorded well with the Victorian business man's belief in the righteousness of commerce and in the spreading of trade everywhere by honest and efficient methods. These beliefs were partly responsible for Gladstone's development of an efficient public accounting system for the House of Commons of his day, and the growth of newer and more efficient accounting methods in business. But long before his day Peel's Government had passed a law (in 1844) which brought into existence the District Auditor much as we know him today. During the next hundred years all sorts of other duties were added to him which helped to destroy corruption in the local sphere; not least, he was given the power to surcharge members of councils for illegal expenditure. The health services, the Highways Board, and Education Boards all became subject to audit, and with the growing techniques of publicity people began to learn more accurately how their money was being spent. It was as well that they did, though many locally elected gentlemen were indignant at this intrusion into their private spheres of corruption and privilege.

Finally, and here we do little more than repeat what has been said at the conclusion of previous chapters, publicity became a great enemy of corruption; publicity brought about by the spread of

[1] J. A. R. Pimlott: *The Englishman's Holiday.*

literacy and by magazines and newspapers, and in the particular case of local government by the admission of the public to council meetings. Corruption usually feeds in private, and upon ignorance.

CHAPTER 6

The Law

'In this country justice is sold, and dearly sold, and it is denied to him who cannot disburse the price at which it is purchased.'
(Bentham)

No department of English life has such a high reputation for incorruptibility as the administration of justice; however conservative, or wrongheaded, lawyers may appear to ordinary mortals, they are not regarded as corrupt, and no English judge has been accused of taking bribes since Francis Bacon was impeached in 1621; in the same way the officers of the law are usually considered a splendid example to the rest of the world. It may seem strange therefore to devote a whole chapter to corruption and the law. When the subject is considered more closely, however, a little of the virtue disappears, and some interesting facts begin to emerge. This chapter will briefly mention four of its main aspects: the judges and the legal profession, the magistrates and their courts, the system of police which grew up during the nineteenth century, and the penal system.

*

The Act of Settlement in 1701 exempted judges from subjection to the will of the Crown and thereby laid a secure foundation for the senior courts of British justice. Judges became, and continued to be, men of great status and adequate income, with enormous power in their own field, and this, together with their complete security of tenure, put them beyond the reach of corruption. Many of them had risen to the Bench through political services, which might lead one to expect corruption, but having reached the Bench there was practically nothing to entice them from the paths of virtue. The profession of the law is undoubtedly conservative, but this conservatism, whatever its vices, does not tend towards corruption. Professional monopoly has been safeguarded from time of entry by those with ample means and status, and unauthorized persons acting as solicitors may be penalized; since its foundation in 1831 the Law Society has consistently endeavoured to raise the ethical standards of the profession. The Judges themselves have been constantly under the scrutiny of the Bar, and the risk and penalty for corruption is so great that few men would ever contemplate it after such a long climb to eminence. This is the credit side of the just accusation that may be made against the English legal system of excessive expense to those who wish to use its services.

What then went wrong in the eighteenth and early nineteenth centuries? Basically, two things. First, the natural conservatism of the system as it developed during the eighteenth century proved quite incapable of coping with the new industrial society and its needs. Second, without a proper authority in the profession itself, countless official people holding sinecures began to interfere with the actual administration of the law. Many junior functionaries began to obtain payments that were greater than those received by the judges[1] themselves, and the delay caused by such men, and by the extreme conservatism of the judges, made a mockery of justice.

Attempts to limit the number of attorneys and to raise the standard of the profession began in 1729 when a Committee of the House of Commons was set up to investigate widespread complaints.[2] An Act which was passed in 1729, however, did not have much effect, for it depended for its success too much on individual judges, and another Act of 1730 probably made matters worse by stipulating that proceedings should be in English, thus allowing many more un-learned scoundrels to participate in the profits. Officials were not always particular whom they employed; Frazer, an attorney of the court of King's Bench, for instance, used a prison turnkey as his clerk in 1757, so that he would be consulted by all prisoners requiring legal help.[3] Much good work was done by the Society of Gentlemen Practisers which was formed in 1739, which often prosecuted those who lowered the standards of the profession, and this is an early example of a powerful voluntary body helping to destroy corruption.[4] In 1753 it secured the removal of one attorney from the Roll of the Courts, who had practised while in the Fleet Prison; at another time of a man found guilty of highway robbery, who had been trans-ported and later returned to practice; in 1757 of a man who had used his clerk as a footman, and in 1775 of a man who had acted as a clerk and a schoolmaster simultaneously. Not all the apprentice lawyers of that time, however, were crooked or corrupt, and such a system did at least enable many men to rise to high positions from

[1] Erskine May, op. cit., iii. 388.
[2] R. Robson: *The Attorney in the Eighteenth Century*, p. 10. One witness to this Committee stated that 'several broken tradesmen and bailiffs do practice as attorneys and often set the people at variance, and have got £10 or £20 out of each party by being concerned, and before the matter come to trial, made the affair up between their clients for a bottle of wine and a treat'. (*Commons Journals*, xxi, 236, 1728–29.)
[3] Sir James Burrow: Reports of cases adjudged in the Court of King's Bench (1776), quoted by Robson, p. 291.
[4] Records of the Society, London, 1897.

lowly beginnings, which was not always possible in later days.

By the end of the century lawyers were becoming men of great importance in local society, and in many cases they added lucrative work, and often sinecures, to their private practices. Some of them too made great sums of money out of managing their employers' estates, or in the quarrels over land that became frequent as its value increased with the industrial revolution. The dispute between the Duke of Portland and Sir James Lowther over the ownership of Inglewood Forest was kept going for ten years from 1767 to 1777 and enormous profits were made. Lowther bought up a great many of the attorneys in Cumberland to help him and in 1770 'legions of attorneys accompanied by all the sheriffs and bailiffs they could lay their hands upon, were informing all whom they thought they could terrify that they must be prepared to quit their tenancies immediately'.[1] Lawyers were also engaged to manage elections, to bribe the voters, to object to opponents' voters and support their own; in 1758, for instance, the attorney Richard Fenton claimed £11,408 14s 7½d for a by-election at York in Rockingham's interest, of which £8,388 8s 7½d was for 'treats, entertainments and other incidental charges'.

The development of the industrial and agricultural revolutions, 'turnpike trusts',[2] the growth of social legislation, the sale of property, the growth of canals, railways, private companies, local government, banks and many other institutions gave the legal profession a great opportunity for making fortunes, and many lawyers did so, not always with due respect either for law or morality.

Much of the weakness of the profession was due to the inadequate system of education. The articled clerk had a great deal of work to do in those days but there was no regular system for training him. As he was so important however the attorney often taught him the trade for a comparatively small sum, and he frequently made a fair amount of money from the clients in the way of tips and 'consideration', for the system of tipping everybody for almost any service was practically universal of the eighteenth century, and only began to die out when there was a surplus of labour in the mid-nineteenth.[3]

The industrial revolution, then, and the developments which arose from it, began to give lawyers wealth, status and power, but it also attracted many scoundrels to the profession. In 1801 there were 5,270 attorneys and in 1832 there were 8,702. Those who had climbed the ladder began hurriedly to pull it up behind them and to increase the qualifications for entry and the educational standards. In 1836 the first examinations ever to be held for attorneys were

---

[1] A. S. Turbeville: *History of Welbeck Abbey and its Owners*, ii. Ch. 6, 1939.

[2] A system whereby highways were maintained by appointed trustees.

[3] See E. S. Turner: *What the Butler Saw*; guests were expected to tip the servants who waited on them at dinner.

announced for June 4th, and November 21st for solicitors.[1]

The basic reason for the growth of corruption was explained by Henry Brougham in a great six hours' speech in the House of Commons, in which he proposed most of the legal reforms which were carried out during the remainder of the century. 'The necessary consequences of not suffering an attorney to be paid what he ought to receive for certain things, is that he is driven to do a number of needless things which he knows are allowed as a matter of course; the expense is thus increased to the client, far beyond the mere gain which the attorney derives from it.'[2]

While Brougham, Denman, Campbell and others reformed the law in succeeding years, many jurists brought forward new ideas.[3] Unfortunately not all the reforms produced cheap litigation; fresh fees were levied to compensate people who had formerly held sinecures, and many unfair taxes kept up the costs. Solicitors suffered more from the reforms than barristers, as they were not so well represented in Parliament,[4] but they looked after themselves fairly well in spite of this. They succeeded in deferring the end of the Turnpike Trusts, for instance, in 1849, because it might damage the thousands of solicitors who were clerks to these trusts. Both professions were becoming more selective, however, and soon more money began to flow to the solicitors from the enormous number of firms that were being set up under the Limited Liability Act of 1855, in which a solicitor often played a prominent part. They came into their own also in the growing number of public corporations such as the Water Board, and in the enlarged field of local government. At the same time some of their work began to disappear, such as that concerned with the discounting of bills (as the banks grew in importance), and accountants, house agents and brokers also took work away from them. An example of the increasing status of the profession, however, is the growing habit of wearing gowns by solicitors when in court, and the usage began to be enforced from about 1850 onwards in the new County Courts.

As in business, the new and improved methods of book-keeping that were being introduced in mid-Victorian times helped to raise

[1] But it is rather difficult to take these examinations seriously, the arrangements being informal and haphazard in the extreme. Fortunately they became harder and better disciplined as time went by.

[2] Speeches of Lord Brougham, ii. 311. An example of what Brougham was talking about is given by H. Michael Birks: *Gentlemen of the Law*, p. 179; a Plaintiff's Bill of Complaint, often several hundred sheets, had to be copied out by clerks and supplied to the defendants; every witness's evidence was carefully taken down, and then had to go to the Six Clerks Office and be copied out again, and issued to all the parties. Cases frequently went on for years, being heard by different judges, and there was always a danger that when a decision had been reached the whole case might be opened once more by a Bill of Review.

[3] C. H. S. Fifoot: *Judge and Jurist in the reign of Queen Victoria.*

[4] Birks, op. cit., p. 212.

H

the standards of probity of the profession, and the clerks in the office began to be better educated men and smarter in appearance than Dodson and Fogg in Dickens's *Pickwick Papers*. By the end of the nineteenth century the general picture had emerged of a legal profession, a large majority of whom had had a grammar school or university education, well controlled by its own professional society, with status, wealth and a growing amount of power. And as we have said, the penalties for corrupt practices had become so great that few were likely to endanger their whole careers deliberately for the sake of a small sum of money.

*

We turn to the junior courts and to the magistrates. From the Restoration of Charles II in 1660 onwards their main duty began to be that of securing the supremacy of the Church of England, and forming a local and national 'establishment' based upon Anglican landed interests. A self-constituted group such as this was inevitably corrupt, and as the population grew and other interests became established (such as the merchants and nonconformists), it grew more corrupt still. The political story of the squirearchy and of its economic downfall has already been mentioned in previous chapters, and this profoundly affected the magistracy. The squire and the parson were usually the pillars of the local magistracy and the damage done to them by the new trading class, by the twenty-five years of revolutionary wars with France, and by their incapacity to deal with the great new urban populations, were ultimately the factors which changed the magistracy as well.

But in the late seventeenth century the magistrates were in a comfortable enough position, punishing severely all who did not share their particular opinions. In 1661 there were 140 Quakers in Warwick gaol[1] and another fifty-eight in Lancashire; in 1662 there were twenty-three dissenters in Middlesex gaol, of whom seventeen had been put there by one magistrate.[2] In 1664 there was a rising at Famley in Yorkshire with the rebels claiming as one of their aims 'a gospel magistracy', but it failed and twenty were executed. The repression continued in the interests of the established Church, fitfully in some places, but occasionally with great severity.[3]

The social status of magistrates, meanwhile, was rising, and the government encouraged this, as a way of stimulating loyalty to itself, by increasing their numbers. In Staffordshire, for example, in 1665 there were fifty-one justices, of whom four were Dukes, six Earls, and nine baronets and knights. In 1679 there were seventy-five, of whom forty-eight had a title. These strangely included the Arch-

---

[1] *Journal of George Fox.*
[2] Middlesex County Records, 1549–1689, iii., p. 329.
[3] F. Bate: *Declaration of Indulgence* (1908), p. 44.

bishop of Canterbury, Prince Rupert and the Duke of Bavaria.[1] Not surprisingly such elevated personages hardly had time to fulfil their duties, and in another county, Warwickshire, seventy-two of the 109 JPs appointed for the years 1674–82 never seem to have performed any duties whatsoever.[2]

Both Charles II and James II made efforts to change the constitution of the local benches of magistrates and justices of the peace, but were resisted by Parliament, where it was able to intervene, or by local opinion. Whoever was in power the wealth of magistrates went on increasing, and as their wealth increased so did their social exclusiveness; in 1732, for example, a law made it illegal to be a justice unless one had property worth at least £100. At the same time they came to be more carefully picked politically—'None were left that did not go with the humour of the Court.'[3] The magistrates then were for the most part country gentlemen, and often clergymen,[4] of whom only a small minority appear to have fulfilled their duties at all conscientiously.[5] As the populations of the big towns grew, however, men who had been justices there preferred to move out into the more pleasant countryside, with the result that more and more merchants took up the post in the towns and the surrounding suburbs, and some of these too seem to have made a healthy profit out of licensing and fees.

This is not to deny that the duties of public life could be onerous; they frequently were so, and some novel forms of corruption arose in order to evade them. One of the oddest was the law of 1699 which offered exemption from public office for life if a man secured a conviction for felony against somebody else. These certificates of exemption, issued by Quarter Sessions, grew to be very popular, and were known as 'Tyburn tickets'; it became possible to buy one for about £5 in the early eighteenth century, but prices rose very considerably in the nineteenth century towns, and were reported to have reached £200–£300. In view of the rapid increase in their duties in the towns, this anxiety not to be a magistrate was understandable, for as the industrial revolution proceeded the justices had to supervise roads, canals, bridges, prisons and the like.

As the eighteenth century wore on magistrates became even more notable for their violence towards anyone not of their own class and creed, and the punishments they inflicted for theft in particular sound incredibly brutal and uncivilized to modern ears.[6] Their ferocity also in enforcing the game laws, their violence when they

---

[1] Bertram Osborne: *Justices of the Peace, 1361–1848*, Ch. xv.
[2] Warwickshire County Records, vii, xxxvi.
[3] Bishop Burnet, op. cit.
[4] In 1832 one quarter of the justices were in holy orders.
[5] Osborne, op. cit., p. 168.
[6] Osborne, op. cit., pp. 184–201.

became frightened by the French Revolution, and the gross in-equalities which grew greater with the industrial and agricultural revolutions and the increase in population, developed a fierce hatred of their authority among the working classes. The period of their decline was however approaching, and reached its conclusion between 1832 and 1848. The 1833 Factory Act put the factories under an independent inspectorate, an Act of 1835 put the prisons under Home Office inspectors, the JPs lost their power over roads in 1835 and the Municipal Corporations Act of the same year still further reduced their administrative functions; while the major reconstruction of their judicial functions took place in 1848, with the Summary Jurisdiction Act.

We have spoken of the narrow-mindedness of the old magistracy, its class structure and its corruption, and of how Parliament passed laws to reform it. This is however an incomplete picture, for the justices began a movement for reform themselves around 1750.[1] This movement was strongly connected with Henry and John Fielding, who were magistrates at Bow Street from 1749 to 1780, but it is difficult to assign exact reasons for this change in outlook. To begin with, the two men were salaried, which may have helped them to be independent; more important, there were great changes in medical knowledge and particularly in midwifery, and the population began to rise; the evils of gin drinking became so notorious that a national campaign was started against it, and it was discovered that crimes of violence tended to decrease at the same time. Much more important, people had grown tired of the corruption of Walpole and of Newcastle's system of governing the country; Pitt represented a new spirit of patriotism; the failure of the 1745 rebellion by the Young Pretender finished any thoughts of further civil war, and England began to think of herself as a great nation. Military victory and imperial pride apparently have the effect of diminishing corrup-tion and stimulating social progress, as in Britain after the Napoleonic Wars, in the welfare state that grew out of Edwardian imperialism, in the measures following victory over 1945, in Bismark's state socialism in Germany after 1870, and in the reforms of Napoleon, introduced in his early years as Emperor.

*

The state of law enforcement under the eighteenth century magis-tracy can well be imagined. Cromwell had made an unsuccessful attempt at a national police force under the control of the Army, but after the 'thief-taking' became a purely local affair, with a high constable in each county and a parish constable appointed by the JPs. The latter was unpaid and every local man was liable to be called on to serve, so that many men were willing to bribe anyone

[1] Dorothy George, op. cit., p. 67.

who would do the work for them. In the country districts, where
everybody was known, the system more or less worked, and the
punishments were so violent that while society remained static so
did crime. But with the rapid increase of the population and the new
industrial cities everything broke down. Thieves and highwaymen
were able to boast openly of their profession and almost anyone with
a grudge against another man could raise a mob at the street corner
by offering it loot in an attack upon his enemy's house. Henry
Fielding introduced paid constables and an organized force which
ultimately became the Bow Street Runners, and the effect was
thought to be miraculous, but efforts to extend the system throughout
the country failed. From 1822 Peel endeavoured to develop a police
force, but he was told by a select committee which he appointed to
report on the subject—'It is difficult to reconcile an effective system
of police with that perfect freedom of action and exemption from
interference which are the great privileges and blessings of society in
this country; and your Committee think that the forfeiture or cur-
tailment of such advantages would be too great a sacrifice for
improvements in police.'[1] Much of the real credit for the reform of
the police can be traced back to Sir John Moore, whose scheme of
army reform is considered in another chapter. The first part of the
scheme was for military training, and the second for moral training,
to replace the old brutalized relationships between officers and men.
This was abandoned after Moore's death at Corunna in 1805, but it
was adopted again by Sir Charles Rowan, one of Moore's officers,
when he became the first Commissioner of Metropolitan Police in
1829, with the military part forming the basis for training, and the
moral part, supplemented by the 'beat' system, forming the basis for
relations with the public.

As a result of the efficiency of the Metropolitan Police, the
London thieves were driven out to the suburbs and provincial towns
where there was no organized system at all. A Royal Commission
(with the inevitable Chadwick as a member) recommended wider
areas and better training, and an Act was passed permitting JPs to
appoint Chief Constables if they wished, but a large number
preferred to save the money. In 1856 Parliament brought in a co-
ordinated system and gave the power of inspection to the Home
Office. There was the usual outcry about liberty, but local authorities
came to accept the increased inspection in return for an increased
grant. The pattern of police reform is thus very much the same as
that of other bodies we have considered: appalling inefficiency and
corruption which a few men tried to prevent from within; an assault
on the old system by a few men who knew what they wanted, helped
by the utilitarians; large scale reform in the second half of the

[1] Quoted from Charles Reith: *A New Study of Police History*, p. 25; to which
acknowledgment is made for the substance of this paragraph.

eighteenth century; and a solution which left most of the status in local hands, most of the power in central hands, the money being supervised by a disinterested group of inspectors.

*

Much of the reform of the police was helped by prison reform. The state of the prisons in the eighteenth century and the treatment meted out to both innocent and guilty is an accurate mirror of the defects of the whole legal system. On the continent of Europe the number of capital offences seems generally to have diminished, but in England it was increased from seventeen in the fifteenth century to 200 by 1800.[1] Every sort of branding, burning on the hands and whipping was practised on men, women and children; but of course crime continued to increase. About half those in prison were there for debt, often for a minute sum, and as they had to pay the gaoler money for necessities their chances of release progressively declined especially as owing to the torpor of the courts it often took a year or so to try a man. Not only the gaolers made money out of the prisons; many of the local prisons were privately owned; the Duke of Leeds, for example, owned Halifax Prison and Lord Derby drew rent for Macclesfield Prison. Gaolers often made extra money by offering their prisoners a choice of chains or irons, but the Bishop of Ely, it seems, would have none of this, for at the prison at Ely which he owned men were fixed to the floor on their backs by iron rings.[2] Usually the gaoler was paid a small salary to feed his prisoners and was left to make what he could out of them, and he was often entitled to a fee when a prisoner was released; if a man had no money he could stay in gaol.

We have seen that the shock of the American War of Independence helped the reform of the House of Commons, it certainly did the same thing to the prisons, for it suddenly became difficult to sentence people to transportation when there was nowhere suitable to transport them. 'Transportation to His Majesty's Colonies and plantations in America is found to be attended by various inconveniences, particularly in depriving the kingdom of many subjects whose labour might be useful to the community' observed the Act of 1776. Both in America and later in Australia a profitable business grew up; contractors could use prison labour for seven or fourteen years and then sell to settlers at inflated prices.

The story of corruption in British prisons is an appalling one, but it follows a familiar pattern once again. The pioneers of reform were people like John Howard, Elizabeth Fry, and, on the theoretical side, Jeremy Bentham himself. Once again Sir Robert Peel took the first measures compelling justices to organize the prisons, to inspect them

[1] See D. L. Howard: *The English Prisons*, p. 5, for details.
[2] John Howard: *The State of the Prisons*, 1777.

regularly and to send quarterly reports to the Home Secretary. Gaolers were to be paid, women warders were to be in charge of women prisoners, and the chaplain and the surgeon were to visit the prisoners, who were to be graded and taught to read and write. In 1835 the Whigs introduced a system of State inspection, but here the parallel with most other reforms comes to an end. Most corruption was ended, but the remainder of the nineteenth century is a sorry record of failure in the treatment of those who lay in gaol. Once corruption had been ended in other spheres, progress was made on many fronts; once corruption had been largely ended in prisons, Victorian society contrived to forget the miseries and squalor behind the grim walls of Pentonville and Dartmoor. Publicity is the greatest weapon against corruption, and once corruption has gone evils may be remedied by the same methods. This happened in other spheres of nineteenth century life, but not in the prisons; for the Victorian did not want to read anything about 'sinners' save that they were penitent or being punished.

CHAPTER 7

The Armed Forces

—◦❧❧◦—

The story of corruption in the Armed Forces in the seventeenth to the nineteenth centuries is both absurd and horrible. If men's lives had not been fruitlessly wasted, one could laugh at the absurdities of Army organization, the purchase of commissions or the stupidities of a man like the Earl of Cardigan,[1] but as it was the British tradition of 'muddling through' in naval and military matters was a tradition of paying for corruption and incompetence with other people's lives.

We begin with the Royal Navy, and at the Board of Admiralty we immediately meet that great personality Samuel Pepys. Pepys came to dominate the Navy Board and by 1664, having bought off his predecessor in 1660, was earning large sums from the fees, gifts and bribes which he was able to demand, putting by £2,000 a year, a very large sum in those days. One bribe 'did so cheer my heart that I could eat no victuals almost for dinner for joy to think how God do bless us, every day more and more'.[2] Pepys was a great administrator who saw nothing wrong in these arrangements, but unfortunately not all those who followed him in the eighteenth century were equally efficient.

Not all the jobbery, however, was done at the desks of the Admiralty. 'There were gentlemen and there were seamen in the Navy of Charles II, but the seamen were not gentlemen and the gentlemen were not seamen.'[3] The gentlemen may have been given lucrative posts at the Admiralty, but there was a great deal of money to be made at sea. One remunerative naval operation was to tout for private cargoes. In the troubled years of the late seventeenth century, with dangers both from enemy warships and from pirates, goods were much more likely to reach port in a naval vessel. A number of captains appear to have made a good profit by taking such cargoes, and the Earl of Torrington is said to have levied a toll on his captains while permitting them to do this.[4] Pepys, who hated Torrington, did

---

[1] C. Woodham-Smith: *The Reason Why*. (The story of the 'Charge of the Light Brigade'.)

[2] See Samuel Pepys Diary and A. Bryant: *Samuel Pepys: The Man in the Making* (1949), p. 228.

[3] Macaulay: *History of England*.

[4] E. S. Turner: *Gallant Gentlemen*, p. 45.

everything he could to discourage this sort of behaviour in others, and also, more importantly, made it necessary for those who wanted to be lieutenants to pass an examination after a specified period of service. This was a quite vital measure which it took the Army at least a century and a half to imitate.

In fact, the difference in status between the Navy and the Army since 1660 is always interesting, with the *Royal* Navy continually ranking ahead of the Army, yet the latter always attracting people of greater status and wealth who could afford to purchase commissions. It is much harder for a navy to usurp a government than for an army to do so; more important as regards corruption, an incompetent sailor might drown the entire crew, officers and admiral, whereas an incompetent soldier usually only caused the deaths of himself or the men under him. There was another interesting contrast between the Army and the Navy. The Army was more attractive in peace time than in war, and the worst corruption took place in peace. The Navy, on the other hand, was cut back and neglected in peace time, but a great deal of money could be made in war; in the years of peace in the eighteenth century the ratings were possibly better off than their officers, for they were able to transfer to the merchant service, and as trade was expanding they did not do so badly; the officers, on the other hand, suffered a great deal, as promotion was blocked by old men in a shrinking service;[1] some overcame the difficulty by standing for Parliament, where, if not given promotion, they could make a nuisance of themselves, or if need be protect their own reputations or attack those of their rivals;[2] but when the Navy went to war promotion was rapid and there were some rich prizes, and it is significant that towards the end of the century, because of the recurring wars with France, there was a great deal of nepotism in the Navy.

Nevertheless, during this century the independence and professionalism of the Navy continued to grow, and on the whole its standards of integrity rose; it would not have been surprising if they had declined, so outdated were the Navy's tactics, so conservative were the old men who controlled it, and so appalling were the living conditions of the lower deck. Its social status was strikingly enhanced in 1779, when George III suddenly decided to send his thirteen-year-old son to sea as a midshipman, thus starting a custom which has been followed ever since. The King asked that no special privileges should be given to his son except that he should have enough light to study by. Not enough is known about this action of George III, which was of very great social importance; the fact remains that it has been followed by every monarch since with regard to his second

[1] In 1744, for instance, Sir John Norris at the age of eighty-four was called upon to repel a full-scale invasion. See Michael Lewis: *History of the British Navy*, 1959, p. 115.
[2] Turner, op. cit., p. 87.

son. The Navy is almost bound to be the Senior Service in an island like Britain, and it was almost bound to have a greater *esprit de corps* than the Army. Nelson could speak of his men as a 'band of brothers'; Wellington called his troops 'the scum of the earth, conscripted for drink'. That may reveal the difference between Nelson and Wellington, but it is also typical of the difference which had grown up between the two Services by 1800.

Our gratitude to George III has to end there, however, for during his period of predominance there was more jobbery than ever before.[1] Under the Earl of Sandwich as First Lord from 1771 there was no public accounting, funds were directed for personal benefit, ninety-seven ships were struck off the list and replaced by fifty-seven inadequate vessels. Ships were built smaller than had been estimated for, or sometimes they were not even built at all. Stores were not up to requirement, and old ships were sold when repairs could have been made, and had sometimes been paid for; great admirals like Howe, Keppel, Rodney and Barrington were passed over and superseded by political nonentities whose votes were needed, and the same process took place all down the line; fortunately the movement for reform came just in time, for although Britain lost America she defeated the French at sea.

The men who sailed in His Majesty's ships were not of outstanding calibre in spite of the romantic halos thrown around their achievements by history. They were not usually transferred from the merchant service (which increased in numbers throughout the period and had much better pay)[2] although in 1795 the Admiralty compelled all owners to release a proportion of their men for naval service; but the 20,000 or so provided in this way were not surprisingly the dregs of the merchantmen. The 'press gang' was another method of recruitment and a very bloody one; among the press gangs' sources of recruitment were the prisons, and local magistrates found it extremely convenient to see that strikers, rioters or anybody at all they disliked could be hauled off by the gangs. This was not enough, and an Act of 1793 allowed three-quarters of a British merchant ship's crew to be foreigners. There were a lot of mercenaries in the Navy too; 'I have some of all the States in Germany, Austrians, Poles, Croats and Hungarians—a motley tribe' wrote Collingwood, Nelson's successor.[3] The officers were rather better. The captains were men with status, power and wealth and were used to authority, and they might at any time have the responsibility of sailing into some foreign port and negotiating with the local ruler on behalf of His Majesty King George III.

Following the King's example from 1779 onwards the middle

---

[1] Lewis, op. cit., p. 140.
[2] E. Halevy: *History of the English People in 1815*, p. 79.
[3] *Life:* i., 43–44. (Letter to J. E. Blackett.)

classes, especially the poorer middle classes, began to try to get their children into the Navy through the kindness (or nepotism) of some well placed relative. Both Nelson and Cochrane, perhaps Britain's two greatest sailors, entered the Navy in this way. Success brought their protegees power and status and also comparative wealth, for officers were well-paid in the money values of the day. But the really profitable work came in capturing enemy merchant ships. When Hood captured the San Lago which carried £25 million of gold, he gained £50,000 for himself and every captain in his squadron received £30,000.[1] When money could not be distributed from 'prizes' status was carefully allotted. A good captain who did his duty well could get a knighthood; a good commander who showed originality while obeying orders a baronetcy; while admirals who did well got peerages, with the money to keep up appearances if they were poor. It is noteworthy that the poor *could* rise, but they had to be very good and usually needed influence as well. 'The whole number of post-captains ... amounts to about 840; of these I estimate about 450 to have attained their rank from merit and long service, leaving 390 who I really believe have risen purely by private patronage and borough interest.'[2]

But the real reason for the string of victories won by the Navy during the Revolutionary and Napoleonic Wars, which contrast with the failures and drawn battles interspersed with occasional successes in the other five French wars since 1688, was the reform of administrative corruption associated with Lord Barham, who was Comptroller of the Navy from 1778 to 1790.[3] He and his followers brutally cut down the staff on land. Howe, for instance, developed a new form of tactics which gave all the real power to the admiral on the spot. There could not be many comfortable or domesticated sailors after Barham and St Vincent: 'when an officer marries he is d ... d for the Service' wrote the latter. One fine letter runs

'Sir, you having thought fit to take yourself a wife are to look for no further attentions from
Yr. humble servant,
J. Jervis[4]

After the Napoleonic Wars, and for the remainder of the nineteenth century, Parliament cared little for the Navy and its forces were regularly cut down. Too many men for too few jobs meant increased jobbery, but there was no general decline into systematic

[1] Brenton: *Naval History*, vol. i., pp. 143–4.
[2] An inquiry into the state of the Navy, by 'An Englishman', quoted by Halevy, op. cit., i., 91.
[3] Lewis, op. cit., p. 154.
[4] *Memoirs of Earl St Vincent*, quoted by E. S. Turner, op. cit., pp. 99–100.

corruption. Sir James Graham reformed the Admiralty from 1832 onwards, and after 1836 cadetships were introduced with instruction at sea. The main battle against corruption had been won, and the influence of the Navy on national life and outlook was almost entirely anti-corruptive from then on.

*

If the Navy solved most of its problems of corruption in the first great period of reform after the American War of Independence, and cleared up more administrative complications in the 1830s, the same is not unfortunately true of the Army, where as late as 1870 all progress depended on influence and wealth. It was not generally a safe occupation to be a general in war time until about 1860; Cromwell and Marlborough expected to lose many of their generals in the front line, and did so, but from 1860 until 1939 the general moved further and further away from the firing line.[1] There tended, therefore, as we have said, to be more attempts at influence or nepotism in the Army in peace time than in war; most of the important naval reforms have tended to be just after or just before a war, and most of the important army reforms *in* war or because of the threat of war, doubtless why Britain usually lost the first few battles.

On the office side of the Army we find the usual story of racketeering and nepotism, and it was not until 1782 that the 'Secretary at War' became answerable (after the War of American Independence) for Army payments formerly handled by Paymasters-General who sometimes netted up to £27,000 a year on the funds at their disposal but left the real work to the office clerks. Everybody had to be given some prize; the Home Secretary dealt with the grant of commissions and the employment of troops overseas; the Treasury looked after Army fuel and victualling and a separate Board of Generals looked after troops' clothing. After 1793 the Commander-in-Chief handled promotions and discipline, the Home Secretary numbers and operations, the Ordinance Board arms, stores and the pay of artillery and engineers, the Treasury provisions and fuel and the Board of Generals clothing. Most of these tasks were taken over by Lord Panmore in 1854 when he became both Secretary at War and Secretary for War, but until 1870 the War Office looked after the 'civil' side and the Commander-in-Chief the military side, and they both hated each other so much that they only communicated by letter—at an average of 30,000 a year or over 100 for each working day. Parliament worked away at the problem and in the seventy years after 1833, 567 different commissions and committees were set up to cure the evils, but the major reforms only came after the Crimean War in 1857, with the growing threat of Germany in 1870, and after the Boer War in 1904.

[1] For details of this see Earl Wavell: *Generals and Generalship*.

The standing army dates from the restoration of Charles II, and even that corrupt age looked askance at the system of purchasing commissions which developed. 'The Guards will soon be full of tricksters, robbers and hackney coachmen, for however stout, loyal or well-born a man may be he will not get in unless he has money to give the officers.'[1] The whole system was in fact a classic example of inviting corruption. Neither troops nor officers were adequately paid. On the other hand the purchase of a commission gave social status and entry into high society, and many a colonel made a large fortune out of his command. Colonel Charteris, for example, received a bounty for raising troops in the reign of Queen Anne, and collected vagabonds and criminals to shield them from the law, and then blackmailed them in return. Money could also be made from supplying poor clothes to the troops or from bribes given by clothing contractors, underpaying the men, letting them out as hired labour, or keeping dead men's names on the Army Lists and pocketing the pay for them.

Recruiting methods were equally appalling.[2] The naval press gang was often employed, and one respectable publican in Dublin, for example, was lured on board ship drugged with alcohol and taken to Holland, where he had to enlist to save himself from starvation; and one thousand recruits in Marlborough's army defected to the French because they had been forced on ship, blindfolded, and compelled to enlist.[3]

The reasons for the state of the Army were based on the fear of a military tyranny or dictatorship. 'To render the executive sovereign incapable of tyranny, the armies entrusted to him should consist of citizens and should be of the same mind as their fellow citizens. . . . There are but two possible means to obtain this. Either those who serve in the army should possess sufficient wealth to pledge their good conduct towards the other citizens, and should be enlisted for a year only as was done at Rome, or if there be a standing army and

[1] *Calendar of State Papers: domestic*, 1666.

[2] Farquahar: *The Recruiting Officer*.

[3] Colonel H. de Watteville: *The British Soldier*, p. 68. But it was also the age of the willing soldier—the mercenary. Col. de Watteville gives the story of one Peter Drake, an Irishman, who was a very good soldier who served under Louis XIV; he deserted and returned to Ireland where he enlisted with the Dutch; after various escapades he escaped from the Dutch to London and asked for a bounty of £5 to enlist in the English army in Holland. However, he was more attracted by the money for enlisting in General Steward's regiment under orders for the West Indies, so took this money but went off to Holland nevertheless. After arriving there, however, he ran into General Steward's regiment which had somehow contrived to end up in Breda instead of the Bahamas. He was arrested but saved his life by enlisting in another regiment; not long after he deserted to Louis XIV. He was captured at Malplaquet, and was wounded, but by catching Marlborough's attention he succeeded in having himself and five colleagues driven back to the French lines in a carriage.

the soldiers be drawn from the worst order of the people, the legislature must possess the authority to disband the forces at pleasure.'[1] The British Army fulfilled both these conditions, and the corruption we have noted was a reflection both of what existed in the remainder of society and a hatred of all types of tyrrany. The laws of England followed Montesquieu's doctrine; the 1694 Mutiny Act gave Parliament the power to discharge the Army, while an Act of 1757, which gave greater powers to the Royal Prerogative, stipulated greater 'pledges' by the military. A colonel had to possess an income of £400 per annum from real estate, a lieutenant-colonel or major £300, a captain £200, a lieutenant £100 and an ensign £50. To minimize the strength of the Army few regular barracks were set up, and throughout the eighteenth century troops were usually billeted in inns.

It is not surprising that conditions in the Army were so bad. Promotion of able young men was nowhere as easy as in the Navy;[2] a private who had served about ten years and shown outstanding bravery might become an ensign, but even this was deplored in some quarters as a 'mixing of the classes'.[3] Men however still continued to join, for it was guaranteed employment with (after 1806) a guaranteed pension, and this was more than industrial England was offering to its inhabitants. Much of the work was less skilled than in the Navy and on many occasions less dangerous.

It followed from the purchase system that all officers above the rank of ensign were financially independent of the government. The senior officers received a great deal more money, but all promotion above the rank of colonel went by seniority, so that if a brilliant young man were to be promoted by the government all those who had purchased commissions before he did had also to be promoted. Representing as they did the landed interest (of twelve generals promoted to the peerage after 1792 all but one, a curate's son, were of noble birth) the officers were much more numerous than the naval officers in Parliament, and in 1812, for instance, thirty-four were elected, the tendency being for the Army and Parliament to perpetuate the corruption which already existed in both of them.

Under such conditions discipline became almost non-existent. 'The Bishop of Killala yields the palm of superiority to the English for their *dexterity* in pillaging and plunder; indeed compared with every European army save the Papal one it is the only excellence, in candour, we can admit them to lay claim to.'[4]

But the reforms of 1780–84 and the work of the younger Pitt had a curious effect upon the Army. Pitt distributed peerages to gain

---

[1] Montesquieu: *Esprit des Lois*, book ii, ch. vi.
[2] Halevy, op. cit., p. 108.
[3] *Quarterly Review:* vol. 13, p. 420.
[4] *Journal of Lady Holland:* 22, iii, 1800, vol. ii, p. 61.

votes as did George III, but the old families still considered themselves superior to richer but socially inferior families; the system of purchase created a plutocracy, not an aristocracy;[1] consequently the social structure had begun by 1800 to be rather different from the military hierarchy to a degree that horrified foreign observers; 'duels between officers of unequal rank, although severely punished, are by no means uncommon'.[2] The social structure also was changing so quickly that the British Army was not quite so hidebound as continental armies, but it was appallingly undisciplined. The Duke of York and Sir John Moore had both helped to reform the Service somewhat, the latter introducing his system of combined military and moral training to keep discipline, preserve order and prevent crime, which, as we have seen, Sir Charles Rowan later used in developing the Metropolitan Police.

But the reformer's life was not an easy one. The moment the struggle with Napoleon was over the old anti-militarist tide began rising once more, this time based upon economics rather than fear of royal despotism. The conservatives wanted army institutions to remain in the same preposterous state that they were; the progressive radicals merely wanted to cut down the size of the Army and save money. With no great war between 1815 and 1914 it is surprising that any reform took place at all.

Because it was not a period of great national danger, the second period of reforming corruption in other spheres (the 1830s) had almost no effect upon the Army. Some progress was possible after the Crimean War, however, because the apparatus of Victorian reform began to come into play; William Russell, perhaps the first great modern war correspondent, was able to report to *The Times* and to the people of England on the atrocious state of the Army; the work of Florence Nightingale showed up the horrible conditions of the supply department and the care of the wounded; above all the fear of royal despotism had faded, and Britain had become proud of her empire, so that people at home were prepared to pay some attention to the sufferings of soldiers abroad. The social structure of the country, moreover, was no longer that of the Army. 'Our merchants had become princes', and the money they spent on their Army had to be well spent, and not for the benefit of an outdated gentry.

Perhaps the best hated man in England, and one of the worst commanders in British military history, was flourishing at this time —James Brudenell, 7th Earl of Cardigan—and his career may be used to illustrate some of the defects of the Army and its organization.[3]

[1] Halevy, op. cit., i. 118.
[2] General Foy: *Guerre de la Peninsule*, i. 244.
[3] For a full account, see C. Woodham-Smith, op. cit.

Born in 1797, he was admitted to Christ Church, Oxford, in 1816, but on coming of age he was given the pocket borough of Marl-borough to represent in Parliament. After an elopement, and a singularly unfortunate marriage, and neglecting his parliamentary duties, he bought the command of the 15th Hussars for about £40,000. In 1833 he stood for Northern Northamptonshire, the family seat, where he successfully spent £30,000 to get himself elected. In 1834, after quarrelling with most of his officers and trying to remove one of them, he was himself removed from command by a court martial; despite protest he then bought the lieutenantcy of the 11th Light Dragoons. Disputes with officers, duels with officers and quarrels with newspapers ended by his being found guilty of intent to murder, at the Old Bailey. The House of Lords, however, found him not guilty. He also survived an action for adultery brought against him, in which he probably bought off the principal witness. He was put in charge of the Light Brigade and proceeded privately to the Crimea, where he lived on his private yacht in great style, and eventually led the famous charge. For a time he was a hero, but his popularity did not long survive official inquiries and news-paper attacks.

For not only the newspapers, but the humanitarians and the statisticians got to work on the sordid state of the Army. Some measures were taken which raised the status of the private—such as the institution of the Victoria Cross in 1856—but the reform was only partial; the system of purchase was only modified and the price lowered. The country had to wait for another thirteen years for the general reform of the Army under Cardwell in 1870. He had abolished flogging in 1868, bounty money to bribe recruits in 1870, and from 1870–71 he encouraged the self-governing Dominions to raise their own forces. These, together with the abolition of purchasing commissions, were the main reforms which concern this chapter, and it is worth looking both at their cause and effect. They came in the third great period of the reform of corruption at a time when Britain suddenly became aware of the German danger; they came just at the beginning of a great period of imperialism when nationalism was rising to its heights, and the reforms were made by men who enjoyed Gladstone's financial confidence, so that they were not stopped on the usual grounds of economy.

Their effect was above all to give the soldier status and the officer a pride in the rank he had achieved; the discipline was enormously improved, the pay was better, and the English officer who conquered native forces abroad in the heyday of imperialism was a man who was attaining status, power and wealth—and as time went on a reputation for incorruptibility. It is one of the tributes to that for-gotten statesman Edward Cardwell that he not only reformed a monstrously ill-formed Army, but that he is largely responsible for creating the 'public image' of the honest English officer on duty abroad; such men might not invariably be good at war but they were magnificent as ambassadors.

CHAPTER 8

The Church

She was honourably descended
And by means of her alliances to
The illustrious family of Stanhope
She had the merit to obtain
For her husband and children
Twelve separate appointments
In Church and State
(Memorial to Mrs Bate, quoted by Addison:
The English Country Parson)

So far we have discussed institutions which were openly, and often unashamedly, corrupt, and have described how this corruption was brought to an end. We now turn to influences of a different kind, embodied in institutions which were themselves involved in corruption but which, once they had shaken it off, were instrumental in its defeat in other spheres of life; we discuss also the influence of science on corruption.

Between 1660 and 1860 the Established Church in England was deeply involved in practices which now appear to us to be corrupt. It is never reasonable to judge the deeds of one age by the moral standards of a later one, and it is charitable to suppose that the nepotism, place-seeking and materialism, to say nothing of the persecution of dissenters, which were acceptable to the Church of England appeared less hypocritical by the standards of the seventeenth and eighteenth centuries than they do to us. With a few notable exceptions it was not until the nineteenth century that there emerged within the Established Church large numbers of men whose lives were rooted in principle, or groups to whom the Gospel meant social activity and social equality.

There was at first some reason for the Church's material self-interest, for it had suffered greatly during the Civil War, and its leaders were resolved to rehabilitate it as soon as Charles II returned. It meant, however, that for a century or more the clergy sought security and a safe income, often by methods which contrasted oddly with their profession, and that the Church was determined to perpetuate special privileges for its members.

The 1673 Act of Uniformity purged the Church itself of Puritans, and further Acts multiplied the disabilities and penalties for not being members of the Anglican Church. The Corporation Act kept nonconformists out of most offices, the Five Miles Act kept them from teaching in the schools, and the Conventicle Act threatened them with imprisonment and transportation if they held religious meetings for more than five people; the Test Act of 1685, prohibiting them from holding all types of public office, was originally aimed at Roman Catholics, but the Church of England found it a most convenient weapon against all other faiths than its own.

Even though all Protestants had joined together to help the Church of England against James II and drive him from the Throne, the Toleration Act which was passed by William III retained many of the hardest features originally imposed upon dissenters, and further measures were passed against Catholics and against Unitarians. These measures were particularly severe in Ireland, where the vast majority was Roman Catholic, but it was a century and a half before the privileges of the Church began to be substantially reduced by laws passed in Parliament and by agitation in the country.

With the arrival of the Hanoverian dynasty in 1714, and later with Walpole as Prime Minister, the Whigs were fully in power, and they made sure that the Church should be controlled by politically safe Whig bishops. This of itself led to a great deal of corruption, which was heightened by the social and economic position of the lower clergy. In the villages and rural areas they and the local squires were almost the only educated men, and it was natural for a declining Church and a largely impotent squirearchy to combine. Both had had considerable power and status, often as magistrates, and all too often they used their position to supplement their wealth. The parson profited from the agricultural revolution which was taking place in England, for it improved the income from his tithes and any land he owned himself, and he often married into the landed families. A good example is the Rev Mr Collins in Jane Austen's *Pride and Prejudice*. What a parson's wife was expected to do in return, for the children, is shown by the quotation at the head of this chapter. A typical outlook at the beginning of the eighteenth century was that of Mrs Adams, the widow of the Rector of Great Baddow in Essex, who wrote in 1700 'my cosen Jack Nicklas is to have his living, so he is to go into orders with all speed; this good living had made him declare his resolutions of being a Minister, and now his next business must be to get him a good fortune with a wife, his parsonage will be a very good provision for a younger brother his own portion besides.'[1] The Churches themselves flourished under the patronage of the local aristocracy and by the end of the century the transformation from a village church to a class

[1] Addison, op. cit., p. 71.

church was complete. 'A stranger would think our churches were built, as indeed they are, only for the rich. Under such an arrangement, where are the lower classes . . . to learn the doctrines of the truly excellent religion which exhorts to content, and submission to the higher powers?'[1] Never was religion better used as an 'opiate for the people'. In consoling some lowly starving labourers Hannah More told them: 'In suffering by the scarcity you have but shared the common lot, with the pleasure of knowing the advantage you have over many villages in your having suffered no scarcity of religious instruction.'[2] If that was an advantage, they certainly had it; Hannah More cared deeply for religious education, but most of the clergy forgot even that: 'Catechizing does not exist; if it does I should like to see the man that ever saw an instance of it. If anywhere practised once or twice in the year, it is such a rarity, so small an exception, as not to be worth naming.'[3]

It would however be a mistake to imagine the clergy as a whole living in affluence, sitting lightly to their duties and allied with the most reactionary forces of their time. The ordinary country parson often lived in the poverty described by Macaulay,[4] because what had been a sufficient payment in Elizabeth's reign was quite inadequate by the eighteenth century.[5] Such conditions encouraged corruption, for among this very real and widespread poverty there were some great prizes, and there were a lot of competitors. Moreover with the right influence a man could take several livings at one time and place a few luckless starving curates to carry out the duties for a nominal fee. In Fielding's novel *Joseph Andrews*, when the squire offered Parson Adams a living with £130 a year: 'He at first refused it, not wishing to quit his parishioners with whom he had lived so long; but on recollecting that he might keep a curate at this living, he hath lately been induced to do so.'

The way in which Walpole kept bribery and the distribution of places under his own control is well known, and the degradation of the Church by place-hunters was intensified when the Duke of Newcastle was in power.[6] The bishops were all political appointees, and the normal method of procedure was to appoint a man to a bishopric in Wales, and then if he behaved himself and supported the government to appoint him to more lucrative positions.[7] They were expected to remain in London throughout the winter and vote for the Government in the House of Lords, and for this reason

[1] Arthur Young: *An inquiry into the state of mind amongst the lower classes*, 1798.
[2] J. L. and B. Hammond: *The Town Labourer*, pp. 226–8.
[3] William Cobbett: *Rural Rides*, 1835.
[4] *History of England*, Ch. 3.
[5] A. T. Hart: *The Country Priest in English History*, Ch. 3.
[6] S. C. Carpenter: *Eighteenth Century Church and People*.
[7] Sykes: *Church and State in the Eighteenth Century*.

Walpole never appointed any bishops in America; consequently the Church of England never established a firm hold in the New World. Perhaps if he had, later governments would have kept in closer touch with America, with a possible postponement of the War of Independence, which had such a profound effect on corruption in Parliament.

Apart from pluralities, the parson began to develop other sources of income as the century proceeded. He had always, from the time of Henry VIII, had his 'glebe', but he was not legally permitted to buy and sell produce until 1805. But all through the eighteenth century many parsons had been practising farmers, using the new agricultural methods to their profit, which may have been justifiable, but becoming also practising landlords, enclosers of land and owners of real estate, which was certainly not. John Leroo, the Rector of Long Melford in Suffolk, did this to such effect that he raised his income from £528 4s 6d in 1791 to £1,219 15s 0d in 1817, and when he died two years later the patronage of his living was sold for £15,000.[1]

Such, then, was the picture of the worst side of the eighteenth century Church of England, with its pluralism, its grasping for preferment and money, and its intolerance of all change and progress for any class but its own. The same materialistic spirit, somewhat more mellow and urbane, is expressed in the following century in the novels of Anthony Trollope. Corruption is not too strong a word for such activity within the Church of Christ. What brought it to an end?

First and foremost there was the great and genuine revival of spiritual religion which must be associated above every other name with that of John Wesley, the greatest Christian leader of eighteenth century Britain. The new spirit which he aroused spread far beyond the Church of England, of which he was a member, or the Methodist Church of which he was the progenitor. When he preached in the fields and byways of England many Christians began to think outside the boundaries of a narrow class, and the religious movements which followed Wesley spread through many levels of society—the Methodist movement among the industrial proletariat and the Evangelical movement within the Established Church itself. Later, the Oxford movement and the Roman Catholic Church developed closer contact with the poorer sections of society, and this too helped to destroy the enervating atmosphere of privilege in the Church.

These movements of reform within the Church itself sprang to some extent from the greater reading of the Bible that was taking place, and which grew with the Evangelical movement. The sudden acquisition of an Empire, and the desire to spread Christianity throughout its length and breadth, doubtless played its part in

[1] Hart: op. cit., p. 121.

bringing the upper and middle classes back to the reading of the Bible, while for the working classes the Sunday Schools, started by Robert Raikes in the 1780s, were often the only places to learn to read and write, so that the Bible became the textbook of the English language. The reading of such a revolutionary book as the Bible is not helpful to a community based on corrupt practices.

But along with this revival, this breaking of new ground, the Church began to lose some of its former allies. To begin with the country clergy lost their natural allies the squirearchy, who ceased to be the most powerful people as wealthy industrial magnates began to settle in the countryside. England too ceased to be a primarily agricultural country and became an industrial one, and the Church paid dearly for its failure to make contact with the masses in the towns, who slowly began to win political power with the vote. But the Church persistently backed the wrong side in its pursuit of privileges for itself; it had been an instrument of political power in the eighteenth century, and tried to remain one long after the secular State became dominant.[1] For the State no longer required the Church as much as it used to. During the days of the Whig supremacy the bishops' votes had often been required to pass measures in the House of Lords, but after the succession of George III they ceased to be needed. The State's need of the Church of England became so much less that it gradually relaxed control, and in 1853 it ceased to supervise the Convocation of the Church. This was in marked contrast to the early eighteenth century, when it seemed clear to many that the Anglican Church was a great bastion against the threat of Catholicism from the Continent. With Marlborough's defeats of Louis XIV, and the series of defeats inflicted under the elder Pitt, France ceased to be a danger.[2] Spain had long since ceased to be one, and although there were a great many Irish in the industrial towns of the North, and in parts of the East End of London, they were an economic rather than a political problem. The danger came, if it came at all, from rationalism and the atheistical beliefs of the French Revolution, and most British people found these so unpalatable that they set back progressive movements in England by a quarter of a century.[3]

The Church's political decline continued throughout the nineteenth century, when it was gradually deprived of its privileges and reformed of its abuses, by the pressure of State and public opinion. The first formal move was the repeal of the Test and Corporations

---

[1] Even as late as 1873 prayer meetings were held to prevent the catastrophe of a dissenting majority on the School Boards in Birmingham.

[2] But until the middle of the nineteenth century the Monument to the Great Fire of London still ascribed the fire to Roman Catholics.

[3] It was Coleridge's opinion that if the Jacobins had been Puritans instead of unbelievers they would have triumphed. (Table Talk, ii. 68.)

Acts in 1828, but they had been long disregarded outside the universities, for annual Acts of Indemnity had saved nonconformists from the penalties theoretically attached to the law. The next great measure was Catholic Emancipation, which was not however the result of generosity on the part of the Church—nineteen bishops voted against it and ten for it. Once the Whigs were in office in 1832 they began to set about curing other abuses, preparing a scheme for a Commission to administer episcopal and cathedral endowments, and proposing new sees, the abolition of pluralities, and the reduction of the incomes of rich bishoprics to help poor ones.

One important point characterizes these reforms. The Church was beginning to lose everything but its social status—apart, of course, from its proper spiritual purpose—and consequently those who came into it did so less and less for reasons of private gain. The men who entered the Ministry came to be a little like those whom Florence Nightingale later recruited for the nursing profession; people of good education and intelligence, sometimes with private means of their own. On the other hand they tended to be less ambitious for power, or to be concerned with economic problems to any great extent, so that the Church's influence in destroying corruption was not as forceful as it could have been. The Church was attracting men of higher ethical standards than previously, but the ancient social message of Christianity still tended to be overlooked. But most of the power and the lucrative attractions of the Church had disappeared, and with them went the capacity to bribe and corrupt on any significant scale; but by this time also bribery and corruption had become intolerable to the Church's conscience.

*

We turn now to other branches of the Christian faith.

The Methodist churches in the early nineteenth century had many weaknesses, but corruption and privilege-seeking were not among them, for they kept much closer to the people of the new industrial towns than the Church of England had succeeded in doing. 'The Church offered no function to the poor man . . . the Chapel invited him to take a hand in the management of the affairs of his religious society.'[1] In industrial Yorkshire one person out of twenty-three was a Methodist in 1824, in affluent rural Surrey one out of 249.[2] Often they taught men and women to concentrate on the next world rather than on this, which is doubtless one reason why Cobbett called them 'nasty, canting lousy Methodists', but they did a great deal to teach the working classes how to exercise power without corruption. Many of the early trade union and socialist movements had connections and training in Methodism, and about half the

[1] J. L. and B. Hammond: *The Town Labourer*, pp. 270–1.
[2] Annual Register, 1824.

original pioneers of the famous Rochdale Co-operative movement appear to have book 'Cookites' or Unitarian Methodists, who had seceded from the main Church.[1] In the rural areas the Methodists were often firmly against the established order of things, and by training men in self-government they helped to sweep away ecclesiastical and aristocratic corruption in its strongest citadels. George Loveless, the leader of the 'Tolpuddle Martyrs', was a Methodist local preacher, and Joseph Arch, founder of the National Agricultural Labourers' Union, was also trained as a Primitive Methodist preacher.[2]

Most of the nonconformist denominations which grew up in the seventeenth century followed a somewhat similar pattern of development; a period of intense vigour and sectarianism under the Commonwealth, persecution under Charles II, disability in the eighteenth century, a 'quietist' period followed by revival in the nineteenth, until about 1870; after which there began a decline. Congregationalists, Baptists, Unitarians and many other groups followed this pattern, and all played a part in destroying corruption in England, and encouraging Parliament to destroy out-dated privileges pertaining to the Church of England; while the so-called nonconformist conscience was a continual threat to bribery and corruption in many walks of life.

But of all the dissenting groups the most effective and the most constitutionally important were the Quakers under the organizing genius of George Fox. He appears to have had an intense awareness of the dangers of seeking power or status, and the Society of Friends was so arranged as to minimize these. There were no clergy and the minimum number of officials, with the 'Clerk' as the main business official of each Meeting. As early as 1675 a separate 'Meeting for Sufferings' was set up to help Friends in their disabilities, and quickly began to form a pattern for all later 'pressure groups'. Such pressure groups as the Anti-Corn Law League not merely trace their ancestry to these early ideas, but have played an invaluable part in destroying corrupt practices, publishing injustices and educating those who were not directly represented in Parliament.[3]

The local organizations were used to stir public opinion, publicity was used to draw attention to abuses, and pressure was put upon local parliamentary candidates. Northallerton Friends, for example, were urged to 'give their voices and make what interest they can' on behalf of two candidates who seemed likely to support Quaker concerns, and both were returned. This in embyro is the modern

---

[1] George Holyoake: *History of the Rochdale Pioneers*.

[2] For much fuller details see W. D. Morris: *The Christian Origins of Social Revolt*.

[3] The full story is told by Norman Hunt: *Two Early Political Associations*, from which subsequent details are taken.

pressure group with its local branches and delegates, public relations and national campaigns, which in numerous cases has helped to bring about changes in the law, and it seems possible that the Quaker Christian tradition has been valuable to English political institutions in this way.

It is interesting, however, that even the austere nonconformists did not wholly escape the peculiar hypocrisy which characterized some Victorians, which could allow corruption, along with many other social evils, to continue without thinking that Christians had any responsibility for them. This attitude was worst among those denominations or sects which had always concentrated upon the life to come rather than upon curing the evils of this world. A good instance of how this outlook encouraged corruption is given in a letter written in 1880 by a nonconformist Minister in Surrey to the Conservative Members of Parliament warning them to increase their contributions to the Church's repair fund, or the congregations might vote Liberal: 'We don't take any interest in politics. It seems to us that there is not much difference between Conservatives and Liberals. But we do take a deep interest in our place of worship, and we are anxious to get it out of debt so that our consciences may not trouble us when we worship God, in the remembrance that we worship Him in a House that is burdened with debt. Those who help us most in our struggle to meet our liabilities are our best friends, and will get our votes be they Liberal or Conservative.' Such ambivalence of conscience was by no means uncommon.

There is little doubt that as a result of the corruption of the eighteenth and the bigotry of the nineteenth century Church of England, and of the manner in which it allied itself to the upper classes of society, the Church promoted nonconformity among the wage-earners. People who had worn themselves out on farm or factory during the week did not wish to sit with their oppressors on Sundays. The nonconformist chapels swelled in numbers as industrial bitterness grew. This was most pronounced in Wales. As we mentioned earlier it was an eighteenth century custom to send a promising Whig bishop to Wales to see if he behaved himself and supported the party. He was almost always an Englishman without interest in the Welsh or their language, with the result that they took very little interest in him. Nonconformity therefore flourished in Wales, together with a fierce hatred of all vested interest, corruption and privilege that has lasted to this day.

Some evidence for what has been said may be seen in the census returns. In an effort to retain her hold the Church of England built between 1801 and 1851 a total of 2,529 churches at a cost of over £9 million, of which nearly one fifth came from public funds.[1] In the same period the nonconformist groups, often without wealth and

[1] 1851 Census: *Religious Worship*, p. 39.

certainly without access to public funds, grew very much faster. In 1801 the Methodists had 825 chapels and in 1851 11,007; Congregational chapels grew from 914 to 3,244 and Baptist chapels from 625 to 2,789. In this way corruption and privilege helped to promote their own destruction in religious affairs, and after 1851 the dissenting vote or the 'nonconformist conscience' was an ever-present element in the battle against the misuse of power, wealth and status.

So much for a brief sketch of corruption, its decline and fall, in the Established Church. We return to an appreciation of the Churches' positive contribution to the defeat of corruption in public life generally in a later chapter.[1]

[1] See p. 166.

Education

'Of all my reflections none was more constantly my companion
than a deep sorrow for the present decay of learning among us and
the manifest corruption of education.'

(Defoe, 1728)

—◦❦❦◦—

During the same two hundred years (1680–1880) education travelled
much the same road as organized religion. Teaching developed in
circumstances which were hardly creditable to a great profession,
and which were not infrequently corrupt, but as an educational
system developed it became an antidote to corruption; the universities offered some remarkable examples of bribery and nepotism,
but later played their part in defeating corrupt practices.

Most of the early schools were religious foundations, descended
from monastical education. As early as the middle of the sixteenth
century, however, other influences began to make themselves felt;
the new merchant classes, for example, wanted to give their sons an
education less grounded in Latin and Greek, and often banded
together to found schools which taught English, reading and writing,
and other more practical subjects. Such schools multiplied during
the seventeenth and early eighteenth centuries, and were often
looked after by merchant guilds, such as the Coopers and Mercers.[1]
At the same time there was a remarkable growth of 'elementary'
education under philantropic and charitable auspices, resulting in
what were broadly called the 'Charity Schools', some founded by
private endowments and some by the subscriptions and support of
churches. Without questioning the benevolent intentions of their
founders, however, the endowments were often grossly inadequate
and the quality of the teachers subsequently poor in the extreme. A
typical case was that of a Mrs Priscilla Gibson, who in 1701 left her
estate for the support of a school at Bow in East London; a husband
and wife were appointed at a combined salary of £50 a year to teach
the principles of the Church of England, the boys to read, write and

---

[1] For a fuller account of what follows see J. W. Adamson: *Short History of
Education*, or S. J. Curtis: *History of Education in Great Britain*. The examples
mentioned in the next few pages naturally emphasize the darker side of the
picture.

'cast accounts' and the girls to read, write and use a needle. It is not surprising that teachers who were paid less than this—and they existed—had to extort what money they could from their pupils. Sir John Mandeville even went so far as to describe the charity school teachers as follows:

'wretches of both sexes . . . that from a natural antipathy to working have a great dislike of their present employment, and perceiving within a much stronger obligation to command, than ever they felt to obey, others, they think themselves qualified, and wish from their hearts to be masters and mistresses of charity schools.'[1]

A typical school in a poorer district of London was the Green Coats (Hamlet of Radcliffe) School.[2] There was one master for sixty boys and one mistress for forty girls. In 1754, besides the 'three Rs', the boys were taught how to braid fishing nets, and those parents who did not wish them to learn this trade were threatened with expulsion. A resolution had to be passed to prevent school subscribers from using pupils in their businesses during school hours, which had apparently been normal until then. Why be a subscriber and not benefit from cheap labour?

Others were less generous. Nelson thought that since 'early and constant labour is the province of this class, there is but small time and abilities for instruction',[3] and Cobbett has a fine scorn for the schools and teachers of his day,[4] which is not surprising when one examines some of them. Dickens's portrayal of Mr Wackford Squeers of Dotheboys Hall does not seem to have been unduly exaggerated; anybody could set up a school without any qualifications at all, and a Manchester Committee investigating one of the best schools of this kind in the 1830s found it 'kept by a blind man who . . . explains . . . with great simplicity. He is however liable to interruption in his academic labours as his wife keeps a mangle, and he is obliged to turn it for her.'[5] Teachers might be paid ninepence a week per child, and Macaulay once described the teachers as 'the refuse of all other callings, discarded footmen, maimed pedlars, men who cannot write a letter without blunders, men who do not know whether the earth is a sphere or a cube'. Corruption was so extensive that parents often preferred not to send their children to school at all, and when they did so attacks upon the teachers by pupils or parents were all too common.[6]

[1] Mandeville: *The Fable of the Bees.*
[2] Sir W. Foster: *Nicholas Gibson and his free school at Radcliffe.*
[3] Kenneth Richmond: *Education in England.*
[4] G. D. H. Cole: *Life of Cobbett*, p. 138.
[5] Lindsay and Washington: *Portrait of Britain.*
[6] Asher Tropp: *The School Teachers*, p. 9.

The worst is not, of course, typical, and as early as 1698 the Society for the Promotion of Christian Knowledge had been founded because of 'the visible decay of religion in this Kingdom, with the monstrous growth of deism, profaneness and vice',[1] and one of their major activities was the founding of schools, especially in the areas around London. Nevertheless, the fact remains that despite these and other efforts to spread the Gospel, education in England was blighted by its charitable beginnings. For knowledge is power, and 'the story of English education . . . is that of an unseen struggle between the fortunate few and the frustrated many, with the few always careful to be one jump ahead in times of crisis'.[2]

Even at the schools attended by the privileged classes the teaching was lamentable. At Eton in 1740 they were still using Lilly's textbook of Latin grammar, which Henry VIII had used, and avoided any subject that could possible be of value.[3] The Puritans and the later nonconformists did a great deal to build good schools, although they were severely handicapped by the government of Charles II, but as the eighteenth century drew on the Churches and the State alike grew increasingly apathetic about education until the period of the Wesleyan revival of religion.

*

But reforms of the profession and of the schools themselves were already beginning by the end of the eighteenth century. The English system of schools owes much to the Sunday Schools, where the teaching was of course fundamentally based upon the Bible, and it was this as much as anything that encouraged honesty and straight dealing in early years. Not all of those who supported the Sunday Schools did so from the highest motives. Many Christian evangelists did, but others merely wanted the children kept quiet after working six days in the factory.[4] The system of Sunday Schools kept many people happy; the clergy knew that the children were being catechized, and the employer and landowner knew that the poor were being kept in their place, and not taught too much that would be harmful. But those who supported these schools from reactionary motives made three miscalculations. First, the Bible is a dangerously revolutionary book when other people read it; second, Sunday Schools proved the possibility of a national educational system; and third, they whetted the appetite for knowledge, the possession of which by the poor meant eventual power for the working classes and the destruction of the old corrupt political systems.

The teachers in these Sunday Schools were usually paid a penny a

[1] Letter from the SPCK to the clergy, 1700.
[2] Richmond, op. cit.
[3] Ibid., p. 49.
[4] Basil Williams: *The Whig Supremacy*, p. 137.

week per child, plus 'extras' if they could get them, so that the standard of teaching was not always very high. But often they were dedicated men, working six days a week themselves, with some money and status of their own, and no longer just 'the dregs of every other profession'.

The next great step forward was when Joseph Lancaster, a Quaker, started a day school in Southwark, at which he charged trifling fees for those who could afford them, and nothing for those who could not. To cope with the flood of children he devised a 'monitorial' system, whereby the older boys taught the younger, and although this meant a limited sort of education it had important advantages, quite apart from the cheapness, which appealed to parents. Firstly, it was almost the only way of coping with the great population increase; secondly it gave the older boys training in using authority under the supervision of a master; and thirdly, inadequate though it was, it established a network of schools which could be developed with proper teachers later on; fourthly, because it failed, it made people realize the importance and difficulty of the true teacher's work; it raised the status of the teaching profession. A similar system was developed by Dr Andrew Bell, when supervising the Madras Orphanage for the sons of soldiers, and with the Church of England behind him he got most of the credit for what was therefore called the 'Madras system'. In the Devenant Foundation in Whitechapel, where Bell's ideas were tried out, the trustees reported 'It completely fixes and secures the attention of every scholar; the indolent are stimulated; the vicious reclaimed; and it nearly annihilates bad behaviour of every kind; besides being very cheap both of time and money it was particularly adapted to instil into and fix practically in the mind the principles of Holy Religion.'[1]

Meanwhile, however, the old grammar schools had been reduced to a parlous conditions, with every kind of vice, bribery, bullying and corruption. One school had a Head but no pupils for thirty years, while another had only one pupil, and they were described by a judge as 'empty walls without scholars, and everything neglected except the receipt of salaries'.[2] Some of the grammar schools (often against the wishes of their long dead founders) turned themselves into exclusive but terrifying 'Public Schools'. At Rugby in 1794 the boys set fire to the school and its books, and the Justices of the Peace were called in; they read the Riot Act and summoned military assistance. At Eton violence and bullying were the rule under the Headmastership of Keate from 1809 to 1834. Perhaps that is why some pupils, like Peel and Gladstone, who survived this régime, became such tough statesmen later in the century; it may also be why they

---

[1] The Devenant Foundation School: *History of the Foundation.*
[2] Lindsay and Washington, op. cit., p. 74.

possessed such a passion for liberty and independence, and a hatred of mob rule and corruption.

But a great new era was opening up, with the first Government grant to education in 1833, the regeneration of the Public Schools and, later, central inspection and control. There is a curious pattern about educational reform which seems to recur about every forty years; for instance the Sunday Schools and the 'Madras' system occur in the 1780s and '90s; state intervention begins in the 1830s; the Forster Elementary Education Act was passed in 1870; the Balfour Act in 1902; and the Butler Education Act in 1944.

Be that as it may, there were attempts to secure state intervention for many years before 1833, but they were always frustrated by vested interests. The Parochial Schools Bill of Whitbread (a nonconformist) was frustrated in 1807 by Anglican opposition. A Bill of Lord Brougham (an Anglican) was successfully opposed by nonconformists in 1820. A Bill by Roebuck in 1833 was opposed by both political parties, but as a gesture the Government granted £20,000 to help schools—'the same Parliament in the same year had granted £50,000 to improve the Royal stables.'[1] Fortunately the Cabinet also set up a Committee of the Privy Council to superintend the distribution of the school grant, with a Dr Kay (later Sir James Kay-Shuttleworth) as its secretary. Here, as with the Poor Law, with public health and with local government, the introduction of central control was decisive. Although he was constantly opposed by religious interests, Kay sent inspectors to all schools receiving grants, and although prevented from setting up a single training college, he helped to persuade the various denominations to set up their own. He told Lord John Russell that he was working for 'the claims of the civil power to control the education of the country'.[2] Meanwhile people were becoming increasingly horrified by the revelations of factory children working appalling hours, and the drive to improve education and the standard of teachers was gaining momentum. In 1843 a Factory Bill was introduced to prevent the employment of children under eight and to ensure that they went to school, and the children from eight to thirteen should receive part-time education and should not work more than six and a half hours a day. But the Bill stipulated that the schoolmaster must be a member of the Church of England, and that the local parson and two of his churchwardens must be among the managers. Nonconformists therefore opposed the Bill and it was thrown out.

Nevertheless, between 1820 and 1840 the number of children at school doubled and an enormous number of schools had been built, and in spite of their tendency to internecine warfare this was greatly to the credit of the churches; if the training and payment of teachers

[1] E. Green: *Education for a New Society*, p. 12.
[2] Woodward: *Age of Reform*, p. 460.

was wretched it was not altogether surprising, for with industrial England expanding at an unprecedented rate the cost of land reached alarming heights, and schools, their teachers and their standards were as much a victim of this as was Victorian housing. Neither was there a genius like Florence Nightingale to raise the social status of the profession; there was always the gibe about 'a man among boys and a boy among men'; one report of a group of school managers gives this engaging description of a teacher: 'He is very incompetent but we like him, for he gives us no trouble and is very civil—duly touching his cap and never troubling us for money for books or maps, etc.'[1]

From the moment that Kay started to introduce his reforms there was, needless to say, opposition. In the minds of many Victorians there was a terrible danger in giving grants to the 'lower classes' to enable them to become teachers, and that was that they might compete with their 'betters' at other work: 'the feeling of the public against persons thus gaining rewards for themselves and changing their station in life, after they obtained assistance only for the object which the State has in education for them—namely to obtain a staff of future schoolmasters—will rise and undoubtedly overthrow this part of the system'.[2] The middle classes often continued to resent the teacher, partly because he knew more than they did, but especially because he had risen from the working class. Some, it is true, thought that advance should be quicker, but the majority thought with J. C. Wigram, the late Secretary of the National Society, that the education of the lower orders might mean 'an inversion of the orders of society', and that unless the middle class were careful they would be 'unable to maintain the superior position which God had given them in society'; a third group attacked the teachers for being over-educated, a fourth (particularly the Congregationalists) wanted to oppose any education that helped the Church of England, a fifth opposed any kind of bureaucracy in education and a sixth, led by Bright and Gladstone, resisted the reforms because of the cost. But the grants rose from £20,000 in 1833 to £150,000 in 1851 and £836,000 in 1859, and Kay's work was bearing fruit. He introduced his pupil-teacher scheme in 1846 and a teachers' pension scheme which was particularly successful among women, who had fewer alternative occupations than men.

Attacks upon reform were renewed in the Report of a Commission (the Newcastle Commission) in 1861, and by the appointment of Robert Lowe in charge of school administration in 1859. It was his opinion that 'the lower classes must be educated to discharge the duties cast upon them. They should also be educated that they may appreciate and defer to a higher cultivation when they meet it, and

[1] Tropp, op. cit., p. 21.
[2] Woodward, op. cit., p. 462.

the higher classes ought to be educated in a very different manner, in order that they may exhibit to the lower classes that higher education to which, if it were shown to them, they would bow down.'[1] It was in this unpropitious atmosphere that popular education had to make its way, for England, unlike Scotland, took a long time to see that education was a right for every child, and the history of education is a history of those with superior power and status asking 'What do we get out of it?' During the early part of the nineteenth century schools for the aristocracy were wanted, and some for training the factory hand; by 1870 it was worth paying for universal literacy; by 1902 it was worth paying for an executive class to be trained at the new grammar schools, and 1944 it was worth paying for universal secondary education. Today in the 1960s the right of all children to equal opportunity is fairly generally accepted, but for a century and a half there was a 'pecking order'—as much as I can for my own children—as little as necessary for everybody else's; traces of this remain even today.

*

It was not the intention of this chapter to attempt a potted history of education in England, but merely to say enough to demonstrate two points: firstly, by central inspection and therefore control (which continued to grow once Lowe resigned in 1869) the corrupt teachers of the eighteenth and nineteenth centuries were gradually removed and replaced by others to whom teaching was more of a vocation and less a way of making a living; secondly, from the eighteenth century until recent times those who have possessed superior wealth and status have consistently attempted to maintain their own interests, regardless of the children who should have been their main concern. Much of the story may seem unedifying, but it has two important consequences for the history of corruption in England. In the first place central control of the elementary schools produced, as it did in local government and in public health, a body of officials who were incorrupt, whose tradition was service rather than exploitation, and who trained succeeding generations in this tradition. Second, and as it might seem paradoxically, the strong religious interests who so resolutely fought for themselves may have hindered the short-term interests of education, but they left the impress of a strict moral code on later generations of children.

Particularly was this so in the regenerated Public Schools where, earlier in the century (1828–1842), Dr Thomas Arnold had so effectively planted at Rugby School the ideals of 'muscular Christianity' and an unswerving devotion to character as exemplified in sportsmanship and fair play. The two centres of the later Public Schools were in fact the School Chapel and the playing-field, and

[1] Robert Lowe: *Primary and Classical Education.*

K

the ethics of the first were applied peculiarly to the second. When the Duke of Wellington said that 'the battle of Waterloo was won on the playing fields of Eton' he was probably thinking of the tough practice in fighting and bullying that the boys received there in his day. But to a later generation of Public School boys, whose parents possessed both wealth and status, and who because of the English educational system looked upon themselves as a privileged governing class, those playing-fields symbolized the ideals of 'fair play', 'playing the game', the 'honour of the side' and (most important of all when they came to govern) a tradition of incorruptibility.

*

The story of the universities of Oxford and Cambridge presents a striking contrast to the schools. Here corruption was more obvious and harder to deal with, for the Colleges were often rich and independent and the 'University' at both places was poor by comparison. A small group of men with security for life, by means of fellowships which they could obtain by influence, and from which they could not usually be removed, had great power over the students, many of whom were wealthy.

By the eighteenth century it was possible for an observer to say that 'The universities, Oxford especially, have been unhappily successful in corrupting the principles of those who were sent to be bred in them; so that few of them escaped the taint of it, and the generality of the clergy were not only ill-principled but ill-tempered.'[1] There was little change during the early part of the nineteenth century; one classic story is told of a don who obtained a life fellowship which was only awarded to the inhabitants of a small town in Lancashire. He selected his wife with great care, and always rushed her to Lancashire when she was pregnant so that the fellowship might remain within the family, but unfortunately all his children were girls except the last, when his wife had given up hope and remained in Oxford.[2]

The nineteenth century brought a new outlook, however, as many merchants and manufacturers had made money and were seeking status, and one way of getting it was to send their sons to universities; they were men who knew the value of money and they did not want to see it wasted on idle or extravagant dons. This feeling was intensified from 1854 onwards when Oxford and Cambridge came to provide the best jumping-off grounds for success in the new competitive examinations for the Civil Serivce. As more and more of the civil servants came from the old universities government pressure for university reform, and for incorruptibility in College administration

[1] Bishop Burnet: *History of his own Times.*
[2] For examples of such eccentricities see Lewis and Fenby: *An Anatomy of Oxford*, 1938.

and examinations, began to have effect. A Commission reported unfavourably on the universities' religious tests in 1850, and from 1853 Bills were introduced annually to try to abolish them; this was finally achieved in 1870. Reform was also accelerated by the development of universities elsewhere. Lord Brougham, Lord Russell and Thomas Campbell the poet, aided by Mill, Macaulay and Grote, all helped to build what later became University College, London, in 1828, and its guiding philosophy was that of the Benthamites, a philosophy in which corruption could not easily take root. The University of Durham was founded in 1832. The Scottish universities had always been more progressive, and less troubled by sectarian warfare, than the English ones, and although the students were usually much younger they were also more numerous, and this meant that more schoolteachers were graduates than in England.

The reform of corruption in universities, therefore, can be traced to many causes, and it is in interesting contrast to its reform elsewhere. It took place because the Church to which they were so closely allied was itself being reformed; because of competition from new universities and technical institutes; because of Government pressure for good civil servants after 1854; because a few strong men like Jowett were Heads of important Colleges; because the new rich who sent their sons there wanted value for money; and because the Public Schools from which the undergraduates came were in the process of reform.

*

In the wider field of education generally, reform, unlike that of parliamentary corruption, was very largely from the bottom upwards; by the working classes acquiring knowledge and breaking the bonds which held them. This applied not only to children but to their parents, for the nineteenth century was the great age of adult education. The Mechanics' Institutes, inspired by Dr Birkbeck, had developed in the industrial towns throughout the first half of the century; in 1827 Lord Brougham, another of the great leaders of the adult education movement, founded and helped to manage the Society for the Diffusion of Useful Knowledge; and the work was extended by the Working Men's Institutes started by Birkbeck, Brougham and Francis Place. Not only does this development in enlightenment coincide with the general decline of bribery and corruption up to the 1870s, but with the development of reading habits mentioned in previous chapters. In 1850, boroughs of over 10,000 inhabitants were allowed to levy a $\frac{1}{2}$d rate for public libraries, providing two-thirds of the ratepayers agreed; in 1855 the permissive rate was raised to 1d and the population clause was repealed in 1866. Together with these Acts went the withdrawal by Gladstone of the taxes on books and publications of all kinds, and the development of countless organizations for the employment of Victorian leisure. The YMCA was founded in 1844, in 1845 the Rev. F. D. Maurice founded the Working Men's College, and the reform of women's education gathered strength from 1850 onwards. All these influences helped in the overthrow of corruption, for they began to give status to those who had neither wealth nor power, and enormously strengthened the agitation for the vote, which was in the long run a powerful influence in itself.

Commerce and Industry

—◦❧ ❦◦—

This chapter deals with the growth of industrial England, and with forces which, though they were often ruthless, were not generally corrupt;[1] and with men who until the late Victorian Age did not regard themselves as public figures or members of the ruling *élite*. Later on they did, and in our own day their power is immense, but we are not concerned with their behaviour after they had acquired national status and political power in the twentieth century, but with the effect of the industrial revolution on various classes of people, and on national institutions and ideas, until about 1880.

Eighteenth century England had long been a capitalist country, with a comparatively large class of able entrepreneurs able to lay their hands on capital.[2] Owing to the high death rate the increase in population did not keep pace with the expansion of industry, and labour was comparatively expensive. There was a good market for manufacturers, both at home and abroad, and a prospect of good returns for the investor, with savings for those who, at a time of high wages, used machinery instead of manpower; it was in this kind of situation that the great investors like Watt, Arkwright, Darby, Kay and Newcomen started to flourish, and the factory age to begin. During the nineteenth century the size of the firm remained fairly small, and the number of firms grew in all industries; population increased, mainly because of the progress in medicine and public health, and profits on investments were sustained.

The foundations of the industrial revolution, however, had been laid by the great progress in commerce which had taken place earlier, and before dealing with the rise to power of the industrialists it is as well to refer to the political influence and social status of the merchants. 'Our merchants are princes, greater and richer and more powerful than some Sovereign Princes', wrote Defoe,[3] and many of

---

[1] The borderline between ruthlessness and corruption is not always easy to define; we assume that it was possible for the early Victorians to have been ruthless, within the moral concepts of their day, without having necessarily been corrupt in the sense of this book.

[2] E. Lipson: *The Growth of English Society*, p. 190.

[3] Quoted by E. N. Williams: Our Merchants are Princes: *History Today*, August 1962.

them indeed possessed not only solid wealth but great influence in the highest quarters. But below the level of the 'princes' was the larger number of ordinary men who had done well enough in business under the Whig oligarchy of the eighteenth century. These were not of the 'Establishment', which they wished to change; they were often men of the greatest intelligence, descended from those who in the previous century had used up their energies in fighting each other in religious wars; but although their religious faith during the eighteenth century was not so aggressive as this, it was often very strong and just as diversified. Many of them were the sons of dissenting ministers and many, possibly the majority, had the Bible as the centre of their education, their training and their lives. As often as not in the later eighteenth century their education had been based upon the Sunday School, and the beliefs that they had inherited from their earliest years were vehemently opposed to corruption and jobbery.

The industrialists who followed them were largely to destroy the society from which they sprang. At the middle of the eighteenth century they were a very small class, but by 1803 Colquhoun[1] refers to '25,000 manufacturers employing labour in all branches and only 15,000 merchants'. These manufacturers were usually men of fairly small means who by using their initiative and intelligence were able to reap the harvest of profit which was theirs for the taking, and in all their work their religion and class background played an important part. Their achievements fill the moralizing pages of Samuel Smiles's books.[2] It is worth glancing at some of them in passing to see the sort of men they were.

Samuel Whitbread, for example, was the son of a freeholder who paid £300 to apprentice him to a brewer, and left him £2,600 six years later when he died.[3] With this and some other money which he borrowed Samuel Whitbread the elder was able to build up a great brewery firm, and his son and descendants became a great radical force in the early nineteenth century. James Child, the third owner of the Anchor Brewery, died in 1696 and his son-in-law, Edmund Halsey, took over, he built up the business and when he died in 1729 his nephew Ralph Thrale, a yeoman's son, succeeded him, followed by his son Henry. This family became important, and Dr Johnson was proud to number Thrale and his wife among his friends. It is clear from Dr Johnson's own statements to Boswell[4] that it was not merely Mrs Thrale's company that he enjoyed but that he had a high opinion of her husband. But in spite of this fact Johnson and those around him do not appear to have grasped the intelligence and

---

[1] Colquhoun, op. cit.
[2] For numerous examples see *Self Help* and *Lives of the Engineers*.
[3] Williams, op. cit.
[4] For details of this see Boswell's *Life of Johnson*.

growing power of those they were dealing with. Mrs Thrale did not manage the brewery very well after her husband's death: 'Do not be frightened,' said Johnson, 'trade could not be managed by those who manage it, if it had much difficulty.' Dr Johnson's follies are often as instructive and delightful as his wisdom. In the end one John Pakins, who had been manager for twenty years, had to take over, and non-conformity extended its growing economic power. For the £135,000 capital was provided by his wife's family the Bevans, their relatives the Gurneys, and *their* relatives the Barclays. All these families were Quakers, they were all bankers with world-wide reputations and they all had a strong tradition of practical Christianity. Even the names of these and similar men were as biblical as many of their counterparts in Africa today. Jedidiah Strutt, who invented the method of making ribbed stockings on machines, was the son of a small farmer and most of his capital came from dissenting relations; with the money he made he backed Richard Arkwright, together with Samuel Reed, another dissenting hosier.[1] The Rev. Edmund Cartwright, who started power weaving, was a country parson. Richard Arkwright died worth about £500,000, Samuel Whitbread had £350,000 invested in landed property and Josiah Wedgwood left about £580,000, as well as a wealth of artistic talent, to his descendants.

Many of these manufacturers and their contemporaries learnt their skill in public work from the political pressure groups started by the Quakers and others in the seventeenth and eighteenth centuries; others from the effect government had on their interests; others from the fact that they became local mayors, aldermen and occasionally Justices of the Peace. They had an interest in good roads and canals and railways to carry their goods; they had an interest in the licensing laws and they undoubtedly had an interest in obtaining a satisfactory Member of Parliament who would look after their interests. The trading and manufacturing interest 'resembled a hog, whom if you attempt to touch, though you were only to touch a bristle, he could certainly cry out loud enough to alarm all the neighbours'.[2]

A point worth noting is that the majority of successful manufacturers and businessmen did not seem to want political status for themselves, though they had to acquire experience of politics in the course of business. In a sense they made the 1832 Reform Act inevitable because they did not want it; if they had been interested in buying themselves peerages or bribing at elections, the cost in corruption would have been immense and reform might have been postponed; but because they did not want political power, preferring the more absorbing pursuit of industrial creation, and because their

[1] Williams, op. cit.
[2] Sir Robert Walpole.

social ambitions also were relatively limited, the political and social system of the early nineteenth century became unbalanced, since the population increased, the nation's wealth increased, but the same small group of increasingly irrelevant people continued to hold political power.

*

The Quakers have a particular importance in this discussion because of their insistence on a 'just price' for all goods. Towards the end of the seventeenth century, with the growth of standardized goods, the Quaker trade developed because they kept the same quality and price in all their dealings. 'Many Friends that were tradesmen of several sorts lost their custom at first. . . . Then things altered so that all the inquiry was "Where is there a draper or shopkeeper, or tailor or shoemaker, or any other tradesman, that is a Quaker?" '[1] The seventeenth century admonitions were strict: 'I beseech you all, dearly beloved Friends, in the bowels of the love of God . . . that you use but few words. . . . After you have put a price on your commodities which is equal, and as you can sell them . . . stand you silent in the fear, dread and awe of God.'[2] As they were barred from most professions and did not employ a priesthood, the best brains of the Society of Friends frequently went into trade and industry; by the eighteenth century a large proportion of provincial grocers were of Quaker origin; Quakers owned the biggest part of the cocoa and chocolate industry (Cadburys, Frys and Rowntrees), about half the banking industry (Barclays, Lloyds, Hoares and Gurneys), Huntley and Palmers and Jacobs biscuits, Bryant and May's matches, Allen and Hanbury's foods and medicines and scores of other prosperous businesses. By the early nineteenth century they were providing capital for larger scale industry and the manufacture of capital goods. Edward Pease, a Quaker woolstapler at Darlington, had become a coalowner and had thought of building a tramway to Stockton. None of the engineers appeared able to help him, but one day 'a tall man of burly appearance arrived and announced "Heard you wants a rail made, and I be come to do it" '.[3] After a short conversation George Stephenson was employed and the Railway Age began.

These examples taken from Quaker experience are striking, but they are not unrepresentative of dissenting families generally. The Church of England found other outlets for the energies of its talented men, and the pages of English history resound with the names of poor parsons' sons: Drake and Nelson in the Navy, Woolaston, Young, Playfair and Bell in science, Reynolds and Wilson in art,

[1] *Journal of George Fox.*
[2] Charles Marshall, 1637–98.
[3] William Beck: 'Friends and the Railways', from the *Quaker Bedside Book.*

Thurlow and Campbell, two great Lord Chief Justices, and Addison, Goldsmith, Thomson, Coleridge and Tennyson in literature;[1] but it is notable that Anglicans did not predominantly flourish in commerce and industry; all the professions were open to them. Industry and commerce were largely the preserves of the dissenting classes.

The influence of these men and their families was remarkable. For the most part, as we have said, they were slow to take to politics or to climb the social ladder, but there were important exceptions. Sir Robert Peel was the third of that name: the first invented a method of calico printing at his home near Blackburn, the second built up a prosperous industry and received a knighthood, and the third became Prime Minister. After he had repealed the Corn Laws he said in his final speech: 'I leave a name which I hope will be remembered with expressions of goodwill in the abodes of those whose lot it is to labour and earn their daily bread by the sweat of their brow, and who when their work is done will recruit their exhausted strength by abundant and untaxed food, the sweeter because it is no longer leavened by a sense of injustice.' This speech may sound a little sanctimonious to modern ears, but it is a remarkable one; it is doubtful whether previous Prime Ministers had ever thought very much about expressions of goodwill from the working classes, and the comment is permeated by a sense of duty, work and fair play which are typical of the business community from which Peel came.

In the years between 1760 and 1832 the wealth of the country increased but so did the population. Some of the newly rich used their wealth to bribe the electorate, but the price grew higher as the size of the electorate increased. Parliament too was becoming more and more a body of men who had arrived there by talent or principle and who were turning against bribery and corruption at elections. After 1832 neither of the two national parties could afford to be suspect morally, or they would lose the vote of a large part of the business community, and of the 'nonconformist conscience' which was strongly represented in it.

But by the 1870s economic conditions began to change for the worse. Hitherto there had been plenty of capital and a shortage of labour, conditions which encouraged labour-saving inventions and economy of manpower. From the later periods of Victoria's reign there seems to be a new spirit in British industry, and perhaps Wesley's words had come true: 'I do not see how it is possible in the nature of things for a religious revival to last long. For religion must necessarily produce industry and frugality. And these cannot but produce riches. But as riches increase, so will Pride, and the love of the world in all its branches.'[2] Certainly ruthlessness began to increase, a great void developed between capital and labour, firms

---

[1] Samuel Smiles: *Self Help*.
[2] Quoted by Dorothy George: *England in Transition* (Pelican).

were becoming larger and less effort was made to save labour by skilful inventions. Moral standards in business and industry started to decline.

At home the small merchant continued to make the manufacturer keep his prices down, and the economists of the period are continually concerned with micro-economics[1] and the economics of the marginal firm, as well as with the diminishing rate of profit which occurs with developing industrialization;[2] and as long as most firms were still small[3] their intimate, often family nature, put a brake upon corruption. But this did not apply in the same way to capital goods and the products of the heavy engineering or iron and steel industries, where the British manufacturer often enjoyed a near monopoly and where he could charge monopolistic prices; and as the nineteenth century drew to a close more and more industry passed into the hands of the large industrialists.

On the other hand, the worsening economic climate had a salutary effect on corruption in *public* life, for the laws against corruption show a marked tendency to coincide with a general shortage of money, and the outstanding period of reform coincided with the depression from the mid-seventies to the nineties. Parliamentary candidates, who were feeling the pinch, must have welcomed the Ballot Act of 1872 and the Corrupt Practices Act of 1883; as for the workers, although unemployment was high the skilled man in regular employment was in fact better off than ever before, because prices were falling while his wages were holding steady or even rising, and in any case he was beginning to feel his teeth in collective bargaining, and in what could be done by state or municipal action.

In the rural areas, where bribery had always been worst, these developments also tended, though less directly, to reduce the power of the landowners to control and bribe the electors. Improved methods of agriculture had encouraged the large tenant farmer, and more labourers were moving to the industrial towns, while those who remained were the more skilled men, and they also were beginning to be able to stand up for themselves, even though their trade union was not a very successful one. Again, the drift from the rural areas encouraged the decline of the smaller parliamentary constituencies and the ultimate abolition of some of them.

In such ways did the industrial revolution and events in the nineteenth century business world tend to reduce corruption in public life, even though in business and industry itself integrity of

---

[1] Stark: *History of Economics in its relation to Social Development.*

[2] G. S. L. Tucker: *Progress and Profits in British Economic Thought, 1650–1850.*

[3] See Cole and Postgate. In 1870 the average cotton firm employed only 180 workers and the average woollen firm no more than 80; the average factory making machinery 85 and the average iron works 209.

the old-fashioned kind was starting to decline.

*

So far we have discussed corruption in terms of morality. But morality apart, Victorian businessmen knew the truth of the homely maxim that it pays to be honest, which had indeed been demonstrated by the prosperity of the Quaker pioneers.[1] Many of the leaders of Victorian business were not factory men nor office men but salesmen. There was a large and growing market, but it was sometimes highly competitive, and their share of it depended among other things upon their personal reputation. To be morally impeccable became a commercial asset. A man could not be corrupt if he were to succeed in the early and mid-Victorian moral climate, and like most other mortals he condemned in others the vices he did not feel tempted to commit himself.

The same thing applied in the wider world of banking and insurance, although these were mainly joint stock ventures by the 1860s. But if the City of London had not also been the city of probity and high ethical standards it would not have dominated European finance in the way it did, nor become the shipping and insurance centre of the world. British trade and commerce depended upon British incorruptibility. (This is possibly borne out by the pattern of parliamentary corruption, which was largely centred in the south of England, and not in the northern areas where industrial and commercial interests predominated.)

Technology also has a great deal to do with corruption. The remark of one of the early manufacturers that he wished to make factory hands 'as efficient as machines' shows how the machines began to set human standards. A machine is not corrupt, and if you tell it what to do it will do it with varying degrees of efficiency but without the human vices of bribery and corruption. One of the reasons for the decline of 'old corruption' was that employers and society began to look for the virtues of machinery from their workers,[2] and this is not unimportant for an understanding of the Victorian decline in corruption.

Another important influence was improved methods of accounting and book-keeping. By the middle of the century most firms had grown large enough (even in retail business) to require a separate

[1] Cp. also a contemporary commentator, Lord Chandos: *Memoirs*, quoted in *The Times*, October 1, 1962: 'They [government officials] do not grasp that in business a reputation for keeping absolutely to the letter and spirit of an agreement, even when it is unfavourable, is the most precious of assets, although it is not entered in the balance sheet.'
[2] The second stage, one may add, came when employers expected mechanical qualities from their men: repetitive work performed uncomplainingly and anonymously. The third stage seems to have arrived in our own automated day and age, when machines are being persuaded to act more and more like men.

department to keep the books, and, as we shall emphasize again, the growth of the profession of accountancy has been one of the most potent influences against corruption. Book-keeping by double entry and the 'Italian method', as it was known, had been developed as early as the fifteenth century,[1] but practice had not kept pace with theory and there was a very large number of bankruptcies in the eighteenth and early nineteenth centuries. As a result, legislation was introduced, in Scotland in 1880 and in England in 1883, which provided for the punishment of bankrupts who had not kept proper books. The standard treatise by Edward Thomas Jones 'The English System of Book-keeping' was written in 1795 and held sway for a century or more, making possible the more accurate auditing of the accounts of small businesses, and making the more obvious forms of fraud and corruption harder than they were. A great many Victorian novels are concerned with young men who go wrong and fiddle the books,[2] just as Thackeray and Trollope reflect the mid-Victorian obsession with young men in debt. It is an example of how until late in the nineteenth century the commercial world set the standard for morality in a way it no longer does. Now perhaps we expect the highest ethical conduct from professional people working in small groups or partnerships. In the period 1760 to 1870 that was the normal size for a business or manufacturing firm, and this may well have been a factor in limiting corruption.

The rise of commerce and industry also had its indirect effects upon the professional, and even the intellectual, world. Many of the earlier merchants and manufacturers in their success displayed the typical attitude of wealth to power and status. Once they had achieved success they aspired to the status of professional men for their eldest sons. Moreover the very growth of their businesses opened the way for the professions of solicitor, accountant, executive and qualified engineer. The number of 'professional' men increased threefold between the fifties and the seventies, and, as we will suggest later, the rise of the professional organization or 'Institute', with its emphasis on ethical standards, was one of the most important anti-corruption forces.

Again, the world of serious journalism was greatly affected by business advertising. Once more the decisive period is between 1850 and 1890, for the advertisement tax was abolished in 1853, the stamp duty on newspapers in 1855 and the duty on paper in 1861.[3] In 1855 there were about 640 newspapers in Britain, but by 1900 more than 3,000. Every kind of political and social viewpoint could be expressed

---

[1] In fact earlier: 'Put all in writing that thou givest out or receivest in'; (Ecclesiasticus, xlii. 7).

[2] A very good example is Stanley Weyman's *Ovington's Bank*, which gives a fine description of the growing banking system.

[3] C. S. Turner: *The Shocking History of Advertising*.

in every hamlet in the Kingdom (and incidentally the slightest hint of corruption would be denounced by a rival paper). The fact is that these papers were being paid for by the advertisements of the new products. Oxo was going by 1867, Bovril by 1884, Nestlé's milk in 1869, Hovis in the 1880s, the Remington typewriter in 1874, and bicycles, Dunlop tyres, Kodak, the gramophone, Pears Soap and the products of Port Sunlight about the same time. The advertising machines which were later to strangle so many newspapers helped them at first to destroy the older corruption.

*

To sum up, the early nonconformists grew up in a society in which their rights were often denied, and they were left to earn their living in trades which were generally regarded as lowly and debasing. Being men of intelligence and character they built a 'nation of shop-keepers' and often advocated a policy of a 'just price'. It was a fortunate creed in an age when standardized goods were beginning to come on to the market, and it helped to make British commercial institutions respected throughout the world. Secondly, Britain was fortunate in the fact that when the time came to develop her financial institutions in the nineteenth century, the sons of merchants with a sound grasp of finance and a training in high moral standards were there to do the work. Thirdly, there was the improvement in account-ing methods; and lastly, the discovery from experience that it pays to be honest.

The influence of merchants and industrialists on corruption was on the whole a salutary one. Their earlier interests lay less with power, which Lord Acton tells us is the supreme corrupter, than with money-making in creative enterprises. The merchants had a professional interest in honest dealing, even if they had not an ethical one, which in fact many of them had. The merchants, bankers and shippers, especially in the City of London, knew that probity was their greatest commercial saset. The inventors and manu-facturers, on the other hand, were too absorbed in their creative work, of which the making of money was but one aspect, to suffer from the temptations of the vote-catcher and place-seeker, and many of them were in any event men of principle.

It may seem paradoxical to speak of religious principle in a situation which brought appalling suffering to the poor, ruthlessly employed child labour and built the industrial slums which are still with us a century later. But, as we have remarked elsewhere, it is always dangerous to judge the actions of one age by the moral standards of another, and these men were working within the un-questioned moral and intellectual framework of *laissez faire*. The idea that industry is only tolerable to the social conscience within a framework of protective restrictions and social services had not yet dawned. But within their narrow frame of reference they were, many of them, upright men, and taken as a class they were not practitioners of corruption, as were so many of their contemporaries in politics and the public service.

CHAPTER 11

Science

'The unequal division of property and labour, the difference of
rank and condition among mankind, are the sources of power in
civilized life, its moving causes and even its very soul.'
>   Humphry Davy (aged twenty-three): Discourse
>   introductory to a course of lectures on chemistry, 1802

— ❧ ❦ —

The progress of science had an indirect, but none the less profound,
effect upon corruption. This happened partly through a gradual
change in the intellectual climate, since although scientists are
subject to the same human failings as anybody else and may as
individuals be no less corrupt, the scientific approach to public
affairs is inimical to corruption; and partly because the effects of
applied science, e.g. in communications, public health and medicine,
printing and publishing, brought about unparalleled changes in the
way in which people lived and thought, and released forces of public
opinion which were no longer as tolerant of corruption as was the
eighteenth century.

*

Science contributed a fundamentally changed outlook to mankind
from the Renaissance onwards. The old Graeco-Roman culture and
the Christian religion slowly ceased to form the heart of European
civilization, and the scientific spirit took their place. Hitherto the
majority of men had looked to previous generations for inspiration,
and had thought that the poets, musicians and artists of other ages
were greater than their own. But science grows from generation to
generation; and every schoolboy ought to know more physics than
Pythagoras. During the early campaigns for parliamentary reform
men still talked as though the golden age of the Constitution was in
the distant past,[1] and Wesley and Rousseau both believed, like their
contemporaries, in the 'noble savage' who had not been corrupted
by civilization; even in the nineteenth century Gladstone, his mind
steeped in the Graeco-Roman tradition, created parish councils
because he thought this was a return to a previous golden age. But
already most of his contemporaries had understood the parallel to

[1] Herbert Butterfield: *Origins of Modern Science*, 1949, p. 168.

the idea of biological growth, and looked for a golden age in the future, not in the past. The first world war was a cruel shock to them. Perhaps too applied science made its greatest advances in Britain, Holland, France and North Germany because these were the civilized countries furthest away from the old Graeco-Roman civilization and the ancient Christian world. These also seem to have been the countries which by the turn of the nineteenth century were doing most to destroy bribery and corruption in government and society.

The history of science also throws light on the history of corruption in another way. During the seventeenth century great progress was made towards what we call democracy both in Britain and abroad; yet somehow after 1688 an age of deadness and corruption seems to descend upon society, and it was only by the blood-letting of the French Revolution that progress was made towards universal suffrage and the struggle for social equality was resumed. Something rather similar was happening in science: Bruno, Napier, Descartes, Huygens, Galileo, Kepler, Harvey, Bacon, Hooke, Boyle, Halley and Leibnitz are a few of the great names which seem to culminate in Sir Isaac Newton, but after 1699 Newton took up an appointment as Master of the Mint, and it was not until the nineteenth century that the fire of English progress either in science or politics was rekindled. Dr Bronowski[1] gives three interesting reasons for this regression in science, which seem to have had their parallel in the history of corruption. Firstly, 'England in the seventeenth century had been a seafaring nation and, like Holland, was therefore dominated by the sciences of navigation, astronomy, hydraulics, optics and the design of clocks'. But because she was a manufacturing nation as well as a maritime one she outstripped Holland and France in the eighteenth century. The Royal Society was a respectable forum of the great, but real scientific progress was being made by simple, practical men of business. There was a parallel in politics. After the turmoil of the seventeenth century, the eighteenth desperately wanted stability, and a Royal society of another kind—a hierarchical society—emerged. But wealth was beginning to pass to the practical merchants and with it, in the nineteenth century, they themselves were buying power and status. During the eighteenth century itself they had become so powerful and independent that they came to be beyond the temptations of corruption.

'The second misfortune of science was precisely the spectacular success of Newton's system in astronomy.'[2] The system was so successful, so simple and so beautiful that scientists gave up thinking about the matter any further. The same might be said politically of the Revolution of 1688. It solved so many seventeenth century

---

[1] J. Bronowski: *The Commonsense of Science.*
[2] Ibid., p. 50.

problems so well that it was difficult to see that it did not solve them all. Almost all the wealth, power and status were in the hands of the Whig nobility, who could solve most of the difficulties by judicious bribery and corruption. The trouble was that when cracks appeared in the perfect system, still more bribery and corruption was needed to paper them over.

Dr Bronowski's third reason[1] is that the eighteenth century scientists were too anxious to systematize before they had enough information, so that the real scientific advances came from practical men like Josiah Wedgwood, James Watt and James Brindley, and from a few simple observers like the Rev. Gilbert White.[2] Two of these examples are particularly apt for our purpose, for Watt and Brindley, besides becoming wealthy men, introduced new methods of transport which were to transform the old hierarchical society in a manner that we shall discuss in a moment.

There was one other field in which science was having a decisive effect. Until the publication of Darwin's *Origin of Species* in 1859, Christianity had been closely identified with progress. As knowledge of the Bible spread, so did trade; England became more liberal, education improved and so did wealth. But the Darwinian controversy and the writings of T. H. Huxley struck at the heart of biblical accuracy, and the book on which so much English education was based. After 1859 it was no longer obvious that the Bible was true, and a rift developed between science and religion which has not yet been fully healed. It may be no accident that three of the great leaders of science in the first decade of the twentieth century were Jewish: Freud, Einstein and Karl Marx.

*

In many ways, then, Englishmen of the nineteenth century were fundamentally different from the predecessors. Their horizons were wider, their understanding of their environment deeper, their belief in unlimited progress more confident; whether they were better, wiser or happier is another question, but they were undoubtedly different, and it was science that made them so. But not only were their intellectual horizons more extensive; their mastery of their physical environment surpassed that of all previous centuries; the applications of science to everyday life were as revolutionary as were their growing religious and political emancipation.

*

The most revolutionary application of science was in communication. As long as generations of men followed the same track in the same village, or worked on the same farm, society remained hierarchical

---

[1] Ibid., p. 51 (Penguin edition).
[2] *The Natural History of Selborne.*

L

and static, and the small governing class which commanded mobility and power was free to practice corruption unhindered. But once canals, roads and railways began to develop it became possible to concentrate raw materials and human beings in urban societies; and in the towns the static order came to an end. The railways were the most powerful of these influences, for it was the railways that created the nation states of the nineteenth century, just as it is the aeroplane which is creating the international federation of the twentieth. Britain was perhaps fortunate in that her communications welded the nation into one, thus incidentally turning local scandals and corruption into national concerns, at a comparatively early stage. Some later developing countries have had to step on to the international stage at their birth, before they have properly become nations at all; they are compelled to 'wash their dirty linen' under the eyes of the world, instead of in decent privacy.

The railways were great equalizers. The London Underground has been called a 'triumph of democracy', because high and low, rich and poor, are jostled on terms of complete equality and struggle for the same seat or strap. Just so in Victorian England, where the notion of equality was strange, the arrival times of the trains were the same for the poor as for the rich (though the standards of comfort were very different), and all could receive a ticket as of right and not because of status. Railways sharpened the battle between the industrialists and the landed interests; the industrialists welcomed the railways for the opening up of markets, and for the supplies of labour and raw material that they provided; the landed interests were by no means so pleased at the desecration of their estates, even if they profited from it financially. The war between industry and property was won by the industrialists, but it is estimated that the money gained for the landowners by a Parliament controlled by landowning interests was about double the real value. This is certainly one of the reasons why Britain became short of capital from the 1870s onwards, and why an outdated social system was provided with the wealth to survive until our own day.

The railways were great publicizers. Railway travellers who saw industrial England for the first time began to understand the evils of poverty, child labour, unemployment, brutality and disease which had been normal in the imaginary 'golden age' of the eighteenth century.[1] The railways themselves, of course, added to these horrors by bringing smoke and dirt wherever they went.

Finally, the railways turned the large towns into even larger cities, and it was in these cities, especially in the North, that corruption in public life came most strongly under attack.

Whether the mere fact of mobility has a healthy influence on corruption, by releasing people from their customary restraints, is

[1] Dorothy George: *England in Transition*, p. 136.

debatable. In the long run it probably has, but at earlier stages of development it may work the other way, since among the restraints that are removed by mobility are the customary moral sanctions.[1]

But railways are only one example of the application of nineteenth century science to communication. Throughout the latter part of the century other kinds of communication were increasing the speed and publicity with which business was done, and this had its effect upon corrupt practice. For corruption usually demands time; time to negotiate in privacy, to exchange 'hospitality'; time for the negotiators to watch each other carefully, to 'square' the affected interests; nepotism requires time to cultivate the 'right people' and to pull the right strings. Time of this order was more freely available in the eighteenth and early nineteenth centuries, for in the later nineteenth century leisure and privacy began to diminish, at any rate in industry and commerce; the telephone, the typewriter, short-hand, modern office methods and the increasing speed with which affairs had to be transacted under the spur of competition—these and a score of other influences caused trade to be carried on over greater distances and by people who did not know each other intimately. There might be bribery and dishonesty in such negotia-tions, of course, but there was less time for the personal intimacy and less scope for the verbal agreements which characterized eighteenth century corruption.

In the towns themselves, which the railways were helping to expand or even to create, the application of other branches of science was beginning to make life increasingly tolerable. It is difficult for us today to understand how life can have been endured in the eighteenth and nineteenth century industrial town, with its total absence of essential services (as we should now consider them), let alone any civilized amenities. It was the application of the dis-coveries in medicine, chemistry and engineering that made civilized life possible, by connecting disease with impure water, by purifying it, by inventing pipes to carry it and machines to pump it, by building sewers and drains, by lighting the streets, and generally by creating urban civilization out of urban barbarism. The physical achievement was impressive, but from the viewpoint of our discussion the administrative achievement was equally important; under Chad-wick's driving influence, the Board of Health, set up under the Public Health Act of 1848, became an instrument of impartial and

---

[1] We have been especially warned, by the Rev. Edmund Ilogu of Ibadan, against applying the argument of mobility to pre-industrial societies. In his view mobility in such societies tends to increase corruption, because moral restraints are strictly local, and if a man moves hundreds of miles away from his ancestral spirits, who keep him in order, their restraints are no longer valid. Mr Ilogu has written an interesting unpublished thesis under the title *The Problem for Christian Ethics in Nigeria: an organic society undergoing change under the influence of technical civilization.*

incorrupt central control, and a channel through which the Benthamite principles of government were practised.

It is interesting, and may be significant, that the cities in which most civic progress was made, and where corruption was pushed furthest into the background, were those in which the scientific spirit was most active and where inventions of the scientific mind were the basis of local prosperity. Liverpool, Manchester and Birmingham have always been in the van of enlightened municipal government.

Another development of great importance was the application of science to the craft and industry of printing, which gave rise to the modern professions of publishing and journalism. We have referred to this in previous chapters and shall refer to it again. It enabled many dark places to be lit up and many corrupt practices to be revealed for what they were. It is significant that in developing countries little progress has been made along these lines beyond a 'popular', which in practice very often means an irresponsible, press. Virtually all books and important journals have to be imported; foreign publishers cannot for obvious reasons indulge in the hard hitting of the Victorian novelists, pamphleteers and journalists; and nearly everything has to be in the English language; the problem of language is in itself, of course, a serious complicating factor.

Finally, in the background, were the immense advances in medical science and the growth of the modern medical profession. Not only were the great Victorian medical reformers publishing their discoveries,[1] but doctors, men of education and standing, were living in the slums and seeing for themselves the results of *laissez faire* corruption. Among the greatest social reformers were the Medical Officers of Health in the industrial cities, whose position, it is interesting to note, was protected by law to save them from victimization if, by their fearless exposure of the breeding grounds of corruption and disease, they ran foul of local vested interests.

*

These examples of the application of science to the ordinary processes of living may at first sight appear to have only a tenuous connection with the subject of this book, and we have already admitted that it is an indirect one; at the same time we have said that it was profound. The advance of science was helping to create a population that was more numerous, more healthy, better informed and more independent with every generation. Corruption, in the sense of the exploitation of the poor by the rich, the weak by the strong and the ignorant by the understanding, was being pushed steadily into retreat. In these matters many developing countries are at the early Victorian stage of progress, which increases rather

[1] Sherwood Taylor: *A Century of Science*, 1952, Ch. 3.

than reduces the relevance of what we have said.

*

Finally, however, in order to give a balanced statement of this proposition, it is necessary to refer to its opposite. Scientific progress continued to rapidly with the dawn of the twentieth century, for example in communications and production, that it became possible for gigantic corporations to control world-wide markets worth millions of pounds. Most people's morality does not extend so far beyond their own horizons, and after 1900 man's economic reach began far to exceed his moral grasp. It is difficult to worry about corruption thousands of miles away across the world, in remote, exotic countries. It was such changes that helped to make the standards of corruption in the business and commercial world the reverse of what was suggested in other fields, in earlier chapters. From about 1870 onwards the moral standards of the electorate, of Parliament and of the Administration were rapidly improving. In business, after having risen for most of the nineteenth century, they were, as we have said, almost certainly declining.

Nevertheless, the gains from the application of science have far exceeded the losses so far as corruption is concerned.

CHAPTER 12

The Victorian Middle Class

—◦❧ ❧◦—

Nineteenth century progress in industry, commerce, science and medicine, which we have discussed in the last two chapters, had an important consequence in the emergence of a middle class which was numerous, wealthy and self-confident. It had no counterpart in previous centuries, and, more important for our subject, it has no counterpart in the developing countries today. Its influence both in destroying corruption and, more positively, in evolving a spirit of disinterested public service, was immense.

We have already noted something of the influence of the men, in an age when women were subservient. Merchants and manufacturers had prospered and become wealthy, by their own hard work and skill; a significant proportion of them were professedly religious, and all of them, as the century advanced, lived under the influence of the strict, if often harsh, morality of the Victorian age. Having spent their early lives in making money, many of them turned in middle age to seek that peculiar combination of power and status which is accorded in Britain to those who engage in unpaid public service; their wealth was important, because it put them beyond criticism and beyond temptation; the fact that they were successful, often self-educated and self-made, was important because it gave them confidence and independence, the fact that they were numerous was important, because they were strong enough in numbers to penetrate Parliament, local government, education and social work, and many were given to philanthropy. They were immensely *responsible* people. In considering solid, middle-class Victorian respectability today it is fashionable to emphasize the smugness and hypocrisy which were its darker side, and to pay too little tribute to its enduring achievement, particularly in the creation of a sense of public duty.

Many such men lived their whole lives in their own towns, speaking their own accents and living among their own workpeople. Others became more socially ambitious, moved to large suburban mansions or country houses as they prospered, and brought up their children after the pattern on the aristocracy; and it was from homes like these that there emerged the remarkable figure of the upper-middle class Victorian spinster, whose influence on corruption in public life, though different from that of the superior sex, was equally profound.

The lives of most of these women were at first incredibly restricted, as they were not expected to do anything useful except to assist in the ordering of their households; their music and needlework were assumed to fill their lives satisfactorily until they married; and though they may have been people of intelligence and culture it did not occur to their parents or to society generally that they had any contribution to make to the welfare of the country. As the century advanced some very remarkable women broke free of this tradition. Their parents or grandparents had usually made their fortunes in industry or trade, and they possessed both wealth and security; they had a better education than their parents had ever known (though it was usually acquired privately or at home), the new possibilities of Victorian high Society (with a Queen, not a King, at its head) were opening out to them, sometimes providing them with influential friends; and they were given some training in responsibility by the size of their households and the abundance of servants whose lives they ordered. What was lacking in their own lives was power and purpose. When such women emerged from the obscurity of domestic life, and became social workers, teachers or nurses, and encountered inefficiency or corruption, they disposed of it with a ruthlessness which sometimes shocked male observers.

Among the greatest of them was Florence Nightingale, who raised nursing from a degraded occupation to a noble profession. Her parents were wealthy, her father a clever but indolent man. His wife was determined to mould his career and persuaded him to stand for Parliament at Andover in 1835; he had thought that a reformed Parliament would usher in an age of political integrity, and was cruelly disillusioned; as he would not bribe the Andover electorate they did not vote for him, and he retired to make the best of his wealth and status. Henceforward his wife appears to have concentrated on her second daughter Florence. By iron determination and utter devotion to her cause she broke down all the barriers in her way; in her first post she received no pay at all and very little status, but she acquired real power and used it in a way that utterly astonished her Committee.[1] Throughout her life she showed the same indifference to wealth and status, but a very strong sense of power and a desire to use it with efficiency and integrity. Eventually, by the standards of the Florence Nightingale School of Nursing as practised at St Thomas' Hospital, the modern profession of nursing grew up.

The system which it replaced had always been prone to bribery and corruption, especially in the workhouses. The insanitary conditions

[1] *Life*, by Cecil Woodham-Smith: Ch. 6.

were so appalling and the danger of contracting diseases so considerable, that only the poorest, strongest and most avaricious would usually undertake the work. Anything, therefore, which replaced the ghastly conditions of Florence Nightingale's day was almost bound to be an improvement, but it was her particular genius that gathered together so many spinsters from affluent homes and raised the nursing profession to a respectability undreamed of a few years earlier.[1] The problem is discussed in St Paul's Monthly Magazine for August, 1871, as quoted by Mr Abel-Smith:

'The want of remunerative occupations suitable for gentlewomen in these days is painfully felt and universally acknowledged, and fresh schemes are continually being started to remedy the evil. It has been proposed to throw open the learned professions to the competition of women, and remove the various disabilities which keep the sex in a position of inferiority. But it appears that there is one department of activity peculiarly their own, which they have hitherto failed to make the vantage ground it might become. We refer to nursing...'

But if Florence Nightingale was outstanding she was by no means unique. The second half of the nineteenth century is starred with illustrious names; Octavia Hill (1838–1912), a granddaughter of Dr Southwood-Smith, one of the pioneers of sanitary reform, who attacked and reformed one of the worst Victorian evils—bad housing —and created a new conception of housing management; Elizabeth Garrett Anderson (1836–1917), who with extraordinary fortitude fought for women's place in the medical profession, and became the first woman doctor; Dorothea Beale (1831–1906) and Frances Mary Buss (1826–1894), who pioneered education for girls; and Dame Millicent Fawcett (1847–1929), who led the struggle for women's enfranchisement. An earlier generation had produced, from the famous Quaker manufacturing family, Elizabeth Fry (1780–1845), perhaps the most honoured name in penal reform. These are but a few of a formidable band of middle class Victorian women who raised the professional, social and moral standards of their century.

*

But it was not only in their public but in their private lives that the middle class Victorians helped to create a moral climate in which corruption wilted. They appear to have had more leisure than we enjoy today, there was no commercialized entertainments, their families were large, and in their own homes they cultivated the arts, especially the art of reading. There was the great new art form, the novel, to read, and there would often be a great deal of reading aloud from Disraeli, Charles Reade, Thackeray, Mrs Gaskell, George

[1] For a full account see Brian Abel-Smith: A Short History of Nursing.

Eliot, the Bronte sisters, Charles Dickens, Charles Kingsley and a host of lesser writers. Almost all these writers were advocating some cause, or exposing corruption, immorality or social evil. In 1839, 2,032 new works were published, in 1875 3,573 and in 1884 4,832; these are not startling increases, but the books were very often read aloud, and read by every member of very large families, and it is interesting to note the considerable increase in the seventies and eighties when the attacks on bribery and corruption were in full swing. In the fifties and sixties, after the abolition of taxes on newspapers and magazines, many new serious publications arose, apart from the daily papers, among them the *Spectator*, *Athenaeum*, *Chambers Journal*, *Saturday Review* and the *Cornhill Magazine*. Many of these had high standards, both literary and moral, and the effect of this was doubtless felt in the attacks on parliamentary bribery and corruption that were being made at the time.

Another point of curious importance may be made. In their leisure time the later Victorians pursued new sports quite unknown to previous generations, and, typically, they imbued them with moral standards, so that British 'fair play' became the rule in all of them. The new Education Act provided schools which, in the tradition of Eton and Harrow, taught the boys to play these games in a spirit of 'sportsmanship', which became a national cult, and survived long after the religious revival of the early Victorian age had collapsed. All over the world where the British played cricket in the blazing heat, planted golf clubs in jungles, tennis courts on mountain sides, and every conceivable game in every possible place, one potent force against corruption or 'unfair play' has been the mid-Victorian conscience, apparently quite fortuitously planted by the Methodist revival, and given expression in the leisure pursuits of the middle class.

*

With it all there developed that curious sense of public obligation, difficult to define and slowly diminishing today, which characterized Britain during her era of outstanding public integrity. In more aristocratic days it was expressed in the phrase *noblesse oblige*—the duty of the well-born to shoulder his duty to his inferiors—a spirit which persisted into much more democratic days. Few people act from motives that are wholly unmixed, and the Victorians and their successors who gave their services—unpaid—to Parliament, local government, education, social work and charity doubtless enjoyed the status and power that these activities conferred upon them; but that they *did* give freely of their services in this way, and that they derived intense satisfaction from it, and that people respected them for it, cannot be questioned. The spirit of public service—in its crudest terms the willingness to do something for nothing—soon creates an atmosphere in which bribery and corruption cannot breathe. Away from family, clan and tribe it is the rarest of qualities in developing countries; where, however, a corresponding class has hardly begun to emerge.

CHAPTER 1

First Impressions

This book was not thought out in advance; that is to say the authors first gave a statement of the problem as it appeared to them in a developing country; they then turned back and looked at the history of bribery and corruption in some major departments of British life, trying in particular to see how and why matters improved; having done this they hoped that Part II might throw some light on Part I. This was unduly optmistic, for the story in Britain reveals no short cuts to integrity, any more than it does to democracy. We have had constantly to refer to currents moving slowly under the surface, to improvements coming to fruition after a century of change, to gradual tendencies. This is not to say that a comparison of nineteenth century Britain with twentieth century Africa cannot be instructive, but it will not be easy and it may not be encouraging.

There are two kinds of critic who tend to think that the effort is not worth making at all, and that the whole purpose of this book is misguided.

First, there is a considerably body of opinion which accepts the existence of bribery and corruption without question, but holds that it does not matter. This school of thought has some unexpected adherents, including members of Christian denominations. They argue that bribery and corruption have existed throughout history; that they are rampant throughout the world today, even among the greatest nations on earth; that this is regrettable but relatively unimportant; that the fact that Britain experienced half a century of extraordinary freedom from corruption is an interesting historical curiosity but that it has no relevance to life as it is lived today in the developing world; that these are growing pains that any reasonable man would have expected; in short that there is a lot of fuss about nothing.

It has to be admitted, in fairness to this criticism, that there is little evidence that corruption and inefficiency necessarily go together. Some of the worst examples of bribery, corruption and nepotism may be found in contemporary America, a country not renowned for its inefficiency; and whether the developing countries of the world would be more efficient if they were less corrupt is pure speculation. One may be less guarded on the question of the cost of corruption, which many wealthy countries can afford to carry without noticing it, but which developing countries can hardly afford at all. The sums involved in some of the proved cases of corruption in Africa would have brought considerable benefits to people for whom 'underprivileged' is too mild a word, if they had been properly spent. It may also be remarked that the agreeable cynicism of Americans, for example, towards corruption in high places in their native land is a luxury that developing countries cannot afford from another point of view. For these countries depend considerably on enthusiasm and on youthful pride of achievement, and the wounds that corruption in high places inflicts upon this pride are as agonizing as the wounds which thoughtless adults can inflict upon the pride of children. The cynicism of many of the African intelligentsia today— civil servants, professional men, students—towards the politicians whom they so recently venerated; the assumption by even larger numbers that local government is a racket which exists to line the pockets of the councillors; the fatalistic acceptance of the power of petty bureaucracy, often accompanied by extortion—these are not the attitudes of progress and development.

Another thing that one can say without reservation is that widespread corruption, especially in high places, is becoming a handicap to foreign aid and investment. Representatives of aid-giving countries lose some of their enthusiasm when they observe ostentatious living by the ruling few in countries where the masses of the people are living in utmost poverty.

We can only proceed, therefore, on the assumption that corruption *does* matter.

The other kind of critic of the moralizing approach which is inherent in a book of this sort is the social anthropologist. It is always unwise to argue with exponents of this formidable science, since they have their own vocabulary, which differs from that of the ordinary man, and their own concepts, which are not readily understood. But their criticism, as we apprehend it, is that although transactions of the kind with which we are concerned take place, they are not corrupt; they are on the contrary essential parts of the culture patterns of people who differ from ourselves, and the offering of a gift in return for a service has the honourable sanction of custom and is part of the cement that binds society together. To condemn it is to misunderstand the nature of the societies we are discussing, and to abolish it would be to add to the bewilderment and disruption of communities undergoing an unprecedently rapid change from the tribal to the global organization of society.

But the Nigerian authors of the Report on Bribes and Customary Gifts did not take this agreeable view of the situation; they knew all about customary gifts but said that they had to a very large extent degenerated into extortion—and this in relatively unsophisticated areas and at the level of the village head. When we move to the higher levels and consider the manipulation of banking accounts and secret negotiations with contractors it is difficult to explain them in terms of traditional culture. In any case this kind of criticism seems to be rebutted by the fact that eminent Africans in public life are continually calling upon their people to eschew bribery and corruption, foretelling in prophetic tones that it will bring about the ruin of their countries.

This last point is important, for if the outcry against corruption came only from foreigners, notably from the British, we should hesitate to add to it, for it could well be argued that it was none of our business. This could be argued in any case, but we feel more confidence in inquiring into the matter when it is so obviously one of deep concern to the most eminent and responsible citizens of the developing countries themselves.

*

The first thing that emerges from our examination of bribery and corruption in eighteenth and nineteenth century Britain is that little that happens today in African or Asia could be any worse. There are indeed striking parallels, but the prizes for what we now regard as iniquitous go to Britain rather than to the emerging nations of the twentieth century.

It is said, correctly, that it is difficult to get a job in Africa today unless you have a relative or patron who will pull strings. In the Britain of yesterday it would have been impossible. It is said that members of legislatures and of local councils cannot hope for election unless they bribe, but at least they do so secretly, and, one may charitably suppose, with a guilty conscience. In British elections bribery was open and blatant. The authors have witnessed many elections in many parts of Africa, but even if they had the literary skill of Charles Dickens they would find it difficult to describe anything like the Eatanswill election, which was taken from real life.[1]

Again, it is alleged in Africa that the police are not always im-

---

[1] Professor Gash believes that Dickens understated the case: 'The traditional Eatanswill picture of early Victorian elections is in fact not so much an exaggeration as a pale and euphemistic version of the contemporary scene', op. cit., p. 147.

partial, and that they favour the political party in power; the truth of this allegation varies as between central and local government police, and there are exceptions to the general rule in both cases; but no one would deny that the allegations are often true. But in 1833 the Royal Commission on Municipal Corporations had this to say of elections:

'At Coventry serious riots and disturbances frequently occur, and the officers of the police, *being usually selected from one political party*, are often active in fomenting them . . .' (p. 43: authors' italics.)

Even the violence and thuggery which has occasionally marred elections in Africa in recent years was once familiar in England's green and pleasant land, and since we did not dwell on violence, as distinct from corruption, in the earlier part of the book, it is worth quoting further from Professor Gash: He tells us that in the same city of Coventry in 1832 the Whigs hired a band of ruffians, paid them heavily and kept them up to the mark with gin, with 'clear instructions to stop the Tories from mustering and keep the Tory voters away from the hustings on the day of the poll. In this task they seem to have been most successful. . . . Electors who cast a vote against the Whig candidate, on coming out of the booths were "most ferociously attacked and dragged backwards by the hair of their heads . . . when they fell to the ground they were kicked and beat; also their clothes were torn off their persons and thrown into the booth. . . ." Other voters known to be in the Tory interest were forcibly prevented from voting by being pulled back from the polling booth as they were about to enter . . .'[1]

At the time of writing there is considerable concern in some parts of Africa about the same political partiality, accompanied by oppression of political opponents, in the native or customary courts. But in nineteenth-century England the Native Court Judgeships, or their approximate equivalent, were 'usually filled by the patron with his underlings. Incompetent and corrupt persons were in many instances appointed to discharge the office of Recorder or Justice of the Peace. In some cases the former, and salaried, office was enjoyed by absentees. Thus the Recorder of Lancaster did not attend the Quarter Sessions once between the years 1810 and 1832.'[2] This is not quite the same thing as the oppression of political opponents, but it is of the same general level from the point of view of integrity.

And so it would be possible to continue, but to do so would merely to be to repeat examples of which a representative selection was quoted in Part II. The simple fact is that nineteenth century

[1] Gash, op. cit., p. 148; this is only one example from a whole chapter entitled 'Electoral Violence' (Ch. 6).

[2] Redlich and Hirst (ed. Keith-Lucas), op. cit., p. 124.

Britain and twentieth century Africa are so alike in these matters that Britain cannot speak censoriously to Africa. Naturally the pattern of bribery and corruption varies in detail. As a purely personal judgment there are two ways in which the situation in the developing countries is in fact worse than in eighteenth/nineteenth century Britain. First, intimidation, as distinct from open violence, is more widely practised, backed sometimes with the threat of force, but more frequently of ostracism; it is an effective weapon among people whose ancestors were accustomed to think as one, and among whom original or rebellious thinking, had it been theoretically possible, would have been the equivalent of disloyalty, or even treachery. Independence does not yet mean individual independence of thought, and moral courage to stand out against the 'herd' way of thinking is a rare virtue. Second, there is almost certainly a greater amount of petty exaction running through society from top to bottom, from the Chief granting a legitimate request from a petitioner to the building foreman hiring daily-paid labour and taking his rake-off from each successful applicant. This is undoubtedly in-fluenced—and here we agree with the social anthropologist—by the recent tradition of exchanging gifts for favours, a tradition heavily exploited by a rapidly growing petty bureaucracy.

The rest can be paralleled or outstripped from eighteenth and nineteenth century Britain.

*

The second point that emerges is that salvation is not to be looked for in statutory legislation. It is true that in our account of developments in Britain we have referred to certain legislative landmarks, the Municipal Corporations Act of 1835, the Secret Ballot Act of 1872, the Corrupt and Illegal Practices Act of 1883 and the Public Bodies Corrupt Pactices Act of 1889; as well as to the establishment of an impartial Civil Service Commission; we have also said that these measures had the effect of 'finally sweeping away' certain abuses. But this is not the same thing as saying that they were responsible for their abolition; the Acts merely stated as a matter of law what majority public opinion had by then made acceptable in practice. The laws may have run a little ahead of public opinion as a whole, but they certainly had majority opinion behind them before they became laws, and the abuses which were finally swept away were the abuses which only a minority were continuing to commit.

But what is so striking in tracing the long and painful path by which Britain reached, for example, electoral rectitude, is that every relevant measure that was added to the Statute Book during the nineteenth century was *already* on the Statute Books of the develop-ing books before their first general elections ever took place—the secret ballot, the penalties for bribing and treating, the adjudication of electoral disputes by the Courts—these were all written into the electoral regulations of a dozen countries as a matter of course.[1] They had almost no influence on the amount of bribing and treating that took place, and little more on other kinds of corruption. Similarly, British local government legislation, or local rules, affecting declaration of interest in contracts, the actual award of contracts, or the disqualification of candidates who try to use influence have been carefully reproduced, but with little effect.

People cannot be made honest by Acts of Parliament or statutory regulations; they will always find some way round them, if *most of them* want to.

We may see some sort of parallel in Britain today in the demand for an Act of Parliament to abolish the colour bar. The reasons in favour of such an Act are obvious, but it is opposed by many people who are no less anxious to see an end of colour discrimination than an Act's supporters, but who consider that an Act of Parliament would be unreal until such time as a large majority of those at whom an Act would be directed have reached a more enlightened state of mind. For although innkeepers, for example, can to some extent be controlled by law through the renewal of their licences by a Bench of Magistrates, no private landlady can be compelled to take as a lodger anyone whom she does not want. Not only would it mean a breach of person freedom to compel her by law to do so, but the law could never be enforced. Nor, it is claimed, is the situation very different in the matter of employment; private employers cannot be compelled to employ somebody they don't like, and large-scale or public employers are in a helpless position if their British employees object to the employment of coloured men, whether the reason be colour prejudice as such or the fear of unemployment and redundancy. Only when the great majority of people have outgrown colour prejudice could legislation be introduced to forbid it, thus sweeping away the final remnants of something which is offensive to the general public conscience; and it could never be forbidden by law in purely private relationships.

Whether the time is ripe to introduce such legislation, or whether the present British Government is unduly nervous at taking a step

[1] A present-day exception to this is the limitation of *legitimate* campaign expenditure by candidates which is imposed by the twentieth century Representation of the People Acts in Britain. So far as we know this has not been attempted in African electoral legislation, although it has been considered. The difficulties in Africa are (a) that such legislation would be virtually impossible to enforce in the present state of accounting, auditing and financial control; (b) that 'legitimate' expenditure in British terms, e.g. hire of halls, printing of election addresses, etc., is not the root of the problem; by far the greatest campaign expense is bribing and treating. 'Treating' at elections ought perhaps to be in a different category. In some circumstances, as when people make a long journey to meet their candidate or to vote, feasting or drinking together would be normal custom, and the British laws concerning 'treating' are cold and unrealistic.

in legislation which would be ahead of public opinion—what indeed *is* the state of public opinion—these are matters for individual judgment.

But the general thesis that legislation cannot run *far* ahead of public opinion is undoubtedly sound, particularly in matters which affect personal attitudes, preferences, prejudices or moral standards. It is not easy for legislation to outstrip public opinion in *any* matter, but it is easier for it to do so in order, for example, to compel people to drive slowly, or keep their homes in a sanitary condition, or pay their rates, than it is to compel them to show Christian brotherhood to all men or to be honest in their personal affairs. Even in the matter of driving slowly the law cannot for long go against the grain of the community's collective common sense, as is shown by the fact that 'thirty' limits are sometimes altered to 'forty' when it becomes obvious that the law is absurdly restrictive, and that people of sober and responsible habits are not observing it.

The developing countries, then, have started their independent and sovereign lives with every accepted British law against bribery and corruption and every normal regulation against nepotism and undue influence. These laws and regulations have not worked. When we come to ask why not, the obvious answer is that the currents of public opinion have not yet flowed strongly enough in their favour. This is the situation which we will now try to examine.

M

CHAPTER 2

Sanctions

—◦❧❦◦—

(a) *The Sanction of Religion*

We use the word religion in its literal, though now subsidiary, sense of the cause to which a man is 'bound', and which normally gives his actions a social and not a selfish motivation; the sense in which a dedicated communist is a more religious man than an easy-going Anglican. It is necessary to make this definition for two reasons: first, because it does not require belief in a spiritual religion (the sense in which the word is usually employed) to hold that bribery and corruption are wrong, for corruption is merely a form of theft, and theft is held to be intolerable in all societies, atheist, animist, Christian, Muslim, and is contrary to the laws of all organized communities; second, because in nineteenth century Britain Christians and rationalists both made important contributions to its defeat.

To millions in the western or 'westernizing' world religion in this sense has now largely departed from the unselfish motivation, and is based on personal acquisition. To other millions, in societies emerging from tribalism, religion has still much to do with fear and superstition, and in its more positive aspect with the communal life of the tribe and the worship of ancestors.

In the developing countries today men are tossed about between the influence of these various religions, and their conduct, in private and in public, reflects this fact. No religion to whose ethic corruption would be intolerable has yet emerged predominant.

The struggle for integrity in public life in Britain, in as far as it was based on a religious faith or a moral code, has been outlined in previous chapters, and we will now try to draw some of the threads together.

*

We have seen that the late eighteenth and the nineteenth centuries were a time in British history when the Christian religion laid a greater emphasis than ever before on conduct and morality. From the Reformation to the Reform Bill the Established Church could hardly have made much impact on corruption, as it was itself corrupt, and its bishops and clergy for the most part idle and un-distinguished men. But John Wesley left his mark on the eighteenth century as few men have left their mark on any century, reviving the Established Church, in which he maintained that he lived and died, through its Evangelical Movement, and leaving behind him the dissenting Church which bore his own name. The Methodist move-and its aftermath coincided with the industrial revolution, and was more largely responsible than any other influence for the integrity and thrift of a large section of the working class—qualities which appear almost incredible against the hard, drab existence of the slaves of the factory system. But it was nevertheless in the dark industrial towns that the Methodist chapels were built and where the austere Methodist religion took root. In reading about the lives of African political leaders one is repeatedly struck by the fact that nearly all of them started life as school-teachers. In reading the lives of the later Victorian and Edwardian trade union and labour leaders one is similarly struck by the large number whose training-ground was the Sunday School and the nonconformist chapel, where they preached the Word, saw how the Word should be translated into industrial and political action, and learnt the arts of speech and leadership. The influence of the Sunday Schools was itself immense, and although their instruction would seem to us today to be formid-ably narrow, they taught thousands to read and write, and moreover were an important influence in encouraging thrift and self-help among the poor.

Before trade unions were established—and indeed before they were legal—the working-class associations known as Friendly Societies had grown up with the industrial revolution, and before the end of the eighteenth century they were on a legal footing and were providing sickness, unemployment, old age and funeral benefits for many of the most insecure and vulnerable of the wage-earners. Some of them—those whose members were all of one industrial occupation —were indeed trade unions in all but name,[1] and the 'friendly society' element in the later trade union movement is perhaps not sufficiently understood by African trade union leaders today. What is of relevance to this discussion is that

'among the local societies in towns, the greater density of population led to the formation of societies of special composition during this period—societies with some religious or moral principle as their mainspring. . . . One of the most numerous was the Sunday School type . . . "the contributions are of course very low, and an actuary would be surprised how they get on at all. For they are very cheaply managed and the members are, of course, among the most steady, provident and respectable." . . . The appearance of these societies

[1] P. H. J. H. Gosden: *The Friendly Societies in England, 1815–75*, p. 71.

based upon some ethical or religious principle was one of the most striking developments among local societies during this period.'[1]

The point we wish to establish is that as the working-class movement gathered momentum in nineteenth century Britain through the friendly societies, co-operatives and trade unions, and eventually through the Labour Party, its leadership was largely religious and its philosophy was impregnated with the strict moral codes of nonconformity; to this it owed its stability, its thrift and its incorruptibility. In the twentieth century it has departed somewhat from its predominantly Christian heritage, and it has required the mid-twentieth century intellectuals of the Party, seeking to re-define the basis of socialism, to reaffirm that it is first and foremost an ethical creed; though to simpler minds this would have appeared self-evident, since we are not fit for socialism until we handle other people's money with the same degree of probity as we handle our own, and this is not often the case.

The influence of the Methodists and their fellow nonconformists was powerfully augmented in mid-century by the group within the Church of England which became known as the 'Christian Socialists', who entered the political and industrial arena in revolt from the 'other-worldliness' of both wings of the Established Church—the Evangelicals and the Oxford Movement. But other-worldly though the Evangelicals and High Churchmen may have been, and remote from the struggles of the poor, they were influencing the minds of the middle and upper classes of English society, and in politics, in local government and in business they joined forces with the prosperous dissenters to create the moral climate which was characteristic of middle-class Victorian England, and which was one of the influences which swept corruption out of public and commercial life. Not least among the formative influences of the time, for a special reason, was the Headmaster of Rugby School, Dr Thomas Arnold, who in the fifteen years before his death in 1842 stamped his character on the English Public Schools, and ensured that the education of the sons of the privileged classes was firmly rooted in Christian morality. The effects of Arnold's influence were far-reaching in a society which for another eighty years was largely governed by a ruling caste of hereditary leaders.

What all this amounts to is that throughout the nineteenth century powerful religious forces were marshalled against corruption at every level of society. Moreover it is important to remember that those who were not Christians in belief were nevertheless inheriting and accepting as normal the Christian codes of conduct, with their emphasis on thrift and integrity. Anyone who lived in Britain between the wars is likely to be familiar with the agnostic or the

[1] P. H. J. H. Gosden: *The Friendly Societies in England, 1815–75*, p. 20.

atheist whose standards of personal conduct and honesty were those
implanted in his forefathers by Sunday School and Chapel, though
he himself would probably be unaware of it. The influence of
Victorian morality persists today, though it is dying; middle-aged
people who grew up under the last of its influence, and who recognize
it in their contemporaries, feel a noticeable gulf between themselves
and the post-war generation which had abandoned it. The purpose
of this slight digression is to establish that the influence of a religion
in society goes far beyond its actual adherents.

It is not easy to locate such an influence in the developing countries
today. The Christian churches are at any uneasy stage. The prevailing
atmosphere in Africa, as elsewhere, is materialistic, the great gods
being money, allowances and consumer goods. The great causes,
capable of arousing selfless idealism, are nationalism, anti-colonial-
ism and industrialization, and nationalist sentiment does not always
look kindly on the religion of foreign missionaries; also the leadership of the churches is still largely 'expatriate' at the top. Some of the
most powerful churches do not regard bribery and corruption as
being matters of first importance; some are themselves corrupt.
Church services are packed, and the need for religious expression
appears to be infinitely greater than in contemporary England, but
religion and conduct are not meshed. The many Christians, clergy
and lay, who try to fight against corruption are voices crying in the
wilderness rather than a close-knit force in politics or public life.

All African culture is based on religion, but the props of that
religion have been knocked away even more drastically than the
props of Victorian morality in contemporary Britain. The great
traditional religious sanctions—'accountability to one's age-grade or
to the spirit of departed ancestors, which exercised some measure of
"spiritual" check on the exercise of authority and leadership'[1] mean
little or nothing to those now exercising authority and leadership, or
to the rapidly expanding élite. And though Christian worship is, as
no longer in Britain, a need as urgent as sport or entertainment,
Christian morals are not yet backed by sanctions as powerful as
those of tribal morals; the desire to avoid individual responsibility
and to do as others do is till the more powerful motivation.

The religion of Islam, a more powerful influence than Christianity
in many regions and growing everywhere, for all its stern personal
disciplines of prayer and fasting, and for all its greater integration
of so many aspects of life with the Faith, appears to be tolerant of
bribery and corruption in secular affairs, and to be more concerned
with private than with public morality.

However, what we were describing in England was not a successful
attack by the Christian religion on bribery and corruption, but an
influence quietly making itself felt under the surface of national life—

[1] Edmund Ilogu: op. cit.

a stream, so to speak, which was continually being joined by new tributaries, and which at the end of a hundred years was flowing strongly enough to have some influence, largely indirect, upon corruption.

Another stream was flowing in the same direction. Perhaps the most important single influence in cleansing and energizing government and administration in the nineteenth century was the religion of the Philosophic Radicals or Utilitarians, a group of men dedicated to a rationalist and scientific creed. As John Wesley and his followers left their mark on the beliefs and behaviour of the eighteenth century so did Jeremy Bentham and his disciples on the nineteenth. This is not the place to discuss the tenets of their religion, any more than we have discussed those of Christianity; we must take them equally for granted, though we shall say a little more about them in a later chapter.

Here it is sufficient to say that the influence of the great Utilitarians, Bentham himself, the Mills, father and son, Place, Hume and Hobhouse upon corruption in public life complemented that of Wesley, Shaftesbury, Maurice, Newman and other great pillars of the Christian faith. In particular the Benthamites were the great opponents of nepotism and sinecures in Parliament, of bribery at elections and of corruption and irresponsibility in central and local administration.

Had not these religious currents flowed so strongly under the surface of national life during the nineteenth century, it is questionable whether corruption would have been virtually destroyed by the century's end. It is questionable also whether corruption in developing countries can ever be defeated until influences as profound as these have worked themselves into the national consciousness of the new States, thus making it possible for anti-corruption laws to become effective and for anti-corruption officers to become redundant. Indeed, it is only such influences that can turn geographical territories, created by the accidents of history, into nation-states in the highest sense.

(b) The Sanction of the Law

We have already said that laws are of little use unless the great majority of people respect them, but at that point we were referring to actual legal enactments forbidding bribery and corrupt practices in particular situations; or, we might have added, the Standing Orders of statutory bodies governing the award of contracts, the procedure of tendering, or the appointment of candidates for employment.[1] But here we are talking not about laws, but about the Law.

[1] It did not come within our province in discussing eighteenth and nineteenth century corruption in Britain to refer to the modern rules governing these matters. Readers are referred to Ch. XIII of Dr R. M. Jackson's book *The Machinery of Local Government*—'Dishonesty and Corruption', p. 337.

The penalties for corruption are laid down not only in individual Acts or in statutory regulations, such as those governing an election, but, if one may extend the meaning of the word corruption to such things as theft, embezzlement and forgery, in the ordinary Criminal Code. The difficulty in developing countries today is that the penalties of the Law do not always appear to carry a stigma sufficient to deter the wrongdoer from doing wrong again. We caught glimpses of the same situation in eighteenth century Britain, as when a Member of Parliament for a pocket borough bribed so blatantly as to be sent to prison and fined, but appeared on his release to stand elsewhere.[1] This cheerful attitude is regrettably common in some African countries today, and one is constantly surprised by the manner in which people who have been punished for an ordinary criminal offence reappear without apparent embarrassment in their private, and occasionally in their public lives. A prison sentence may mean discomfort, inconvenience and loss, but it does not always mean social ostracism. This may of course be an excellent thing from' one point of view, for do not our most enlightened criminologists in Britain constantly urge this attitude upon us? On the other hand, although no one would advocate that society should take a pro-longed revenge against a man who has purged his offence, an attitude commonly found in Africa is that he was not in fact offended against society, but that he has been unlucky in a sort of lottery.

In colonial days this was an even commoner attitude, for offences against the law were often thought to be offences against the colonial power that made the law, and were thus political offences, and accordingly commendable. This attitude, incidentally, has not yet worked itself out, even after self-government. One of the authors was recently asked what were the voting rights in Britain of a man who was in prison for a political offence, and was given to under-stand that this had some bearing on a local case. On inquiring what the offence had been the answer was 'forgery'; how, then, was this a political offence? The Court which had sentenced him was a court of his political opponents!

We do not deny that these things are altering for the better, or that pride of nationhood is increasing respect for the law, which is also enhanced by the great dignity, wisdom and integrity of the higher Courts. But fundamental disrepsect for the laws of the State, deriving partly from their confusion with the laws of the white man, is still an obstacle to the growth of honesty. Mr N. U. Akpan, a civil servant of great integrity, wrote recently of his mournful experience of visiting in prison three young men who had been his pupils at school; 'My experience about the attitude of these prisoners was common; it was an attitude not of repentance or regret, but of self-pity and of curses either of their star or of some enemy. To my expressions of

[1] p. 68.

sorrow and disappointment about what they had done, each of the first two replied "I've just been unlucky, that's all. After all, everybody does it".[1]

In a comparison of Britain and Africa, this example loses some of its force when one remembers that the identical words might have been spoken by thousands of frustrated and rudderless young men in English prisons at the moment. But it serves to express a common attitude in Africa *which has never yet been seriously challenged*.

Respect for the Law is also lacking, especially in the lower courts which deal with the ordinary run of offences, because of the obvious foolishness of some English legal concepts in an African society. Laws which allow an obviously guilty man to go free because of some incomprehensible rule of evidence, or which find a man guilty and fine him without compelling him to make restitution to the offended party or his family, are obviously not meant to be obeyed by sensible men. This lack of respect does not extend to the jurisdiction of the native or customary laws, *unless they are vitiated by political partisanship*; indeed, many folk are ready to submit their disputes to an informal court of their own creation, in clan or union, rather than brave the unpredictable hazards of the English law.[2]

The fundamental point here is the engagement of loyalties. Africans are as law-abiding as any people in the world when the commission of a crime means offending against the *mores* of society, and within the ambit of family, clan or tribe where the divorce between law and religion is not yet complete honesty is as high as anywhere in an imperfect world. But loyalty to 'the State' is a concept which takes time to grow, and while it is growing the sanctions of the State's laws are imperfect; many people break them with no profound sense of guilt, and endure their punishments with no deep feeling of stigma.

*

It is convenient here to say something of a related problem, that of law *enforcement*. Even if respect for the law is deficient it can be inculcated by steady and impartial enforcement, since even in the most law-abiding citizens the elements of respect and fear are interwoven; most of us, if we indulged in honest self-examination on this point, would find that we obey the law partly because we have been brought up to respect it, but partly because we fear the consequences of breaking it; and we might find it disconcerting to realize how large a part is played by fear rather than respect in determining our behaviour. But when the consequences of the law are evaded, either

---

[1] Speech by Mr Akpan on Bribery and Corruption, reported in the *Nigerian Outlook*, September 26, 1962.

[2] It is fair to add that most African professional lawyers will not agree with these views.

by influence or by bribery, and when it is widely known that this is done, the law falls into further disrepute. In the developing countries we have no evidence, other than common gossip, that the law is evaded by influence. It is, however, well known that it is evaded by petty but widespread bribery, and we refer here not only to the bribing of the police to overlook traffic offences, but the bribing of sanitary inspectors to overlook insanitary conditions, housing inspectors to overlook overcrowding, and so on down the line of officials whose duty it is to inspect and to assess. That corruption of this kind is widely practised no one will seriously dispute. Until it is brought to an end there is little hope that the prestige of the law will be enhanced, but presumably it can only be brought to an end by better pay, and increase in professional self-respect and the rigorous punishment of offenders.

Unfortunately, corruption of this kind is not confined to the minor, and doubtless underpaid, officials; it extends to elected representatives who have special judicial responsibilities, for example local assessment committees for income tax, to whom it is worth while for a wealthy man to pay considerable sums in bribes for his assessable income to be reduced.

It is difficult to think of anything helpful or constructive to say on this particular matter, other than what we hope to say in a wider context in the next two chapters.

CHAPTER 3

Disciplines

—◦❧❧◦—

(a) The Discipline of Commerce
In Part II of this book we contended that the influence of business, commerce and industry on corruption in Britain had been a healthy one. It is possible that we overstated the case, and excused too readily the more brutal aspects of the industrial revolution and the more ruthless money-making of the Victorian capitalists. The following passage, for example, would hardly seem to bear us out:

'A comparatively small body of men found themselves, as a result of luck, cunning or merit, in control not only of new vast sources of wealth, but also of an almost unlimited power over the destinies of their fellow-men. As is well known and universally recognized today, the conscience of the new holders of power proved unequal to the strain that the new power laid upon it. The wage-earners were unmercifully exploited; wages were forced down below starvation level; hours of work were stretched to a point which seems incredible . . . Worse still, children of any age from four or five upwards were put into the mills and the mines, and strained and tortured so that they grew up mere caricatures of humanity. In fine, the warfare between Capital and Labour, from which society still suffers today, was begun by the great crime committed by Capital.'[1]

Even so, we believe that commercial influence on corruption was on balance good, for three reasons: first, because the merchant and industrial classes, especially in the pioneering days, included a significant proportion of men of religious principle, and while many of these men acted ruthlessly in the prevailing atmosphere of *laissez faire* exploitation their motives and actions were not necessarily corrupt in the context of this discussion; secondly, because the discipline of commerce leads to the inescapable conclusion that it pays to be honest, and that probity is a commercial asset; and thirdly, that commerce cannot be conducted without the efficient keeping of accounts, which militates against corruption.

The first of these reasons may have been peculiar to English social

[1] D. C. Somervell: *A Short History of our Religion*, p. 259.

history, especially the fact that the exclusion of the religious dissenters from the professions drove them into trade, and later into
industry. The second and third reasons are, we believe, universal and
inevitable.

Although there are many more African merchants, businessmen
and contractors than there were a generation ago, Africans have as
yet made no large or significant entry into these fields in comparison
with the overseas competitors.[1] African governments, in so far as
they control this activity, are in a dilemma, since although they wish
to encourage local enterprise they want, above all else, rapid development, and this is only possible with the superior resources of overseas
capital and skill. This they are bound to encourage, and the furthest
they can go in controlling it is to make conditions whereby Africans
are trained for managerial and technical posts within the expatriate
enterprise; or in developing public enterprise through some such
device as the Development Corporation, which is in effect a partnership between an African government and overseas firms. This is
excellent as far as it goes, and will undoubtedly pay dividends as
time goes by. On the other hand it acts as a temporary brake on fully
responsible African enterprise, whereby Africans learn in the hard
school of trial and error. So far as industrial enterprise is concenred,
either in mining or manufacturing, processing or assembling,
technical and managerial control is largely in expatriate hands; while
the production of capital goods has not begun. Banking and insurance
are mainly in expatriate hands also, though in West Africa there is
now a fairly long, but extremely chequered, history of African banks.

All this is no doubt temporary, and in any case most expatriate
firms employ Africans in responsible positions, often in those of the
highest responsibility; moreover this process is accelerating, as is
clearly visible to anyone who visits Africa at regular intervals. What
we have called the discipline of commerce is therefore making itself
felt, though its effect is, so to speak, cushioned by the fact that
ultimate responsibility is usually not African responsibility; there is
nothing, that is to say, which quite corresponds to the merchant and
industrial classes who had to stand on their own feet, and who, we
have maintained, had a salutary influence on corruption in Britain.

Nevertheless, some headway is being made. Although the countries
of Africa are not great commercial centres, as was the City of
London in the nineteenth century, they nevertheless have to sell
their goods overseas in order to live, and with the expansion of this
trade African merchants are learning in a hard school that honesty
pays, since dishonest practices and trading in inferior goods simply
mean that it stops altogether. A common form of corruption has
been practised by produce inspectors, who would pass adulterated
or sub-standard goods in return for a bribe. This has not unnaturally

[1] This is of course less true of the undeveloped world of Asia.

backfired, and customers have ceased to buy. Again, African traders have on occasions failed to meet their bills with overseas creditors, so that their firms have been black-listed by overseas Chambers of Commerce, and this had rebounded on the general creditworthiness of the countries concerned. There is evidence that African governments, their overseas representatives, and the more responsible businessmen in Africa itself are determined to fight these tendencies, since, while internal corruption may be bad for a country's health, corruption in international trade could end all hope of development.

Internally, too, business corruption is being attacked by more rigorous competition and more thorough inspection and control. The building contractor who takes a few inches off the agreed floor measurements of a house, or whose materials are below specification, or whose foundations are skimped, is also finding that dishonesty does not pay, since his reputation spreads and people go elsewhere. This is nevertheless the sort of field in which corruption is still widely practised, and one way of defeating it is to train and employ more qualified technical inspectors.

The third way in which commerce influenced corruption for the good was through the necessity of keeping clear and detailed accounts, subject to audit. Here there is still tremendous leeway to make up in Africa, and one urgent priority, among dozens of others, is to train more accountants and to try to raise the prestige of accountancy as a profession. At present large numbers of educated Africans, certainly university students, do not realize the importance or the creative possibilities of the accountant's work, which they regard as mere book-keeping, something which is done by a clerical officer. This is in part a legacy of earlier colonial days, when accounts had to be kept in a very simple *pro forma* style, so that they could be managed by people of limited education. Although great changes are taking place, a good deal of government and almost all local government accounting is still carried on by obsolete methods. Moreover government auditors never have a fraction of the staff they need in order to keep up with the volume of their work, let alone to use audit as an opportunity for education in accounting, as it ought to be in the circumstances of much African administration.

*

If one may digress from the main subject for a moment, this is a particularly crying need in local government throughout English-speaking Africa, as the startling inefficiency of local authority accounts is almost an open invitation to corruption. In Sierra Leone in a recent year every major local authority, including the old-established Freetown City Council, was criticized by the Government Auditor for a mixture of dishonesty and incompetence, with dishonesty the major factor. For some years almost all the local authorities in Eastern Nigeria have failed to satisfy the auditor, and the councillors have in theory been subject to heavy surcharges. In the financial year 1961/62 a serious attack was in fact made on this problem by the Government and the surcharges, which had for some years been withheld because of the seeming impossibility of surcharging everybody, were for the first time made on a very large scale. A great deal of the money owing was in fact paid, and the moral effect of this demonstration that the Government meant business in attacking corruption has had a sobering and salutary effect.

It is of course a negative rather than a positive solution to the problem of corruption to enforce the full rigours of the law and to impose widespread penalties for dishonesty, but it is not one that can be ignored in present circumstances, and is certainly one line of attack, even if it is not the most promising. Control and inspection were after all essential to the administrative practice of the utilitarian reformers in Britain.

*

We have digressed a little from the subject of this section, which is the influence on corruption of strict accounting, which is a more immediate and unavoidable need in commercial life than in local government. Official peculation can continue without disaster as long as there is the docile taxpayer to make good the deficiencies, but business peculation quickly brings its own nemesis. We argue from this that the spread of business and industry will automatically, if slowly, raise the standard of accounting in developing countries, since business survival will depend on it, and that one important anti-corruption influence will correspondingly grow. But, what is more to the point of this argument, this influence is one that could be deliberately strengthened by up-grading accountancy in the list of skills that are needed for development, by awarding it more scholarships, teaching it in technical colleges and universities, and regarding it as a creative factor in development rather than a tiresome overhead which should be paid for as cheaply as possible.

For a generation or more progress will necessarily be slow, since many African businessmen (and more particularly women) are not sufficiently educated to keep accounts, even though they may be very good businessmen. The large credits given by expatriate firms to illiterate market-women are proverbial; their accounts exist, in great detail, in their heads, and they are hard but honest bargainers. But we have to try to consider the pattern for the future, not the exceptions and oddities of the past.

*

There is, finally, another, less direct way, in which the growth of an independent African commercial class could assist in defeating corruption, though nobody could compel it to do so—that is by their voluntary participation in government or local government; or in the idiom which we have employed, by their willingness to exchange wealth for power and status.

What we had to say about the 'nabobs' in Chapter 2 of the first Part of this book is very relevant here.[1] Though they were themselves often corrupt in the manner in which they gained election, their general influence once elected was salutary, because they were more able, more wealthy and consequently more independent than the aristocrats, office bearers and sinecure holders whom they replaced. The middle-class businessmen now arising in Africa have not the great wealth of the nabobs, nor do we suggest that they should buy their way into Parliament or local government as the nabobs did; there is little doubt, however, that even now they have the kind of ability which is often so strikingly lacking in African legislatures and local authorities.

But the curse with which African politics have saddled themselves at the outset is that politics itself is the recognized road to wealth, and for many an extremely easy road. Men who have made, or are making, money in other ways are not on the whole attracted to politics; so far as local government is concerned, the more substantial traders would hardly think of involving themselves in such a dubious activity. Solid businessmen, however (and there is a small class in every African country of very solid businessmen) are more fitted than most to assist in the work which local government, or even Parliament, is supposed to do. This becomes apparent when, as often happens, a council is suspended for malpractices and their place taken by an *ad hoc* 'caretaker committee', including generally a fair proportion of businessmen and local managers of firms; the quality of administration invariably improves; when democracy is restored their services are lost, which is a most serious comment on democracy. As such men become more numerous in the community one may at least hope that more of them will bring to parliamentary and local government the disinterested (i.e. uncorrupt) approach and the practical experience which characterized so many of their kind in eighteenth and nineteenth century England.

(b) The Discipline of the Professions
In his book *The Machinery of Local Government* Dr R. M. Jackson writes: 'There is no single explanation of why a state of general laxity and corruption gave place to an honest civil service with ministers who no longer regarded their office as an opportunity to grow rich and secure their family's fortune. One factor of great

[1] p. 67.

importance was the growth of the professional class' (p. 345). Indeed he appears to think that this may have been the most important factor of all, for a little later he writes 'The discipline of professional men by their professional organization has probably been the biggest single factor in inducing high standards of conduct.'

The number, range and variety of professional associations in Britain is so immense that it is probable that no one person can be regarded as an authority on the subject, and the student can do no better than turn to the invaluable pages of *Whitaker's Almanack*. Here, under two sections called 'Societies and Institutions' and 'Professional Education', he will find a positively awe-inspiring catalogue, and a little imagination will lead him to realize the force of Dr Jackson's contention, for there appears to be no profession, however remote and exotic, whose members are not subject to the scrutiny and in some cases the discipline of their peers.

We are here concerned with those fields in which corruption was once so rampant, and more particularly with those associations which came into existence in the great age of corruption, which they were partly instrumental in destroying. But before giving particular consideration to these it may be useful to make some general comments on the catalogue as a whole.

Whitaker (1961) lists the astonishing total of 1,255 Societies and Institutions, demonstrating one of the deepest traits in the British character—the love of voluntary association—but the vast majority of these are charitable, religious, cultural, propagandist or educational in a broad sense. There are however 150[1] which we may identify as professional in the sense of this chapter. The largest single group is within the engineering profession, which accounts for 30;[2] in the teaching profession there are about 20, in local government 18 and in medicine 17; the rest cover accountancy (11), the actuaries' profession, advertising, agriculture (7), arbitration, architects (5), auctioneers and estate agents (3), banking (3), building (2), the Civil Service (2), clerks of works, grocers, hoteliers, housing managers, industrial artists, insurance (4), journalism, metallurgy, publishing, quantity surveying, the secretarial profession (3), statistics, surveyors, university teachers, valuers and veterinarians.

It is worth looking at the local government associations in a little

---

[1] This 150 admittedly includes a number of separate associations for Scotland, and it is a remarkable fact that the Scottish associations preceded their English counterparts, often by a long period.

[2] It may be of interest to record the astonishing variety of professions within this profession. There are four associations of a general nature, and separate institutes (sometimes more than one) dealing with the following branches: aeronautical, chemical, civil, consulting, electrical, design, fire, inspection, gas, heating and ventilating, highway, illuminating, locomotive, marine, mechanical, mining, municipal, naval, radio, road transport, ship-building, structural and water.

detail, as we have devoted a chapter to the subject of local government in Part II, and have mentioned some of them in passing. There is first the all-embracing NALGO;[1] this is first and foremost a general trade union, but it goes further than most trade unions in insisting on high professional ethical standards from its members; its fundamental document on *Conditions of Service* gives prominence to the duties, as distinct from the rights, of local government officers, and it is so much to the point of this discussion that it is worth reproducing it in full, in spite of its length:

'The first duty of a local government officer is to give his undivided allegiance to the authority employing him. With his private activities the authority in general is not concerned, so long as his conduct therein is not such as to bring discredit upon the service in which he is an officer. For that conduct public service is entitled to demand the highest standard.

'The maxim laid down for a court of law, that it is of fundamental importance not only that justice should be done, but that it should manifestly and undoubtedly be seen to be done, applies with equal force to the local government officer. Public confidence in his integrity would be shaken were the least suspicion, however ill-founded, to arise that he could be in any way influenced by improper motives.

'From this it must follow that the local government officer, as a public servant, must not only be honest in fact, but must be beyond the reach of the suspicion of dishonesty.

'He is not to subordinate his duty to his private interests; or to put himself in a position where his duty and his private interests conflict. He should not make use of his official position to further those interests; but neither is he so to order his private affairs as to allow the suspicion to arise that a trust has been abused or a confidence betrayed.

'He should be courteous to all with whom his duties bring him into contact.

'The public expects from a local government officer a standard of integrity and conduct not only inflexible but fastidious. It is the duty of the service to see that the expectation is fulfilled.'

There are then a number of Associations of different kinds of local authority, Municipal Corporations, County Councils, District and Urban Councils and Parish Councils. Their function is more akin to that of the pressure group, and they are concerned to some extent with defending or furthering their own interests, but the more positive aspect of their work is largely parliamentary, and consists

[1] The National Association of Local Government Officers, later the National and Local Government Officers Association.

in informal consultation with, and advice to, the Legislature on all matters which affect their respective types of authority.

Finally there are a number of institutes which cater for the interests of the many professions which work under the 'umbrella' of local government—of Clerks, Treasurers, Engineers, Education Officers, Surveyors, Medical Officers, Planning Officers, Rating and Valuation Officers and so on. These largely promote consultation on matters of common professional interest.

But although it is primarily NALGO which concerns itself with professional ethics, these other nation-wide associations with their different purposes have the indirect but very real effect of heightening the status of the profession of local government as a whole.

As we shall see in a moment, the legal and medical professions stand somewhat apart from the rest, but of the seventeen medical associations that we have mentioned, one is the professional trade union, the British Medical Association, one is an ancient Royal Society and two are Royal Colleges; but within the profession as a whole there are institutes dealing with many of its separate branches, almoning, dental, general practice, midwifery, nursing, obstetrics and gynaecology, optical, pharmacological, pharmaceutical, radiological and technical.

Taking the 150 professional societies as a whole, it is significant to the general argument of this book that fifty of them, spread over a representative professional field, were founded between 1834 and 1897.

*

The other list to which we have referred, under the general title of 'Professional Education', is equally instructive, although it overlaps a good deal with the first. The word 'profession' is not always very precisely used in England, but a reasonable definition would be an occupation for which there are nationally recognized qualifications, both upon entry and for promotion, and for which there is a nationally accepted code in such different matters as professional fees and professional behaviour.

The ancient professions of Medicine and Law are in a special category, since not only were their professional associations first in the field,[1] but they possess statutory powers of adjudication. The General Medical Council, the supreme controlling body of the profession, was given power under an Act of 1858 'to erase the name of any registered medical practitioner judged by the Council to have been guilty of infamous conduct in any professional respect, from the Medical Register, which is the instrument created by Parliament for the purpose of marking the distinction between qualified and

---

[1] The Royal College of Surgeons of Edinburgh was founded in 1505 and the Royal College of Physicians in 1518.

N

unqualified medical practitioners. A sentence that a doctor's name be erased may thus entail deprivation of professional income.'[1] Moreover, there was no appeal from such a sentence to the courts. Under an Act of 1902 the Central Midwives Board was given comparable powers, though in this case an appeal lies to the High Court. Under the Solicitors' Act, 1919, the Discipline Committee of the Law Society (the controlling body of the solicitors' profession)[2] may also strike a solicitor off the Roll, though again subject to the right of appeal to the High Court.

Other professional associations are not in this privileged position, but in all the leading professions they supervise standards of entry and promotion and approve examinations, and establish professional codes of conduct. Any member of a professional body found guilty of corrupt practices would, in effect, be ostracized by the profession and would be unable to practice it.

*

We have looked at these matters in some detail, as the development of professional bodies would seem to offer a more specific opportunity for a frontal attack on bribery and corruption than any other development we can think of. The main watershed in the history of Britain in these matters was perhaps the Reform Act of 1832, because it transferred power from the aristocracy to the middle classes, who quickly consolidated their power in government, business and the professions; the revolution in public morality was largely a middle-class revolution, or at least was led by the middle classes. All the present indications are that it is the new middle classes, if anyone, who will effectively tackle bribery and corruption in the developing world.

The process has of course already begun, though the authors cannot unfortunately lay claim to a comprehensive knowledge of how far it has developed. Doctors and lawyers are in a somewhat complicated position, as their original allegiance may have been to the British General Medical Council, or to the General Council of the Bar or the Law Society; or to their counterparts in the country where they qualified—America, Canada, India, etc.—and not all countries recognize each other's qualifications. But Societies centred on Medicine and Law in the developing countries themselves are certainly taking shape, however the conflict of loyalties may be resolved, and this is a development which needs to be accelerated. The teaching profession is following suit, or in some cases had led the way.

[1] Report of the Committee on Ministers' Powers (Cmd. 4060)—Specialized Courts of Law, p. 83.
[2] The controlling body of the barristers' profession is the General Council of the Bar.

It is not, however, in the higher branches of medicine, law or teaching that corruption is rife, but in some areas of government, of public corporations, building contracting, income tax assessment, the award of scholarships, local government and the native courts. It is in fields like this that professional codes need to be established through association.

In so far as attempts have been made they appear to be subject to a common danger. Local government is a good example, because beginnings have been made both with unions of local authority staffs and with associations of local authorities as corporate bodies. They quickly tend, however, to become enmeshed in the trade union aspect of their work to the exclusion of all else; pay, privileges, allowances, promotion and status are all legitimate aspects of what they ought to be doing, but if they do nothing else they fail to make any impact on the problem of corruption or standards of professional conduct. Many of them study the constitution of NALGO, and their leaders visit the Association in London, but they do not seem to attach importance to the unique aspect of this trade union, that it emphasizes duties as well as rights, and endeavours to raise employment in local government to a high calling.

It may be that there *is* no short cut to professional integrity, and that professional bodies, like legal enactments, do not initiate improvements but reflect them. But this would be a disappointing conclusion, and we do not believe that it is historically true. The developing countries all say that they can short-circuit development in the western world, or in a fashionable phrase of the moment, that they can 'by-pass the nineteenth century'. Here is an admirable opportunity for them to do so.

CHAPTER 4

Uneducated Democracy

—o⧉⧉o—

In theory the self-regulating processes of democracy ought to banish bribery and corruption from public life, for if public men are corrupt they will not survive the next election; in practice, few democracies are of a quality which would ensure this. Freedom means freedom to do wrong as well as to do right, and lacking the discipline imposed by an educated electorate many governments and local authorities in developing countries have chosen to go on doing wrong because they know that the voters either will not care, or will not understand, or will not find out.

Edward Gibbon has a striking sentence in the *Decline and Fall of the Roman Empire*[1] when he is describing the intrigues which surrounded the persecution of Athanasius by the Emperor Constantius: 'Corruption,' he says, '*the most infallible symptom of constitutional liberty*, was successfully practised.' What he meant by this enigmatic remark is not altogether clear—presumably that if people have enough freedom under a constitution they will *inevitably* become corrupt; an uncomfortable thought if carried to its logical conclusion, for it seems to suggest that the best way to abolish corruption would be by an honest dictatorship; and there has indeed been evidence in recent years that where ruling families or politicians have been intolerably corrupt the military *coups d'etat* which have succeeded them have had a cleansing effect. It is hardly for us, however, to recommend this! What we can more properly do is to consider the relationship between education and democracy, and its bearing on our problem.

A characteristic feature of developing countries, in comparison with the more developed world, is that they are having to live in several centuries simultaneously. There are admittedly great extremes of wealth in Britain, great differences in education, and, perhaps greatest of all, differences in culture and styles of living. It is doubtful, however, whether any of these differences are as fundamental as those between the huge mass of family farmers, living very like the English peasant of the middle ages, illiterate, superstitious, handling very little money, their world bounded by the family or

[1] Ch. **XXI**. Quoted in standard Dictionaries of Quotations.

clan; the wage-earners and urban proletariat, living like their counterparts in nineteenth century Britain, semi-literate, underpaid, badly housed, but beginning to understand their rights and to feel their power; the growing middle class of traders, teachers and officials, whose styles and standards of living approximate to those of the privileged classes of the twentieth century; and the top professional and business men, whose material and often professional standards equal or exceed those of the western world. It is metaphorically possible in many parts of Africa to span the centuries in the course of a short walk.

In this situation it has become necessary to give every adult person the vote. This is not questioned, at any rate by us. It is no argument to say that in Britain it took more than a century after the first Reform Act to achieve a democratic franchise, for that sort of process will never happen again. Attempts have been made in some parts of the world to devise a qualitative franchise, which would give the vote to those capable of exercising it; some of these have been ingenious and sincere, and have, looked at objectively, corresponded to the common-sense facts of the situation. But the forces working against such attempts are overwhelming. In any case, who is really entitled to distinguish between one man's fitness and another's? Who can say that an illiterate man who has paid his taxes and brought up a family shall not vote, while an educated but untried young man shall do so? Moreover, these questions are not settled by reason alone, and the twentieth century has more or less decided that every man and woman shall have one vote.

Nevertheless, this presents special difficulties which were not experienced in Britain, where the franchise roughly kept pace with education, or as others would argue, education roughly kept pace with the franchise. The principle of 'one-man-one-vote' has now to be applied to societies which we have described as spanning the centuries, and this produces its own kind of democracy.

If one started with the tribal aboriginies of Australia, or the pygmies of the Congo, among whom ballot box democracy would be premature, and proceeded to the most educated and civilized society that the twentieth century can show, wherever that may be, we should have an ascending line. Somewhere along that line would be a point below which elections would not result in democracy, but might even tend to produce its opposite, since what would emerge would not be the wishes of the many but the wishes of the few, by whom the ignorant majority were manipulated. Similarly, within developing countries, with their widely disparate societies, democracy is more valid in the upper than the lower reaches of these societies, as is shown by the fact that in many 'bush' constituencies members are elected to Parliament, and may become influential national, or even world, figures, for reasons connected with ancient local feuds which have nothing to do with the twentieth century at all, let alone with a political platform. All this amounts to no more than stating the obvious—that democracy and education are closely linked, and that the quality of democracy improves as education increases.

We therefore need a vast expansion of education before the automatic controls of democracy could have any chance at all to work upon corruption. In what we called the 'upper reaches' the controls do work to some extent already, for men and women who are tired of corruption will employ the ballot box to destroy it, or, if the ballot box only presents them with alternative kinds of corruption, public opinion will be generated which cannot be ignored, and which will call 'A plague on both your houses'. But this kind of public opinion is less effective than it ought to be in a democracy, as long as there are vast numbers of electors to counter-balance it to whom corruption causes no great concern, either because they do not understand it or because they take it for granted. Unfortunately, millions *do* take it for granted; they do not see why a man should take the trouble to get himself elected to Parliament or to a local council unless there is something in it for him, and if there is also something in it for *them*, in the shape of a bribe, everyone is happy; exactly as they were in nineteenth century Britain.

It needs to be said at this point that governments in the countries under discussion, which contain men of the highest calibre, do not appear to give much of a lead in this matter to the unenlightened electorate. Some of them seem capable of an extraordinary 'double-think' which is indistinguishable from hypocrisy. It is obvious from their excellent platform speeches and statements of policy that they fully grasp the concept of public service; members of the House of Commons could not explain more eloquently that they have entered politics with the sole object of serving their fellow-men, by raising their living standards and ensuring their happiness and prosperity. Having made these admirable speeches they then proceed to line their pockets and provide for their families in an apparently cynical manner (though they sometimes explain disarmingly that this is necessary because the cost of getting elected has impoverished them).

It is important to understand this phenomenon, and the explanation is in fact extremely simple. Most first-hand observers are agreed that the governments under discussion include men of first-rate ability, who would reach comparable positions in any country. The same is true of their civil services. But there are not *enough* men of experience, ability and character to fill *all* the positions in a modern government; talent is too thinly spread. Accordingly, the difference between the best and the average, and between the average and the worst, is far greater than in more developed countries. This is exacerbated by two things: the 'spoils' system, whereby faithful members of the party have to be rewarded with high office; and also by the need to distribute high offices *geographically*, so that every area has its share. The spoils system operates in some degree in more advanced countries, notably in America; in Britain its operation is not blatant, as there are generally ways of rewarding the faithful with positions of status rather than of power; while geographical distribution of power is not an important factor in a small, integrated country in which the idea of the 'son of the soil' no longer carries weight. If power in the developing countries were concentrated in the hands of the best, or if the talents *within* governments were less differentiated, we should hear less of corruption in high places.

Bribery apart, a vast uneducated electorate hampers the automatic control of corruption, as people tend to believe anything their political heroes tell them, and even more anything that their favourite newspaper prints. (We assume, of course, that education and the ability to read a newspaper are not synonymous.)

This kind of discussion appears to have no end and to offer no hope, and there are of course no quick solutions. But there is no doubt that the more rapidly education spreads the more quickly will bribery and corruption diminish, provided always that education means more than the ability to read and write. Here is another of the endless dilemmas in which developing countries find themselves; social justice demands that everybody should be given primary education; but there is a point below which education, like democracy, is scarcely worth having, and large numbers of semi-literate people will benefit neither their country nor themselves; moreover, and this is the other horn of the dilemma, while social justice may demand primary education for all, planned development would benefit more directly from higher education for a few, since a thousand men with advanced professional or technical skill would make a greater impact on development than a hundred thousand who could read and write, but could do little more. To plunge for one or the other, or, on limited budgets, to strike a balance between the two, is the painful problem of every developing country.

But formidable though the problem seems, there is no doubt at all that it is in education that the ultimate solution lies. In Part II of this book we were repeatedly compelled to end a chapter (e.g. on elections, the civil service or local government) by saying the same thing in different ways, namely that the final spurt in the struggle against corruption was brought about by the spread of knowledge among the millions instead of only among the thousands—the increase of newspapers and journals which kept pace with the ability of people to read them, the improvement in their quality as people became able to read them more intelligently, the development of the scientific attitude and the consequences of applied science; followed by increasing movement about the country, which gradually gave people so much wider horizons than they had before.

We also said that the growth of responsible political parties was one of the major factors in defeating corruption, but the essential word there was *responsible*. Parties cannot be responsible to an electorate in the abstract; they are responsible to it for carrying out specific electoral promises. The reason why we said that in Britain they were an increasingly good influence on corruption was that they were increasingly having to put forward responsible programmes which they would be capable of carrying out, and which the electors would understand and criticize. If the electors are incapable of understanding, as they are over large areas of the developing world, parties are in the literal sense of the word *irresponsible* or responsible to a small group among themselves. The only way of causing them to be more responsible is to have a more educated electorate.

It is no use leaving the subject with a few pious platitudes, particularly if they happen to be pessimistic ones as well. If education is in fact a pre-condition of the destruction of bribery and corruption, what hope does the future hold?

There is first the mass-attack on ignorance, the 'crash programme', in the modern idiom. Forward-looking Africans are fond of saying that whereas Europe and America gave the world the industrial revolution and the agricultural revolution, Africa will be associated with the educational revolution; that she will make and apply new discoveries in educational techniques which will be comparable in their field with the eighteenth century discovery and application of power and machinery, and which will transform the problem of education as they transformed the problem of production. They do not profess that they will do it unaided, as the financial resources are beyond them, but given aid on the scale to which the developed world is now committed, their own belief in the paramount need for education, and their dedication to the destruction of ignorance, will transform ignorance into knowledge at a greater pace than mankind has ever achieved before.

This goes far beyond our present scope, and is relevant only in that the hope and determination exist. Of more relevance to our argument is not the large-scale mass attack, but the small-scale personal penetration.

In situations where whole societies have to be transformed, it is easy to under-rate what can be achieved by individuals, or by particular schools or colleges, or, as we have earlier suggested, by professions. If the transformation is not material or economic, but is concerned with values and attitudes, it is indeed only from such sources that transformation can start to flow.

The British colonies were led to independence by an extraordinarily small number of dedicated men; what is less obvious is that many of them owed their original fire and integrity to an even smaller number of great headmasters, for example Fraser of Achimota and his right-hand man Aggrey. Later, with the coming of political power they have been caught up in the web of corruption, but the great pioneers among them were not personally corrupt. People dedicated, as they were, to a cause so much greater than themselves are not corrupt. Great headmasters are rare, but if we are looking for people to lead us out of the wilderness of corruption they are among the men who could achieve most. We have remarked earlier how Dr Arnold, because he lived in the days when England was governed by an élite and because his influence and character affected other privileged schools, set an indelible mark on the character of nearly a century of British government.

It is a platitude of innumerable public speeches, which does not of course make it any less true, that education is worth little unless it includes education in character and integrity. No great progress has been made in translating this excellent precept into practice, and the difficulty of doing so is probably greater in the developing countries than elsewhere. A few generations ago education, in tribal society, was a corporate responsibility, in which the whole extended family shared; within a narrow context it was an education in responsibility and morals. In the swiftly changing circumstances of today education is increasingly becoming the responsibility of parents alone, and their influence is overshadowed by the schools; when, as must happen for some time to come, the literate child shows so much more than his illiterate parents, respect is undermined.[1] Moral behaviour is not taught in the school curriculum as effectively as it was in the extended family, but one negative tradition of the old education survives— the discouragement of individualism, the shrinking from individual responsibility. It was of course said of the English public school system also that its purpose was to make boys conform to type, and that the worst sin was to be unconventional; but the family tradition behind the public school boys was of a different order, the 'prefect' system encouraged responsibility, and in adult life decision came easily, and moral courage was accorded only a little less respect than physical courage. One of the permanent exasperations of life in Africa, that no one will accept responsibility but will always seek to pass it higher up if he can, may well stem from the tradition—still recent enough to be powerful—of tribal education. It makes the task of educating for character in a non individualistic world vastly more difficult.

It is the complaint of teachers all over the world that all the most difficult and unwanted responsibilities get thrust upon them, and nowhere is this truer than of Africa today. In addition to the chores which descend upon his English colleague the African teacher must, if there is an election, act as presiding officer, if there is a census, as a chief enumerator, if there is to be a committee he must lead it, if a

[1] Edmund Ilogu: op. cit.

community development campaign, he must inspire it; on top of all this—and of course on top of teaching—he must supply a large part of the leadership in government and administration, and this finally takes him away from teaching altogether. But all these things that he does are of little weight in the ultimate scale of values compared with his potential influence as a maker of honest citizens. In no occupation is it more important that the trade union should not swamp the profession.

In the contemporary situation a few dedicated men in law, medicine, teaching, the civil service and local government may seem no more than a few Davids hurling their pebbles at Goliath. But they would not for long lack reinforcements, for no one who has lived in Africa for any length of time can be unaware of the passionate longing for leadership of this kind. The best elements in these countries, quickly disillusioned with internal power politics, tired of bribery and corruption at every level, and above all conscious of the selfless idealism of recent years, are in a mood to follow anybody who will lead them against corruption, provided only that what he preaches he also practices in his private life. For a few false prophets have appeared upon the scene, who make things infinitely worse.

At the level of the very ordinary man, it sounds a little comic to sophisticated ears to hear of the various Leagues of Bribe Scorners who have at one time or another set out to grapple with this problem especially as they have flickered in and out somewhat ineffectively, and have indeed provided a stock joke, apocryphal or not we do not know, of the League secretary who absconded with the funds. But the early Christians also caused considerable amusement, and had occasional backsliders.

Meanwhile, there is one simple, if apparently negative, way in which those who deplore corruption can make their witness, and that is by resignation. Some of the reports on corruption in local government which were quoted in Part I stated that councillors who had silently acquiesced were as guilty as those who took an active part in corruption. 'Not one councillor resigned in protest . . .' phrases like this recur.[1] The weight of the pressure brought to bear on bribery and corruption is likely for a long time to be the combined weight of such individual actions. We do not, of course, underestimate the degree of moral courage required to resign, and to suffer the subsequent persecution.

It is possible that we have, after all, achieved no more than a little easy moralizing, and in any case we, as passers-by, can have no influence on the situation whatsoever. But it seems justified to write in this vein, since nothing ever happens if everybody waits for the next man to start.

[1] p. 21.

CHAPTER 5

Power, Wealth and Status

—◦❖❖◦—

We said earlier[1] that in Britain power, wealth and status had always tended to be in somewhat different hands, and that although the desire of people to exchange one for the other had been the cause of a great deal of corruption, it had also had its beneficial side, as it had kept the classes who possessed them fluid, and had been one of the reasons why Britain had managed to change peacefully and not violently. The separation still persists, though it is not (and never has been) at all rigid. Many professional people, for example, and especially clergy and doctors, have little wealth or power but considerable status; others, among whom we may include various kinds of speculators and promoters, have considerable wealth but almost no status and little power; a few, for example senior civil servants and higher technologists, have only modest wealth, their status is obscure as they work largely in the background, but they wield very great power. The number of people possessing all three is very small; even the mysterious—possibly mythical—group which has in recent years been nicknamed 'The Establishment' is associated with power and status, but not necessarily with wealth.

But in the developing countries, with their highly disparate societies, there is a remarkable concentration of power, wealth and status in the hands of a few, among whom politicians are predominant. For the equation of politics with wealth is the outstanding, and terrifying, feature of these countries. In Britain people enter politics today from various motives, not all of them necessarily commendable; but the motive of direct financial gain is not among them (though as we have tried to show in Part II it *used* to be).

We said in the last chapter[2] that the new political parties tend to be 'irresponsible', using that word in its literal and not pejorative sense, because there is not an educated electorate to whom they *could* be responsible in the normal way. Through no fault of their own they are largely responsible to themselves, and such criticism as comes their way is often foolish and ignorant; they cannot adjust themselves to the tides of public opinion, because informed public

[1] p. 58.
[2] p. 200.

opinion is not articulate; this does not mean that there are not large numbers of informed people in these countries, but that they are concentrated in positions, and especially in civil service positions, which do not allow them to be articulate in public. Politicians therefore wield quite exceptional power, and fallible human nature often leads them to abuse it. We do not support the common criticism that they are 'dictatorial', because this tendency is thrust upon them by circumstances; an immature democracy faced with huge problems of development needs strong, decisive government if it is to survive, let alone advance. They do however quite frequently fall into the temptations which beset their British predecessors, of feathering their own nests and providing for their families at the public expense. The most obvious symptoms of this are the lands, houses, cars, allowances and privileges with which they endow themselves, and which would take away the breath of their counterparts in wealthier countries;[1] all this, however, is legitimate if they choose to make it so, and of their frequently alleged illegitimate earnings, or acquisitions of land and property through influence, it is impossible to speak, since gossip is not evidence.

The point is that politics means not only power but wealth, and not only wealth but status, since politics is not only, as the Oxford Dictionary suggests, an art or science of government in these countries, but a national obsession. It is difficult to think of any question outside private family life which is not liable to become political; even a charity can become a party political issue; even a local council whose actual activities are confined to cutting the grass and sweeping the market will be fought for by the parties, though these tasks hardly lend themselves to ideological interpretation. More important, the apparatus of political control reaches out into almost every sphere of public activity—Boards, Corporations, Committees, provincial, district and local administration.[2]

The professional politician, i.e. the man who depends on politics for his income and his livelihood, is still a comparatively unfamiliar figure in British politics. Most members of the House of Commons earn their living in some other trade or profession, and are, so to speak, 'amateur' politicians. Their income as an MP, set against the expenses incurred, is not considerable, and indeed is very unfair as between individuals, since to some it may mean gain and to others net loss. Owing to the great claims which Parliament now makes on the time of its members, the disappearance of a leisured class, the fact that business and professional men themselves work harder than ever before, and the desire of some members to do their parlia-

[1] In one aid-seeking country in Africa, Ministers are provided with houses with seven bathrooms, free of rent, rates, electricity and certain services.

[2] Public Services Commissions are an important exception; nepotism in filling appointments takes place in spite of, not because of the PSCs.

mentary job either properly or not at all, the professional politician is, however, coming more to the fore. Unless he has previously established himself in another career he is not usually a popular figure, since there is a healthy instinct which leads people to suppose that a man should prove himself in some other direction before claiming that he is fit to govern the country.

But in the developing countries, in spite of the relatively small amount of time during which Parliament meets, the professional politician has established himself at the outset of self-government, and he cannot always be said to be a man who has earned his fitness to rule by his outstanding success in some other sphere of life.

Irresponsible tendencies are increased by the fact that rival political parties in the developing countries are not based to any large extent on opposing programmes, based on different social and economic beliefs; they are in varying degrees tribal, regional or religious, and extraordinarily little is said in election campaigns—almost nothing in local government election campaigns—about policies. In the less developed of the developing countries this is inevitable—as Mr Julius Nyerere said of Tanganyika, in a country like his own one-party government accords with common sense, because when all the problems are elemental there is nothing for parties to disagree about (except who should wield power), and there seems little to be gained from pretending that there is. 'Except who should wield power'—that is really the root of the matter, for the power sought is the power to rule in general and not according to particular policies or beliefs as to how society should be organized; power, moreover, which is not, as we have already said, subject to the criticism of an informed electorate.

This importance of power as distinct from political belief is further illustrated by the ease with which members of parties perform the feat which is usually known as 'jumping on the band-wagon', that is switching parties when it is obvious that power and its consequent patronage is going to the other side.

In our study of political extravagance and corruption in Britain we saw that the most effective remedies at one time or another were the accession to Parliament and to local councils of men of substance and standing in their own right, generally from commerce and industry; severe financial crises which brought Parliament to its senses and showed up corruption as something that could not be afforded; the effects of the utilitarian philosophy of Bentham and his disciples, which brought a more scientific attitude to bear on government and produced a more rational and efficient administration, closely controlled from the centre; and the growth of an impartial civil service.

The first of these we have already commented on; the second is not one that any friend of the developing countries would wish to

206 CORRUPTION IN DEVELOPING COUNTRIES

recommend, though there can be no doubt about its salutary effects, and in some countries financial stringency has already put a brake on the grosser forms of extravagance which are on the borderline of corruption. The last two are closely linked.

It is difficult to exaggerate the debt which nineteenth century Britain owed to the Benthamite utilitarians for sound and economical administration; to Jeremy Bentham himself for the theoretical framework, and to his disciple Edwin Chadwick for the translation of his theories into administrative practice. It is impossible here to try to summarize the philosophy and achievements of the utilitarians,[1] but for the purposes of this study it is relevant to say that Bentham pioneered a scientific approach to the problems of government, laying them open to the scrutiny of investigation, of exact knowledge, of statistical information and to a ruthless pursuit of the utilitarian doctrine of the greatest good for the greatest number. The consequence in administrative terms were economy, efficiency, inspection and control. Chadwick was the great driving force who, armed with these principles and these criteria, hacked his way through the jungle of the unreformed Poor Law and explored the unchartered wastes of public health and sanitation. From the point of view of bribery and corruption it was the Benthamite principle of 'inspectability' and central administrative control that is most relevant. Chadwick's massive reports and unanswerable proposals compelled the Government to accept, in spite of the expected opposition from vested interests and advocates of a strictly local democracy, a degree of central control and inspection which would have been unthinkable at the beginning of the century, and which steadily wore down inefficiency and laxity on the one hand and private selfish interests (in other words nepotism and corruption) on the other. This was the beginning of the Crown's acceptance of responsibility for 'welfare' which blossomed a century later into the British Welfare State.

It is unnecessary to argue the need for central control as such in most developing countries, for as we have seen the political parties in power need no persuasion on this subject.[2] But the control for which Chadwick and his associates fought was control by experts and civil servants, and not by politicians, a very vital difference; a control, moreover, exercised at all times in the interest of the 'greatest number', and not in the interests of a party or a ruling clique. The modern doctrine that Party, State and People are inseparable and

[1] Of the vast literature on the subject see esp. E. Halevy: *The Growth of Philosophic Radicalism*. There are various lives of Chadwick, notably by S. E. Finer and R. A. Lewis. For a briefer and more general account see Redlich and Hirst, ed. Keith-Lucas, op. cit., Chapters 1–3 of Part II.

[2] Though it should be added that in some countries the new Governments at first gave far greater autonomy to local authorities than was wise, and a control of a stricter kind than obtained under colonial administration was sometimes reimposed as a matter of necessity.

indistinguishable had not, of course, taken root at the time, and our argument has less relevance to the one-party states, especially those where the boundaries between politicians and civil servants have been redrawn. But if the possibility of bribery and corruption is to be lessened, or until the millenium when the controllers of the state are free from human corruptibility, control and inspection by an impartial civil service and by disinterested experts are vital if the full benefits of taxation are to reach the taxpayer. What degree of impartiality and disinterestedness is possible in developing countries is a large question which takes us out of our context. It is not necessary to suppose, nor is it necessarily desirable, that this independence should be as great as it is in contemporary Britain. It is however desirable, if undue influence is to be minimized, that political leaders should respect the rights and professional expertise of the Civil Service to the greatest possible extent, control it only in matters of policy and not of administration, and refrain from interfering in its normal work in the interest of their friends, their families and themselves; and that the civil service should so organize themselves professionally that they stand as far as possible above politics, so that they can speak if necessary with a strong and united voice.

This does no more than state the obvious; it is possible that the whole of this part of the book does no more.

*

In countries which we have described as 'spanning the centuries' it is obvious that there must be for a long time to come a greater concentration of power, wealth and status in a very few hands than is the case with countries which have enjoyed a longer history in the commercial and scientific era. But reviewing the story of bribery and corruption in Britain we are forced back to the conclusion that an important underlying element in its defeat was the *diffusion* of these attributes. It is significant that when men are sought for public positions in developing countries today it is often virtually impossible to find a person of any standing who is not politically committed. This cannot be regarded as a healthy state of affairs in a democracy, if democracy is the aim. An interest in politics, amounting to an obsession, is inherent in any country seeking to throw off colonial rule and become independent. The phrase 'Seek ye first the Kingdom of Politics'—though it offended Christians because it parodied one which they held to be sacred—obviously contained an important truth, the validity of which has been proved over and over again since Dr Nkrumah first coined it. But if with independence politics continues supreme in status over the sciences, the professions, the arts and all the other manifold activities of man, it seems unlikely that these new civilizations will reach their full potentiality.

Conclusion

—◦❦◦—

The cures for corruption in developing countries are these:

The passage of time, during which, given steady economic progress, loyalties will gradually move from family, clan and tribe to nation-state.

The spread of education, which will enable people to understand what politics are about, instead of regarding them as a tribal or partisan form of excitement; which will help also in the development of a scientific approach to the problems of government and administration.

The evolution of a public opinion, which must follow the spread of education, which rejects corruption either because it is morally wrong or because it is scientifically inefficient, or both.

The growth of commerce and industry, which will strengthen an element in the middle class which is at present weak, and which, historically, has been opposed to corruption.

The further growth of the professional class, and its resolve to raise its ethical standards by increasing association.

The diffusion of power, wealth and status now enjoyed primarily by politicians through society as a whole.

The recognition of the fact that democracy which is worth having is a mature concept, and that in developing countries *local* democracy must by definition be immature; and, consequently, calls for a continuance of central control and inspection, exercised by the civil service.

The raising in prestige and the increase in the number of skilled accountants and auditors, and the recognition of their equal status in development programmes with administrators, engineers, industrialists and agriculturalists.

The rigorous enforcement of the laws concerned with inspection.

The personal witness of individuals who are opposed to bribery and corruption.

There are no shorter cuts than these.

INDEX

Accountancy, profession of, 188–9
Achebe, Chinua, 16, 41
Acts of Parliament (British): against corruption, 67–8, 71–3, 175; against dissenters, 130–1; on local government, 103–5; Ballot Act, 73; Education Act, 1870, 76, 107; Act of Settlement, 1707, 88, 92
Administration (British): generally, 87–97; corruption and reform, 88–94; Board of Trade, 80, 90–2; Exchequer, 88; Excise, 87; Post Office, 90
Adult education, 147–8
Advertising, 156–7
Agrarian revolution, 69, 80, 83, 84, 90, 118, 122, 124
Akpan, N.U., 183
Aldermen, 105
Annual Abstract of Statistics, 92
Arnold, Dr Thomas, 146, 180
Army: generally (British), 120–9; award of contracts to, 80; *coups d'etat*, 58, 196
Audit, 188; District Auditor, 108

Ballot box democracy, 197
Banking and insurance, 155
Bell, Dr Andrew, 142
Bentham, Jeremy, 97, 108, 182
Book-keeping, 113, 156, 188
Boroughs (English), 63–4, 98, 101, 182
Bribery and corruption: definition of, 56; difficulty of proof, 14–16, 82; effect on development, 16, 172; effect on morale, 13, 25–6, 27, 29, 45, 172; reaction to, 11, 12
Bright, John, 87, 93, 96
Britain and Africa: similarities, 173; differences, 196;
British institutions in Africa, 19
Bronowski, Dr J., 160–1
Burke, Edmund, 77, 79, 80n, 85, 87, 89, 90, 94

Cardigan, Earl of, 120, 128
Central government control, 92, 103, 108, 143, 145, 163–4, 206–7
Chadwick, Edwin, 92, 97, 108, 117

Charity Commissioners, 92
Church, The, 130–8, 178–82
Civil servants (Africa), 11, 16, 46
Civil Service (British), 87–97
Civil Service Commission, 95
Coleman, Professor J., 48
Colonial government: influence on corruption, 46; influence on respect for law, 183
Commerce (and industry), 149–58, 186–9
Communications, influence of, 161–4
Contracts, 24, 80, 100
Courts, Customary, 19, 174
Craig, Sir John, 87n, 93, 96
Creech-Jones, Rt Hon Arthur, 15
Customary gifts, 35–7; Report on Exchange of Customary Presents, 36, 39

Defoe, Daniel, 98, 139, 149
Democracy, relation to education, 197–8
Dickens, Charles, 70, 94, 114, 173
Division lists, publication of, 85

Education: generally (Britain), 139–48; connection with democracy, 197–8; connection with character, 201; mass attack, 200; primary and higher, 199; traditions in Africa, 40, 201
Elections: generally (Britain), 63–76; corrupt practices in Britain, 63–76; corrupt practices in Nigeria, 26–31; violence in Britain, 174; violence in Nigeria, 27; cost of, 74, 176n
'Establishment', The, 61, 150, 203
Examinations (civil service), 95

Family obligations, 33–6, 41–2
Franchise, 63, 65, 105, 197
French Revolution, 69, 116, 160
Friendly Societies, 174
Fry, Elizabeth, 118, 168

Gambia, audible voting, 28
Gash, Professor Norman, 70n, 173n, 174

GEORGE ALLEN & UNWIN LTD
London: 40 Museum Street, W.C.1

Auckland: 24 Wyndham Street
Bombay: 15 Graham Road, Ballard Estate, Bombay 1
Bridgetown: P.O. Box 222
Buenos Aires: Escritorio 454–459, Florida 165
Calcutta: 17 Chittaranjan Avenue, Calcutta 13
Cape Town: 109 Long Street
Hong Kong: 44 Mody Road
Ibadan: P.O. Box 62
Karachi: Karachi Chambers, McLeod Road
Madras: Mohan Mansions, 38c Mount Road, Madras 6
Mexico: Villalongin 32–10, Piso, Mexico 5, D.F.
Nairobi: P.O. Box 4536
New Delhi: 13–14 Asaf Ali Road, New Delhi 1
São Paulo: Avenida 9 de Julho 1138-Ap. 51
Singapore: 36c Prinsep Street, Singapore 7
Sydney, N.S.W.: Bradbury House, 55 York Street
Tokyo: 10 Kanda-Ogawamachi, 3-Chome, Chiyoda-ku
Toronto: 91 Wellington Street West, Toronto 1

DATE DUE

OCT 1 4 '64		
NOV 2 4 '64		
DEC 1 8 '64		
JAN 1 5 '65		
MY 6 '69		
APR 1 5 1998		
GAYLORD		PRINTED IN U.S.A.